A HOUSE FOR THE STRUGGLE

A HOUSE FOR THE STRUGGLE

The Black Press and the
Built Environment in Chicago

E. JAMES WEST

**UNIVERSITY OF
ILLINOIS PRESS**
Urbana, Chicago, and Springfield

Furthermore:
a program of the J. M. Kaplan Fund

This publication is made possible with support from
Furthermore: a program of the J. M. Kaplan Fund.

Library of Congress Cataloging-in-Publication Data
Names: West, E. James, author.
Title: A house for the struggle : the Black press and the
    built environment in Chicago / E. James West.
Description: Urbana : University of Illinois Press,
    [2022] | Includes
bibliographical references and index.
Identifiers: LCCN 2021041071 (print) | LCCN
    2021041072 (ebook) | ISBN 9780252044328
    (cloth) | ISBN 9780252086397 (paperback) | ISBN
    9780252053313 (ebook)
Subjects: LCSH: African American press—Illinois—
    Chicago—History—20th century. | Chicago
    (Ill.)—Buildings, structures, etc. | Newspaper
    buildings—Illinois—Chicago. | Architecture
    and society—Illinois—Chicago—History—20th
    century. | African Americans—Illinois—Chicago—
    History—20th century. | Chicago (Ill.)—Race
    relations—History—20th century.
Classification: LCC PN4899.C394 W47 2022 (print) | LCC
    PN4899.C394 (ebook) | DDC 071/.308996073—dc23/
    eng/20211123
LC record available at https://lccn.loc.gov/2021041071
LC ebook record available at https://lccn.loc.gov/
    2021041072

Contents

Acknowledgments

Writing is hard at the best of times, and the completion of this book was made considerably harder by precarious employment and the COVID-19 pandemic. While its faults rest with me alone, its strengths are indebted to the people and institutions who have made it possible.

I am grateful to Eithne Quinn for encouraging my early interest in Chicago's Black press buildings and helping to give my ideas form and focus. These ideas were sharpened further by Sue Currell as part of a postdoctoral application to the University of Sussex. Although the application was unsuccessful, Sue's advice played a critical role in securing a Leverhulme fellowship at Northumbria University, where the bulk of writing for this project was completed. I am proud to call both Eithne and Sue colleagues and friends.

In many ways the Black Metropolis Research Consortium, based at the University of Chicago, has been my intellectual home away from home. BMRC fellowships in 2013, 2015, and 2017 enabled me to conduct research for this and other projects and connected me with a broader network of scholars, journalists, artists, and archivists working on and fighting for Black Chicago, including Anita Mechler, Amy Mooney, Sonja Williams, Amani Morrison, Beth Loch, Cynthia Fife-Townsel, Ethan Michaeli, John Woodford, Beverly Cook, Raquel Flores-Clemons, Chris Reed, Barbara Karant, and Tim Black. I'm grateful to Adrienne Brown, who made time during my 2017 fellowship, listened politely to my inane ramblings, and provided some incredibly useful leads to follow.

My first sustained attempts to make this project a "thing" came during a Fulbright Scholarship at Elon University in 2017–18, where I was made to feel welcome by Rod Clare, Shayna Mehas, Woody Pelton, and other colleagues—not least the "OG" herself, Marnia Gardner. At Northumbria, I benefited from the wisdom and warm collegiality of Brian Ward and other members of the American Studies group. I've also benefited from feedback at various workshops and conferences, including at Stony Island Arts Bank in 2017 and at the 2018 *Chicago Design* conference at the Art Institute, in which I was generously invited to participate by Jonathan Mekinda and Bess Williamson.

Thanks to ElDante Wilson for giving me the scoop on John Moutoussamy; David Hartt for providing me access to architectural drawings of the Johnson Publishing Building; Geoff Georges for use of Alexandre Georges's architectural photographs; Frank Lopez, Courtney Chartier, Katie Levi, Adele Cygelman, and Verlon Lloyd Stone for helping me track down other image permissions; and Saima Nasar, Megan Hunt, Nicholas Grant, Hannah Parker, Hilary Francis, and the Lipman 118 crew for making the bleak hellscape that is twenty-first-century academia slightly more bearable.

Thanks to my anonymous readers and to Jean Lee Cole, who provided invaluable feedback on key sections of the book through *Ideas on Fire*. Dawn Durante has been an enthusiastic supporter, a voice of reason, and a welcome ray of sunshine throughout. Since Dawn's departure from the University of Illinois Press, Alison Bassford has stepped up admirably to help get this book over the line. Thanks to Jill R. Hughes for judicious copyedits and the Illinois design team for a heavy cover.

Thanks, finally, to my family for their support, to Skye for keeping me company, and to Candi for her love, faith, and friendship.

A HOUSE FOR THE STRUGGLE

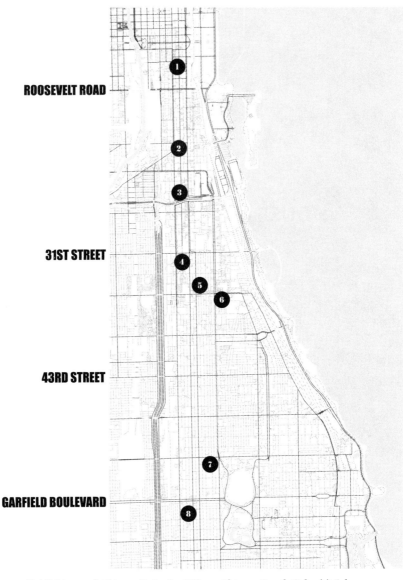

ROOSEVELT ROAD

31ST STREET

43RD STREET

GARFIELD BOULEVARD

Johnson Publishing and *Chicago Defender* Offices, Chicago South Side: (1) Johnson Publishing, 820 S. Michigan Avenue; (2) Johnson Publishing, 1820 S. Michigan Avenue; (3) *Chicago Defender*, 2400 S. Michigan Avenue; (4) *Chicago Defender*, 3159 S. State Street; (5) *Chicago Defender*, 3435 S. Indiana Avenue; (6) Johnson Publishing, 3501 South Parkway; (7) Johnson Publishing, 5125 S. Calumet Avenue; (8) Johnson Publishing, 5619 S. State Street. (E. James West / Mapbox / OpenStreetMap)

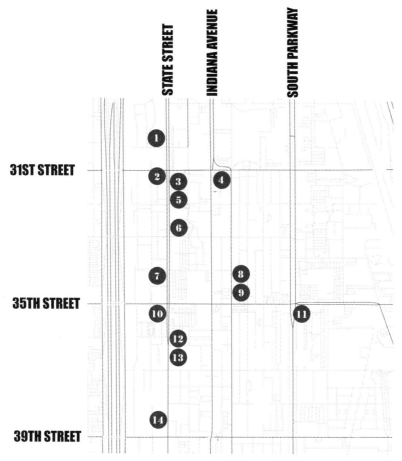

Chicago's Black Newspaper Row: (1) *Chicago Conservator*, 2952 S. State Street; (2) *Afro-American News* office, 3104 S. State Street; (3) *Chicago Searchlight*, 3153 S. State Street; (4) *Chicago Defender*, 3159 S. State Street; (5) *Chicago Enterprise*, 3116 S. Indiana Avenue; (6) *Chicago Leader*, 3245 S. State Street; (7) *Chicago Whip*, 3420 S. State Street; (8) Associated Negro Press, 3423 S. Indiana Avenue; (9) *Chicago Defender*, 3435 S. Indiana Avenue; (10) *Favorite* Magazine, 3518 S. State Street; (11) Supreme Life Building, 3501 South Parkway; (12) Overton Hygienic Building, 3619 S. State Street; (13) Chicago Bee Building, 3647 S. State Street; (14) *Chicago Advocate*, 3824 S. State Street. (E. James West / Mapbox / OpenStreetMap)

Introduction

In June 1922, on the occasion of its seventy-fifth anniversary in print, the *Chicago Tribune*, the leading daily paper in the "Midwest Metropolis," revealed plans for an architectural competition to design its new headquarters on North Michigan Avenue. Its goal was both simple and extraordinarily ambitious: the creation of "the most beautiful building in the modern world."[1] When the Tribune Tower—a soaring 470-foot Neo-Gothic skyscraper designed by John Mead Howells and Raymond Hood—was opened to the public in July 1925, scores of visitors besieged the building, gazing in awe at its steel-framed and limestone-clad exterior and vying to take turns in its high-speed elevators.[2] In the same year, Walter Strong, the recently installed owner of the *Chicago Daily News*, began his own efforts to construct an elegant new headquarters that would rival the architectural splendor of the Tribune Tower. Completed in 1929 and occupying an entire block of West Madison Avenue adjacent to the South Branch of the Chicago River, the Art Deco Daily News Building provided a similarly striking addition to the city's skyline.[3] Full-page advertisements printed in outlets such as the *Pittsburgh Press* declared that the combination of its "splendid location" and the "mass and form" of its twenty-six-story façade cemented the structure as another "masterpiece of this modern age."[4]

As architectural historians such as Katherine Solomonson and Thomas Leslie note, upon their completion, the Tribune Tower and Daily News

buildings stood as compelling examples of Chicago's dual status as an architectural center and media capital.[5] Beyond providing concrete evidence
of journalistic influence, their unveiling appeared to consolidate Chicago's
emergence as the nation's "Second City," a status that, over the previous half
century, had been carefully curated by the publications contained within
them.[6] Like other major American newspapers during the nineteenth and
early twentieth centuries, the *Tribune* and the *Daily News* sought to synony-
mize the character of their content with the character of their buildings,
utilizing the built environment as "a chosen instrument in the battle for
civic authority and public relations under the guise of public interest."[7] Accordingly, their opening was championed as a public good that would allow
each periodical to "render a greater service to Chicago" and simultaneously
reaffirmed the enduring relationship between journal and community.[8] Just
as these publications helped to write the city—or at least their own itera-
tion of it—into existence, so too did their headquarters work to reconcile
parallel histories of media and municipality, demonstrating, as *Tribune*
editor Robert McCormick declared, that their inhabitants were "truly part
of Chicago and merged with its destiny."[9]

And yet what might we discover if we reorient the intersecting histories
of Chicago's print media and built environment away from these familiar
edifices and toward more marginalized communities and media houses? After all, it was not to the city's leading dailies or their gleaming headquarters
that many of Chicago's Black residents first looked during the 1920s as a
means of orienting their literary and literal worlds. Instead, it was to the
South Side, home to the majority of Chicago's African American population
and the publications that served them. It was to sites such as the Chicago
Defender Building at 3435 Indiana Avenue, where, when it opened in May
1921, thousands gathered to hear publisher Robert Abbott discuss "the mys-
teries and problems of a modern printing plant."[10] It was to locations such
as the Overton Hygienic Building at 3619 State Street, home of *Half-Century*
magazine, or to the nearby headquarters of its successor the *Chicago Bee*,
each standing as "a monument . . . to negro enterprise" and an extension of
the tasteful editorial tone advanced by the publications they housed. It was
to these and other locations along the South Side's Black "newspaper row,"
which emerged in the shadow of the Tribune Tower and Daily News Building, but which provided tangible evidence of Chicago's significance as a Black
media capital and the role of its Black periodicals in shaping both the real
and imagined boundaries of the city's emerging "Black Metropolis."[11]

Tribune Tower Building, Chicago. (Library of Congress Prints and Photographs Division Washington, D.C.)

Moving these locations from the margins to the center, *A House for the Struggle* provides a dynamic rereading of the history of Chicago's Black press—a term I use here in relation to Black-owned and -oriented newspapers and magazines—through its connections to, utilization of, and relationship with the built environment.[12] At the heart of this analysis are two of the city's most influential and enduring Black media concerns: the *Chicago Defender*, one of the nation's leading Black newspapers, and the Johnson Publishing Company, best known as the publisher of *Ebony* magazine. The physical sites used and inhabited by these institutions provide the temporal and theoretical framework around which this study is constructed, beginning with the *Defender*'s inauspicious origins at 3159 State Street in 1905 and ending with the design, construction, and unveiling of, as well as the public reception to, the Johnson Publishing headquarters at 820 Michigan Avenue during the early 1970s. Building outward from this foundation, *A House for the Struggle* draws on a diverse range of Black Chicagoan periodicals and publishing enterprises, including the Associated Negro Press, the *Broad Ax*, the *Chicago Bee*, the *Chicago Whip*, the *Half-Century*, and *Muhammad Speaks*.

The central premise of this book—that the buildings of Chicago's Black press matter—is rooted in the literal and performative role of the many Black publishing sites that proliferated across Chicago throughout the twentieth century. When compared to the splendor of the Tribune Tower and the buildings of other white-owned or "mainstream" publications within and beyond Chicago, the structures used by the city's Black periodicals may have seemed inconsequential. However, as this study demonstrates, they loomed large in the minds of their publishers and patrons. Just as the Black press pushed back against racist characterizations of Black people in the nation's mainstream media and advanced the economic and political interests of their readers, so too did its buildings become their "own loud protest."[13] If Black journalists and the publications they created were soldiers without swords, then the buildings they inhabited were both castle and refuge: a sanctuary from the storms of racial injustice and a house for the struggle toward Black equality.[14] Concurrently, they functioned as arbiters of racial uplift and exemplars of Black cultural and economic power—as physical monuments to the rise of Black Chicago and "the upbuilding of the race in America."[15]

However, such grand performances and ambitions often sat awkwardly alongside the more quotidian form and functionality of Chicago's Black press buildings as well as the shifting editorial and ideological priorities of their owners and readers. As they struggled to navigate what Julius Taylor's *Broad Ax* described as "the very dangerous and perilous sea" of Black journalism, many publishers discovered that the buildings they inhabited did not necessarily provide a safe harbor.[16] Accordingly, the spaces inhabited by Black media concerns played host to and came to embody the highly contingent and heavily contested relationships between Black literary and cultural production, business development, civil rights, and urban politics across the United States. This was particularly true in Chicago, where African American migration and white backlash not only helped cultivate one of the nation's most rigidly segregated Black urban communities but also underpinned its emergence as the "undisputed business capital of Black America" and a major center for African American print culture.[17] Placing these stories in conversation, *A House for the Struggle* traces the history of Chicago's Black press through a new lens that has the potential to reshape our understandings of race, space, media, and the modern American metropolis.

Building the (Black) Press

The relationship between print and place has long been central to the development of the American press. For colonial-era newspapers, this relationship was predicated on the intersections of personal and professional space, with private homes and public houses serving as de facto editorial offices for many a budding publisher. The precarious nature of early print enterprises was as evident through their modest and constantly moving addresses as it was through their flimsy appearance and often fleeting circulations.[18] During the Revolutionary period, this spatial peripherality became a positive for some, helping to preserve the livelihoods of radical or dissident publications and their editors. By contrast, more established newspaper offices emerged as symbols of protest, important rallying points, and targets of backlash. The Boston offices of the *Massachusetts Spy* were a regular meeting place for the Sons of Liberty; British soldiers attempted to intimidate publisher Isaiah Thomas by marching outside the *Spy*'s building on Union and Marshall Street.[19] During the War of 1812, the offices of antiwar publications such as the Baltimore *Federal-Republican* came under siege, as critics expressed their discontent at editorial content by attacking the sites in which such content was produced.

A range of factors contributed to the rapid growth of America's newspaper networks, and newspaper buildings, throughout the nineteenth century. As the nation's population expanded westward, the formation of new towns created space for fledgling publications. These trends were abetted by new technologies: modern printing presses, steam railroads, and the electric telegraph. At the dawn of the century, the total number of newspapers in the country stood at around two hundred. By its midpoint this number had reached more than two and a half thousand.[20] Driven by the popularity of the "penny press," mass-produced tabloid-style newspapers gained enormous followings. Success provided the capital to upgrade style and space, and the transition from bulletin sheets to broadsheets was paralleled by the pursuit of increasingly impressive publishing headquarters. Building on the symbolic and communicative function of earlier locations like the *Spy* offices, the "singularly bold and striking" appearance of structures such as the New York Times Building at 41 Park Row became highly visible public landmarks.[21] As media historians such as Aurora Wallace and Julia Guarneri articulate, newspaper buildings provided evidence of past importance, current relevance, and future ambitions. Architecture played a key role in the battle for cultural and political legitimacy and bolstered claims to editorial supremacy. In short, the built environment "supplied a 'definable shape,' a hook on which to hang some news about the media itself."[22]

Beyond advancing the cause of individual publications, media buildings collectively reinforced the press's centrality to the development of the modern American nation. As the towers of the fourth estate overtook the spires of the first estate, this transition was seized upon as evidence of its newfound dominance as sources of authoritative information. Perhaps more importantly, just as media outlets helped to shape popular notions of citizenship, nationhood, and individual and collective identity, so too did their headquarters serve as "a delivery mechanism for notions of patriotism [and] nation building."[23] This role was canonized at the Philadelphia Centennial Exposition of 1876, where a dedicated newspaper pavilion celebrated America's status as a nation of news readers. In an accompanying catalog, detailed illustrations linked the significance of "some of the great newspapers of the day" to their headquarters. Thus, the role of the *Public Ledger* in promoting "the prosperity of Philadelphia and the welfare of its citizens" was tied to its office's status as one of the city's "grandest structural embellishments," while the contributions of the Boston *Daily Advertiser* in advancing "the interests of our great nation" were rooted in its "handsome building."[24]

These linkages between nation, community, and media building were not limited to native English-language periodicals but also included America's thriving ethnic press. While the content of foreign-language publications was organized around a shared heritage, they promoted American patriotism for the millions of European migrants who crossed the Atlantic during the nineteenth century.[25] In turn, ethnic periodicals utilized the built environment to advance claims for inclusion within American capitalist democracy. When the New York *Staats-Zeitung* moved to Chatham Street in 1858, its proximity to the English-language papers of Park Row was celebrated as the physical manifestation of its goal of cultural pluralism, while in the Midwest, the rebuilding of the Illinois *Staats-Zeitung* after the Great Chicago Fire in 1871 was celebrated as a testament to the combined power of German American enterprise and thought.[26] Just a few years after its offices were burned to the ground, the newspaper moved into an impressive new headquarters on the northeast corner of Washington Street and Fifth Avenue that reportedly melded modern American building techniques with the "chaste and massive style of modern renaissance" found in the great cities of Europe. Statues of American publisher and founding father Benjamin Franklin, and Johannes Gutenberg, the German inventor of the modern printing press, were placed above the two main entrances—ornamental flourishes that spoke to the dual "character and purposes of the building" and emphasized the *Staats-Zeitung*'s reputation as "one of *the* representative newspapers of this country."[27]

But what of the nation's African American print concerns? While the buildings of newspapers such as the Illinois *Staats-Zeitung* took their place alongside the offices of white-owned English-language dailies in the 1876 Centennial Newspaper Exposition catalog, there was no mention of periodicals catering to the concerns and demands of America's Black populace. This history can be traced to late 1826, when M. Boston Crummell, a prominent leader within New York City's Black community, invited a group of freemen to his home at 139 Leonard Street in Lower Manhattan. Huddled inside Crummell's residence, all agreed on the need for an organ to help combat the racial slights and stereotypes of the white press. The following spring, in the same year that New York finally abolished slavery, John Russwurm and Samuel Cornish released the inaugural issue of *Freedom's Journal*, the first Black-owned and -operated newspaper in the United States. The editors declared, "We wish to plead our own cause. Too long have others spoken for us. Too long has the public been deceived by misrepresentations in things which concern us dearly."[28]

As Roland Wolseley, Jane Rhodes, and other scholars of the Black press contend, these sentiments provided a blueprint for subsequent publications, with the Black press directed by a desire to defend Black interests and uplift Black concerns.[29] In the imagination of documentary filmmaker Stanley Nelson, Black publishers and their publications were "soldiers without swords," using the pen as a mighty weapon in the ongoing struggle for racial equality.[30] More broadly, Black periodicals offered a forum for debate and a critical space for representations of Black life and culture long ignored by white media outlets. Building outward from the work of German philosopher Jürgen Habermas, a growing body of scholarship has interrogated the role of the Black press in creating and curating Black counter-publics and public spheres. From this perspective, the Black press was not just a "fighting press" but a vital medium through which Black publishers could define and redefine key arguments about Black identity, restage debates around race and nationhood, and "reset the terms of public conversation."[31] In time, this role would position the Black press alongside the Black church and the Black school as one of the most significant institutions in African American public life.

The offices of *Freedom's Journal* were initially housed a short walk from Crummell's home at Five Varick Street, although by mid-1827 the newspaper was based out of the Mother AME Zion Church at 152 Church Street, half a mile closer to the Battery. This transition is an instructive example of the intimate connections between Black religious and print concerns; many early Black newspapers relied on the Black church as a vital ally in the struggle to establish an independent Black press.[32] The shared mission of print and pulpit to uplift the race was unified through sites such as Mother Zion, which became important spaces "for the purposes of social justice, political action, and identity formation."[33] Where publications were able to establish a degree of spatial and literary autonomy from the Black church, their offices continued to function as symbolic extensions of the Black press's role in advancing African American rights. Just as the editorial content of Frederick Douglass's *North Star* championed the cause of abolition, so too did its offices on Buffalo Street in downtown Rochester, New York, become a guiding light for fugitive slaves, where "early morning arrivals could be found sitting on the steps until opening time."[34]

Although Black print enterprises were dwarfed by mainstream press concerns, the acquisition of brick-and-mortar buildings gave notice to their growing influence during the aftermath of the Civil War. As literary scholar Eric Gardner argues, for newspapers such as the Philadelphia-based *Christian Recorder*, "walls and a door offered some protection from the outside world; such physical features made (slightly) safer spaces for the spiritual, the emotional, and the intellectual."[35] At the same time, the simple act of building ownership or inhabitation was a form of protest, helping to broadcast messages of Black pride and racial militancy into the world beyond the page. Perhaps nowhere was this more evident than at the *Richmond Planet*, a Virginia-based weekly headed by "fighting editor" John Mitchell Jr., where the masthead logo of a muscular Black arm holding a lightning bolt between a clenched fist was boldly reproduced on its building's façade.[36] This indelible link between "physical space and metaphysical mission" was welcomed by Black readers but also drew white backlash. The burning of media buildings provided a highly visible warning to other Black publications that threatened to unsettle the color line. At times, specific attacks on Black newspaper offices provided the spark for more widespread acts of white terrorism. In 1898 a white mob in Wilmington, North Carolina, burned the offices of Alexander Manly's *Daily Record*, precipitating a sustained assault on the city's Black community that left dozens dead and hundreds more homeless.[37]

Despite such dangers, Black periodicals, and their buildings, persisted. In Chicago the humble-origin stories shared by early Black publications were crafted into compelling narratives of racial protest and collective struggle. Forged in makeshift offices and rented storefronts, the homes of publications such as the *Defender* were indicative of the myriad challenges facing the city's fledgling Black community. Conversely, as this community rapidly expanded during and after World War I, the circulation and influence of Chicago's Black press, as well as the size and stature of its buildings, grew in tandem. If sites like the Tribune Tower had emerged as chosen instruments "in the battle for civic authority and public relations" by the mid-1920s, so too had the offices of publications like the *Defender* become powerful tools in the fight for Black representation and equal rights.[38] When the paper moved into its new headquarters on Indiana Avenue in 1921, the event was celebrated as a tremendous victory for "the race." A little under four decades later, its move to an even larger plant at 2400 Michigan Avenue was used by John Sengstacke, Abbott's nephew and successor, to reassert its role in the ongoing struggle for racial justice.[39]

The performative function of Chicago's Black press buildings—as symbols of racial uplift, Black protest, and community advancement—would be most dramatically realized through the opening of the Johnson Publishing Building at 820 Michigan Avenue during the early 1970s. An instantly recognizable eleven-story structure, the building was a striking home for leading publications *Ebony* and *Jet*, whose names were emblazoned across a huge billboard spanning the length of its roof. Its public unveiling was seen as a testament to the company's status as the nation's largest Black publishing enterprise and Chicago's enduring role as "the black publishing capital of the world."[40] More significantly, 820 Michigan Avenue reified the self-appointed role of Johnson Publishing and its magazines as "a vehicle for building and projecting the image of Black people in America."[41] The combination of its bold exterior façade and lavish interior design led publisher John H. Johnson to label the plant "a poem in marble and glass which symbolizes our unshakable faith that the struggles of our forefathers were not in vain."[42] Former *Ebony* editor Eric Easter reiterates this sentiment, describing the building as "its own loud protest—a visual pronouncement that black America had arrived in all its striving, outrageous, hip and fashionable glory."[43]

Building the (Black) Metropolis

More than a totem for cultural and political power, media buildings are often closely connected to the broader role of media enterprises in shaping the boundaries of public debate and, indeed, of the city itself. Newspaper offices have long served as centrifugal sites that draw in people and information.[44] Through the use of bulletin boards and other communicative displays, media buildings attracted huge crowds and complemented the periodical's material presence on the city streets. In doing so they enforced and expanded the role of their inhabitants in crafting Benedict Anderson's "imagined community" and curating the contours of urban life.[45] Some publications explicitly embraced their buildings' role as a public square by integrating communal spaces into their design. This included the *Chicago Daily News*, whose Madison Street headquarters became the first private building in the city to incorporate a public plaza.[46] Concurrently, media buildings operated as centripetal sites from which information and ideas were disseminated outward.[47] Across the country, newspaper offices became crossroads where a range of different political networks and social ecosystems converged, while neighborhoods such as Park Row in New York City emerged as "central site(s) in the urban cultural geography of communications."[48]

Proximity to major political, civic, communicative, and transport centers such as city hall or the telephone exchanges on Nassau Street not only offered a practical advantage for publications like the *New York Times*; they also reinforced the relationship between media buildings and the making of the modern American city. As media theorist Scott Rodgers notes, newspapers are both urbanized and urbanizing machines "with an unpredictable gravitational push and pull on city life."[49] Within the context of Chicago, the construction of the *Daily News* and *Tribune* buildings helped to affirm the primacy of the Loop—the downtown business and entertainment district that dominated the pages of the city's daily press and on whose northern and western boundaries these buildings respectively sat—as the organizing axis around which its cultural and political life rotated. North Michigan Avenue proved an ideal location for the *Tribune*, one that provided an opportunity to remake the surrounding neighborhood in its own image.[50] Similarly, the construction of the *Daily News* headquarters was part of a larger plan to advance the South Branch of the Chicago River as a civic asset, providing a literal example of the newspaper's power to reshape the city's geography and reflecting editorial efforts to link Chicago's urban core with its expanding suburbs.[51] Following the building's completion, publisher Walter Strong noted that "its site is focal. . . . Sixty-five thousand suburbanites pass through The Chicago Daily News concourse twice daily. . . . Like the great journal it houses, it is a monument to service rendered and a pledge of greater service to come."[52]

However, away from the bustling confines of the Loop, Chicago was a city less defined by "the architecture of utopian universality" than by its reputation as an urban jungle where densely knit ethnic communities struggled for survival.[53] This was particularly true on the South Side, which by the 1920s had become the focal point for Chicago's African American community. At the turn of the twentieth century, Chicago's Black population numbered around 30,000, a figure that represented less than 2 percent of the city's total population. Three decades later, Southern migration had seen this population swell to nearly 250,000 and its share of the city's population quadruple.[54] As the African American presence in the "Midwest Metropolis" expanded, it became more geographically prescribed. While earlier

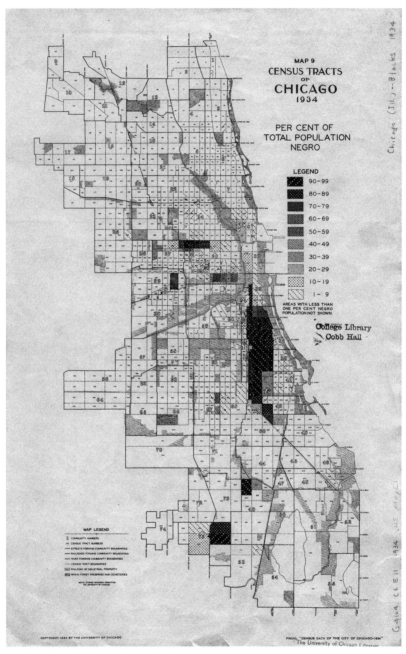

Census tracts of Chicago, 1934. Percent of total population Negro. (Social Science Research Committee, University of Chicago)

generations of Black residents had settled with relative freedom, restrictive housing covenants and white violence ensured that by the early 1930s the overwhelming majority of Chicago's Black population was contained within a thin strip of land stretching from around Twenty-Sixth Street to the lower boundary of Washington Park at Sixtieth Street and from the railroad lines west of State Street to the eastern border of Cottage Grove Avenue. Outlining the emergence of this "Black Metropolis" in their landmark 1945 study of the same name, African American sociologists St. Clair Drake and Horace Cayton described a community of dizzying contrasts, at once "an impoverished ghetto" and a vibrant city within a city "boasting its own cultural and economic institutions, its own business, professional and political leadership, and its own intellectual and artistic elite."[55]

And yet, as journalist Clarence Page attests, this complexity was largely forsaken by the daily press's representation of "the other Chicago."[56] Even before Black in-migration began in earnest, the *Tribune* had helped to popularize a pejorative name for the South Side's emerging racial enclave, where "the great majority are either coffee-colored [or] out and out smoky."[57] Initially restricted to a section of the Rock Island and Lake Shore railway tracks that lay between Sixteenth and Thirty-First Street, the newspaper's description of the "Black Belt" would expand in tandem with Chicago's African American community, coming to include any of the predominantly Black neighborhoods south of Eighteenth Street. The reductive term was synonymous with notions of racialized urban pathology, as the *Tribune*'s columns detailed an area "thickly infested" with crime and populated by Black slums.[58] Perhaps no event would reveal the fraught boundaries of these different Chicagos more than the destructive race riots of 1919, when the *Tribune*'s sensational coverage detailed how white mobs "intended to 'wipe out' the Black Belt" altogether, just as "the Loop had been denuded of Negroes."[59]

While Drake and Cayton hoped that an upswing in Black migration into Chicago during World War II would help Chicago's racially distinct cities converge into a "complete democracy" where "all their counterparts are intertwined and interdependent," the residential and business segregation that had framed the early development of the Black metropolis expanded instead. In his 1983 study, *Making the Second Ghetto*, Arnold Hirsch tracked the proliferation of "massive black ghettos" during the years following World War II, which were aided, not abetted, by large-scale urban renewal and the efforts of Chicago's white business and political elite to remake the city.[60] For historians such as Hirsch, Allan Spear, and Thomas Lee Philpott, this trend was linked to a longer history of African American social and political incarceration within the Black Belt. Such sentiments reflected a broader preoccupation with the so-called urban crisis by postwar social scientists, one that built on earlier characterizations of the Black Belt by the city's daily press to focus on the "ghetto" as an organizing principle for twentieth-century Black urban life.[61]

However, more recent scholarship from writers such as Davarian Baldwin, Adam Green, and Anne Meis Knupfer has pushed back against this reductive preoccupation with the Black Belt or the "Black ghetto," not as an attempt to underplay the severity of racial oppression in the Windy City but instead as a means to understand how segregation and racial injustice created a fertile climate for cultural and artistic expression that underpinned the emergence of Chicago's Black metropolis.[62] Similarly, scholars such as Christopher Reed and Robert Weems have eloquently traced the rise of a vibrant Black business and commercial sector on the South Side. While this activity arguably peaked during the 1920s—a period Reed describes as "the golden age of black business" in Chicago—the city's reputation as the "business capital of Black America" would endure well after World War II.[63] This was a terrain quite different from that presented through the pages of the city's daily press—a community defined not by squalid slums, abandoned homes, and delinquent lots but by thriving networks of Black banks, funeral homes, publishing concerns, and other race enterprises.

Linking such work to that of scholars such as Andrea Burns, Clovis Semmes, and Jeffrey Aaron Snyder, who have explored how institutions such as Black museums, Black theaters, and Black schools became "the lodestars of black communities," *A House for the Struggle* demonstrates how the practical role of Chicago's Black media buildings stretched far beyond their prescribed function as production sites for Black print.[64] Echoing the role of mainstream media edifices, the offices of Black publications became centrifugal sites that drew things and people in. Just as absconders from slavery had congregated on the steps of the *North Star* building, so too did many Southern Black migrants, following the clarion call of Robert Abbott's publication, make a beeline for the *Defender*'s offices after their arrival in the Windy City. The newspaper actively promoted such visits, inviting one and all to complete a "pilgrimage of gratitude" to its headquarters.[65] Similarly, journalist Carl Sandburg highlighted the development of a Black "newspaper row" along the State Street corridor south of Thirty-First Street, a spatially concentrated "propaganda machine that directs its appeals or carries on an agitation that every week reaches hundreds of thousands of people of the colored race."[66]

As the circulation and influence of Chicago's Black press grew, the civic function of its buildings expanded. By the 1950s the offices of enterprises such as the *Defender* and Johnson Publishing had become important political and activist hubs, community centers, art galleries, educational institutions, and tourist attractions: vibrant public squares that complemented the Black press's role in the creation of Black counter-publics and public spheres. In this regard, Chicago's Black media buildings functioned as "free spaces"— a term used by Andrea Burns to describe locations where "marginalized groups can acquire greater self-respect, strengthen their sense of dignity and independence, and work toward a heightened sense of communal and civic identity."[67] Yet at the same time, the location, usage, and appearance of Chicago's Black media buildings remained heavily prescribed—not only by restrictive housing covenants; discriminatory business practices; and the quotidian politics of race, class, and gender but also by the aesthetic choices and editorial philosophies of the Black media barons who controlled them. Thus, Chicago's Black media buildings simultaneously functioned as spaces of a different kind—first, as spaces of regulation (for the heavily mediated visions of Black identity, modernity, and respectability produced through the publications they housed) and, second, as spaces of resistance (for internal agents and outside agitators who challenged the editorial message or philosophical vision these buildings came to embody).

More broadly, the visibility of Chicago's Black press buildings intersected with the role of their periodicals in shaping the real and imagined geographies of the African American city. As *A House for the Struggle* makes plain, Chicago's Black press helped to write new landscapes of Black urban life into existence. Through their editorial content, advertising features, and opinion pieces, Chicago's Black periodicals documented and helped to direct what Baldwin describes as the "larger spatial transformations, class conflicts, and ideological struggles that took place in both the physical and conceptual space of the emerging Black Metropolis."[68] If the "South Side" was a relatively neutral geographic description and the "Black Belt" conjured images of Jim Crow segregation moved north, then "Bronzeville"—a name coined by the *Bee* and popularized by the *Defender*—became synonymous with cultural vibrancy, political agency, and "community pride and self-definition."[69] In this regard, we can connect Chicago's Black periodicals and their buildings with the efforts of Black writers and intellectuals to remap the city and retheorize the relationship between artistry and place—something that arguably reached its apex during the 1930s and 1940s alongside the rise of Chicago's Black Renaissance.[70]

Perhaps most provocatively, the relationship between Chicago's Black press and the built environment provides space within which to both extend and critique scholarly efforts to read the Black metropolis as "a site of creativity, rather than constraint: a space of imagination as much one of brute fact."[71] As *A House for the Struggle* illuminates, Chicago's Black press sat at the intersection of two contrasting, if not necessarily contradictory, narratives: the city's status as a Black business and media capital and its reputation as the most segregated city in America. In turn, the buildings they inhabited provided evidence of Black creativity and a reminder of continued restraint. Even as they offered concrete symbols of African American social and economic mobility, their inherent staticity pressed against the city's constantly shifting racial geography, rendering these structures a fascinating but ultimately flawed lens through which to critique the relationship between Chicago's Black communities, the periodicals that claimed to represent them, and the city that surrounded them.

On Structure and Speculation

A House for the Struggle is split into six broadly chronological chapters. Chapter 1 focuses on the early development of the *Chicago Defender*, which began life in the State Street home of Henrietta Lee, the landlady of publisher Robert Abbott. Unable to afford an office of his own, Abbott relied on Lee's patronage, with her residence serving as the *Defender*'s home for more than fifteen years. These intersections of domestic and professional space helped to cement the *Defender*'s reputation as a "community" newspaper and led to the gradual annexation of Lee's abode. However, by the end of World War I, the disparities between the newspaper's living arrangements and its self-anointed role as the "world's greatest weekly" had become too obvious to ignore. Accordingly, chapter 2 begins with the *Defender*'s move to Indiana Avenue, a moment that affirmed its status as the nation's leading Black newspaper and the South Side's emergence as a booming Black metropolis. Just as the *Defender* sought to center its new offices within Black Chicago's literary and literal worlds, so too did its competitors utilize architecture to undermine the *Defender*'s reputation and increase their own visibility. This included the *Half-Century* and the *Bee*, publications associated with leading Black businessman Anthony Overton, whose editorial appeals to Black middle-class respectability were embodied in their elegant building façades.

Chapter 3 examines the early development of the Johnson Publishing Company. Launching his first magazine, *Negro Digest*, out of a corner office of the Supreme Liberty Life Insurance Building at 3501 South Parkway, publisher John H. Johnson climbed the print and property ladder throughout the 1940s, finally securing a noteworthy headquarters at 1820 Michigan Avenue at the end of the decade. The difficulties Johnson faced during the building's acquisition provide a reminder of the rampant discrimination that continued to affect Black businesses but also helped to bolster Johnson's reputation as a Black publisher who would stop at nothing to "succeed against the odds." However, when the *Defender* announced that it had purchased a nearby site during the mid-1950s, the move appeared to place greater distance between Chicago's premier Black print institutions and the heart of the local Black communities they ostensibly served. Chapter 4 explores how, in an attempt to mediate their move away from the shifting center of the Black metropolis, both enterprises championed their new offices as important civic sites for Black people within (and increasingly beyond) Chicago. As exhibition spaces, social hubs, and tourist hotspots, 2400 Michigan Avenue and 1820 Michigan Avenue expanded Abbott's longstanding dream for Black media buildings to be "the meeting place of all the people."[72]

Chapter 5 details how the coalescing civil rights movement impacted Chicago's Black media buildings and the editorial content of its publications. The *Defender*'s move to Michigan Avenue was designed to provide better coverage of, and evidence of its support for, the Black freedom struggle.[73] This came to bear in a more literal sense than anticipated: cohabitation by the Chicago Urban League placed it on the physical as well as editorial front lines of the movement. However, the building's status as a house for the struggle was complicated by ongoing squabbles over labor politics and editorial direction that threatened to split the newsroom. Similar tensions engulfed the offices of Johnson Publishing, where the arrival of more progressive contributors disrupted the everyday politics of the workplace and the editorial content of the company's magazines. Externally, a series of pickets highlighted how the public visibility of Black media buildings could be strategically used to critique the literary and cultural politics of the publications they housed. At the same time, the growing influence of Black radical publications such as the *Black Panther* and *Muhammad Speaks* reflected the shifting ideological terrain of the Black freedom struggle and threatened to once more reshape Chicago's Black literary landscapes.

Chapter 6 focuses on the design, construction, and unveiling of, and the public reception to, the Johnson Publishing headquarters at 820 Michigan Avenue. Against the backdrop of a peak in Black radical activism during the late 1960s and early 1970s, the building's completion was celebrated by both white politicians and some Black leaders as a constructive (rather than destructive) form of Black Power. Through features such as its extensive Black art collection, a "Soul Food" Canteen, and a research library for Black culture and history, 820 Michigan Avenue appeared to fulfill a diverse range of civic duties, representing a progressive merging of Black business acumen, media production, and corporate responsibility. To Johnson it was a house that triumphantly proved "the struggles of our forefathers were not in vain."[74] However, the building's interior design and layout reinforced institutional gender hierarchies and Johnson's rigid leadership style, while its lavish amenities and downtown location revealed widening fractures between lower- and middle-class African Americans on both a local and national scale. For some detractors, the building was not "its own loud protest" but an empty shrine to Johnson's status as a Black publishing patriarch and to the false promise of Black capitalism and the self-invested desires of the Black bourgeoisie.

Although this study ends during the mid-1970s, readers should not interpret this as an endpoint for Chicago's Black press or its buildings. To be sure, the fortunes of many Black periodicals faded during the latter decades of the twentieth century, and more recent economic and technological upheavals continue to exact a heavy toll on Black publications. However, while disparaged in some quarters as "an outdated protest medium," the Black press remains a vital weapon in the ongoing fight for racial equality.[75] In turn, we need only look to the role of Black press buildings in the creation of the historic Black Metropolis–Bronzeville District during the 1990s, the *Defender*'s celebrated return to the South Side during the 2000s, or the furor surrounding the sale and redevelopment of the Johnson Publishing building during the 2010s to see the oversized role such sites continue to play in public debate.[76] Although it is beyond the temporal and theoretical limits of this book to discuss such case studies in detail, they offer ample opportunities to both complicate and critique the "rise and fall" narrative that continues to dominate Black press scholarship and to address the ongoing impact of and relationship between media consolidation, urban renewal, political activism, and racial and class inequity for Black communities across the United States.[77]

In building a history of Chicago's Black press buildings, I lean heavily on the rich archival collections and institutional knowledge of its public library system and staff—most notably at the Vivian G. Harsh Research Collection of Afro-American History at Woodson Regional Library and the Special Collections and Microfilm Divisions at the Harold Washington Library. My use of these collections is supplemented by research at other institutions, including the University of Chicago, the University of Illinois–Chicago, Chicago State University, the DuSable Museum of African American History, and the Chicago History Museum. Moving further afield, this project benefits from access to material housed at the New York Public Library, Emory University, the Library of Congress, the British Library, Atlanta University Center, Howard University, Duke University, and other institutions, as well as major African American oral history collections such as The History Makers.

I highlight these collections not simply to demonstrate the breadth of my efforts to reconstruct the building history of Chicago's Black press but also to acknowledge the limitations and challenges of such reparative work. *A House for the Struggle* does not claim to be a comprehensive account of the interior workings of Chicago's Black media buildings, the personal and professional networks they housed, or the everyday politics of the workplace. To be sure, I introduce an eclectic cast of characters here, whose experiences provide a fascinating and important insight into the development and day-to-day function of Chicago's Black press. However, this is a story that is less invested in the experiences of individual actors than how their actions contributed to, and helped to complicate, the broader framing of Black media buildings as critical sites in the real and imagined landscapes of Black Chicago. To adapt Adam Green's formulation, I am as much concerned with the roles of these buildings as sites of imagination as spaces of brute fact.[78]

This approach is partly directed by questions of accessibility. In some instances, such as that of Johnson Publishing, corporate archives are not accessible to the public. For other periodicals, archival material simply does not exist. In what Enoch Waters describes as perhaps the "great tragedy" facing scholars of Chicago's Black press, the archival holdings of the *Bee* were sold as wastepaper when the Overton Hygienic Company closed during the 1980s.[79] Such tragedies resonate outward from efforts to recover the histories of specific Black publications, speaking to broader issues of archival erasure and political marginalization. It is not difficult to trace a direct line between the lack of value prescribed to the artifacts of Black life and the lack of value prescribed to Black life itself—past and present, within and beyond the United States. To address such disparities, *A House for the Struggle* argues for the necessity of creative and occasionally speculative approaches to writing history that challenge the boundaries of the archive and the ways we examine and rely on documentary evidence—a reading between the bricks, as it were, as well as the lines.[80]

Furthermore, just as Julia Guarneri argues for the treatment of periodicals not merely "as historical records but also as historical actors, not just as repositories of information but also as instruments of change," so too can we consider the active role played by their offices in shaping the course of history.[81] In this spirit, we can identify other ways in which the buildings of Chicago's Black press matter: as institutional records, archival interventions, and archeological sites. In the case of the *Bee*, its building—now a branch of the Chicago Public Library—represents arguably the most enduring record of its original occupant's commercial orientation and editorial mission. For organs such as the *Defender* and Johnson Publishing, the built environment serves as an alternative archive through which to address the historical significance of these landmark Black publishing enterprises and their representation of, and relationship to, Black communities on a local, national, and international scale. From backstreet storefronts to custom-built corporate edifices, the spaces and places used by Chicago's Black media institutions offer fertile ground to assess the complex and highly contested histories of the publications that resided within them, the Black communities that consumed them, and the city that surrounded them.

1

A Card Table and a Kitchen Chair

In 1893 the world arrived on the shores of Lake Michigan. Coming a little more than two decades after the Great Chicago Fire, the Columbian Exposition provided an opportunity to celebrate the city's emergence, phoenix-like, from the ashes of disaster. Indeed, although the 1871 conflagration had destroyed much of central Chicago and left close to a third of its population homeless, it did little to slow continued expansion. The year before the fire, the U.S. Census had pegged Chicago's population at 298,977. By the eve of the exposition's opening, in May 1893, this number had swelled to more than 1.25 million.[1] The city moved upward as well as outward, with the fire providing Louis Sullivan, Dankmar Adler, and other proponents of the First Chicago School with an opportunity to craft a new urban land-scape centered on that most potent symbol of industrial modernity: the skyscraper.[2] Chicago's ascent was a symbol of the nation's broader capacity for regeneration. Less than three decades after the end of a devastating civil war, the 1893 World's Fair served not only as a defining moment in the history of Chicago but also as a key marker of the United States' emergence as a truly global power.

This ambition was dramatically embodied through the scale and scope of the exposition. As historian David Burg notes, the Chicago World's Fair took its inspiration from earlier gatherings, most notably the 1889 Paris International Exposition. However, while European expositions had seen cities such as London and Vienna temporarily transform their landscapes, Chicago went one step further to create "a veritable new city . . . not only larger than any previous exposition but also more elaborately designed, more precisely laid out, more fully realized, [and] more prophetic."[3] The exposition grounds, located in Jackson Park, seven miles south of Chicago's central business district, and overseen by leading urban designers and landscape architects Frederick Law Olmsted and Daniel Burnham, offered an alternative vision for what the modern city could be. It was a sprawling patchwork of Neoclassical and Beaux Arts design organized around the colossal Manufactures and Liberal Arts Building, reported to be "the largest building . . . ever erected under one roof." For many of the exposition's estimated 27 million attendees, it was nothing short of a miracle, a dazzling "White City" located alongside and within the Second City.[4]

However, while the exposition's characterization as the White City was primarily a reference to the gleaming exteriors of its grand buildings, it also gestured toward the fair's highly prescriptive racial and gender politics. President Benjamin Harrison neglected to include any nonwhite or female representatives among the fair's 208-strong board of commissioners, drawing the ire of prominent Black leaders and women's rights activists. Continued African American demands for representation, either as part of the fair's organizing committee or within the walls of the White City itself, were repeatedly denied. This exclusion stretched to employment; Black workers were shut out from all but the most menial of fairground jobs.[5] Accordingly, the modern city imagined by the exposition's organizers "constructed civilization as an ideal of white male power," with its coded architecture underpinning a vision of the future organized around "the advanced racial power of manly commerce and technology."[6] For many African Americans, then, the White City stood not as a symbol of American progress but of continued oppression, with its stucco-like façades mirroring the determination of its organizers "to keep the fair personnel and exhibits white."[7]

This appearance was rendered even more stark by its contrast with the Midway Plaisance, a narrow, one-mile-long avenue between Fifty-Ninth and Sixtieth Street that connected the western boundary of Jackson Park to the eastward perimeter of Washington Park. A privately sponsored extension of the exposition, the Midway offered a plethora of "ethnic amusements" ranging from mock South Sea Island villages and West African settlements to a Moorish palace. Here, away from the "quiet and good order" of the

White City, was the opportunity to see "people of every hue . . . to listen to their barbaric music and witness their heathenish dances."[8] Chicago's daily newspapers eagerly documented each new addition, helping to further fetishize the racialized spectacle of the Midway for their predominantly white audiences. Particular fascination was reserved for those of African descent, with the *Tribune*'s coverage of arrivals from Dahomey helping to reinforce the racial otherness of both the "genuine Africans" and their African American brethren: "Black as the shades of night . . . they shivered from the cold, raw air and groaned along under heavy trunks which they balanced on their heads with as much skill as the Southern negroes 'tote' smaller bundles."[9]

Against this backdrop of racial exclusion by the fair's organizers and racist representation by the mainstream press, African Americans used their own publications to debate the exposition's merits. While earlier Black periodicals had found their way to Chicago, the city's first "native" African American newspaper was the *Conservator*, founded in 1878 by Black attorney Ferdinand Lee Barnett. As historian Christopher Reed writes, the *Conservator* marked "a major institutional advance in black Chicago's communal maturity," providing an important voice for the city's growing African American populace.[10] Other publications followed, including homegrown institutions like the *Chicago Advance*, as well as local editions of newspapers such as the *Indianapolis Freeman* and the *Western Appeal*.[11] By the time the Columbian Exposition opened its doors, Chicago had cemented its reputation as a small but lively center for African American print culture. Local Black newspapers described the fair as "the great American white elephant," critiqued problematic representations of the Midway issued by white dailies, and remained alert to potential instances of racial discrimination.[12]

The fair also drew the attention of leading Black activists and journalists like Frederick Douglass, the legendary abolitionist and social reformer, and Ida B. Wells, an intrepid young African American reporter whose strident antilynching editorials in the *Memphis Free Speech* provoked the ire of white opponents.[13] In 1892, after Wells had attacked "the old threadbare lie that Negro men rape white women," a white mob destroyed the newspaper's offices and threatened retribution if its editor ever returned to the city.[14] Undaunted, Wells continued her campaign on the pages of Black newspapers such as the *New York Age* before embarking on an international speaking tour. Upon her return to the United States, Wells headed to the Chicago

World's Fair, seeing the "ironic possibilities in forcing visitors, who came to celebrate the progress of white men, to confront the blood-lust of white lynch mobs."[15] Wells's presence helped draw further attention to the exclusion of African American achievements from the fair's exhibits, something that was reinforced by the physical marginalization of Black people within the walls of the White City.

These efforts found voice through a pamphlet that offered a counternarrative to the fair's erasure of African American achievement. Black newspapers helped to advertise and fund-raise for the endeavor, and Wells solicited the help of Douglass, who wrote the pamphlet's introduction; *Conservator* editor Barnett; and prominent Black journalist and author I. Garland Penn, whose landmark study *The Afro-American Press and Its Editors* had been published two years earlier.[16] Pointedly titled "The Reason Why the Colored American Is Not in the World's Columbian Exposition," Wells's pamphlet placed the blame for such oversight squarely at the feet of "the race which holds Negro life cheap, which owns the telegraph wires, newspapers, and all other communication with the outside world." Critically, if white control of communications was a root cause of racial oppression, the pamphlet intimated that Black media ownership could offer a strategy for racial advancement. Through his own contribution on "the progress of the Afro-American since emancipation," Penn celebrated the emergence of an independent Black press and stressed the need for African American publications to be "made in their own offices and on their own presses."[17]

Becoming a Black Newspaperman

If the Columbian Exposition brought Wells to Chicago, then other factors convinced her to stay. The journalist had grown close to Barnett, and less than two years after the exposition's conclusion, the pair were married at the Bethel AME Church on the corner of Thirtieth and Dearborn Street.[18] While their partnership was by most accounts a happy one, it was perhaps Chicago's potential as a Black print capital that ultimately persuaded Wells to settle on the shores of Lake Michigan. In her later biography, Wells described journalism as "my first, and might be said, my only love." She had already purchased a stake in the newspaper prior to her nuptials and recalled that "the following Monday morning, after my marriage, I took charge of the *Conservator* office."[19] Wells quickly became a vocal spokesperson for

Chicago's Black press and a mainstay in a "generation of black editors, politicians, business people, and ministers" who helped to drive Chicago's development as a thriving hub for Black print culture and political activism during the decades following the Columbian Exposition.[20]

Another figure in this generation who was present at the Columbian Exposition, albeit one who would not become a household name to Black Chicagoans for some time, was Robert Sengstacke Abbott, an ambitious young student from the Hampton Normal Institute in Virginia. During his time in Chicago, Abbott attended speeches by Douglass and Wells, with the latter's description of how a white mob destroyed her newspaper offices and drove her from Memphis leaving a clear impression.[21] Abbott returned to Hampton imbued with a new sense of purpose and convinced that Chicago "was the perfect place to realize his dreams."[22] Four years later he returned to attend the Kent College of Law, renting a room on Twenty-Seventh Street, close to the Dearborn Corridor south of Twenty-Second Street, which was quickly becoming the hub of Chicago's Black community.[23] However, Abbott's dark complexion and Southern accent limited his opportunities in the legal profession and his standing within Chicago's Black community, where clear divisions existed between an "old settler" class and more recent Southern transplants who allegedly lacked the necessary markers of Black respectability and refinement.[24]

Seeking new avenues for advancement, Abbott turned toward journalism. His ambition was a newspaper that would fight for Black rights and help to expose instances of racial injustice—whether it was across the segregated South or in what scholars now describe as the "Jim Crow North."[25] To this end, he sought inspiration from Chicago-based journalists like Wells, long admired as a "famed defender of the colored race."[26] He may have been stimulated by the creation of new and more militant Black publications, such as Sheadrick Turner's *Illinois Idea*, which began publication in 1898 with the slogan "Justice is what we advocate—more we do not ask—less will not content us," and Julius Taylor's *Broad Ax*, which, after its relocation to Chicago from Salt Lake City in 1899, gained notoriety as the most controversial Black newspaper in the city.[27] Abbott gave "considerable study and thought to the mapping out" of his publishing ambitions from his lodgings at 3159 State Street, where he had moved after graduating from Kent College of Law, and also gained valuable experience as a volunteer for the *Conservator* and other Black media concerns.[28]

By early 1905 Abbott was finally ready to begin his own publishing endeavor. He named it the *Chicago Defender*, an embodiment of his desire to see it become "one of the strongest weapons ever to be used" to advance the race.[29] Abbott's lofty ambitions were not matched by his finances, so his first challenge was to convince Harry Robinson, a part-time printer who operated a press at 3436 State Street, to publish his newspaper on promise of later payment. A second obstacle was securing office space, with Abbott seeking help from real estate agent George Faulkner, who was based at 2935 State Street. The publisher moved in his office "equipment"—in reality little more than "a folding card table and a borrowed kitchen chair"—and it was from this address that the first issue of the *Defender* was published in May 1905.[30] The paper's State Street address was listed in that year's edition of the *Colored People's Blue Book*, a local business directory published by the Celerity Printing Company at 4926 State Street, which identified the *Defender* as a "clean, newsy and reliable newspaper."[31] However, Abbott quickly fell into arrears and, with no other way of reducing his overhead, abandoned his office at 2935 State Street for the confines of his rented bedroom.

Abbott's landlady at 3159 State Street was Henrietta Lee, a woman who, despite not contributing a single word to the newspaper's pages, would do more than almost any other person to advance its early fortunes. Born in New Orleans, Louisiana, and raised in Columbia, South Carolina, Lee had moved to Chicago during the early 1890s following the death of her husband.[32] It appears that she moved into 3159 State Street not long before Abbott; the earliest mention of Lee's connection to this address I was able to find appeared in the *Broad Ax* in October 1903, and earlier city directories and census records list other locations on Dearborn Street and East Twenty-Eighth Street as her residence.[33] A prominent member of the Quinn Chapel congregation and the Hyde Park Women's Charity Club, Lee was part of a generation of "race women" who helped to direct Black social and political activism in Chicago during the first decades of the twentieth century.[34] With Abbott facing professional homelessness and the *Defender*'s potential cancellation, Lee allowed him to piece together copy at her address before taking it to the print shop to be made up.[35] While no formal record of their agreement survives—perhaps none existed to begin with—it was in all likelihood conceived as a short-term solution to Abbott's office situation. However, 3159 State Street would ultimately remain the *Defender*'s home for more than fifteen years, forming the bedrock for its unlikely transformation into the nation's most powerful Black newspaper.[36]

Abbott later recalled that the entirety of the *Defender*'s early copy was created on a folding table within the confines of his compact lodgings: "The small room in which I slept was, at the same time, office, composing room and parlor combined."[37] However, the publisher quickly convinced Lee to allow him use of her dining table and kitchen. As the *Defender*'s presence at 3159 State Street expanded, Lee appears to have established some basic parameters. For example, Abbott was reported to have been given access to the kitchen only "between breakfast and dinner times," while the telephone remained in Lee's name despite the growing number of calls intended for the *Defender*'s publisher. Nevertheless, the arrangement persisted as an ad hoc and decidedly amateur enterprise, with a lack of formal office equipment meaning that "an empty egg crate turned up on its end would be the improvised typewriter table or stand."[38] Despite such idiosyncrasies, Abbott and Lee were able to reconcile the building's dual function as personal residence and newspaper office, something embodied by Lee's decision to allow Abbott "a sign on the transom of the door designating the place as: THE CHICAGO DEFENDER."[39]

A Golden-Starred Mother

It is possible to piece together some information about the *Defender*'s first significant home from city directories, census data, and other scattered details. The three-story red-brick building at 3159 State Street featured white stone trim and had been built in the early 1880s for an estimated five thousand dollars.[40] Like many of the surrounding buildings, it was a mixed-use structure, with apartments on the upper floors and street-level offices rented to local businesses. At the time of the *Defender*'s launch, this space was inhabited by Jacob Parks, an African American undertaker described by the *Broad Ax* as one of the city's leading Black public figures.[41] Abbott's bedroom was at the rear of the building's second floor, and Lee harbored a number of other lodgers, including Jennie Lineberger, a "fashionable dressmaker" and a prominent member of the Quinn Chapel congregation.[42] During the newspaper's early years, the State Street Corridor between Twenty-Sixth and Thirty-First Streets remained residentially and commercially mixed. In the 1910 U.S. Census, Lee's neighbors included a

Russian émigré family at 3157 State Street and the household of Justus Emme, a German immigrant and whiskey merchant who resided at 3143 State Street.[43] However, the neighborhood's demographic profile would continue to shift as Black Southerners followed earlier migrants such as Lee and Abbott north of the Mason-Dixon Line.

Beyond such anecdotal information, much about the *Defender*'s unconventional offices, at least during its early years, remains hidden. However, through Abbott's archival papers, the newspaper's coverage, and our own imagination, we can delve deeper into its daily usage and performative function. This begins with the role of Henrietta Lee, whose intervention quickly became central to a gendered corporate narrative of the *Defender*'s origins. Abbott framed the newspaper's founding in explicitly gendered terms, as a process akin to raising a child.[44] As the "father" of the *Defender*, Abbott made the kind of sacrifices expected of any responsible parent, beginning with his decision to abandon 2935 State Street and instead work from Lee's home under "the feeble, flickering light of a kerosene lamp."[45] *Defender* biographer Ethan Michaeli contends that the newspaper provided Abbott with "another mouth to feed when he could barely feed himself," with the publisher often skipping meals to ensure that he had money for ink and paper.[46] Such evocative descriptions frame Abbott's choices as a "grand Victorian gesture of self sacrifice" typical of early twentieth-century "race men" who claimed to subordinate their own desires, and even their physical health, for the collective advancement of Black people.[47]

If Abbott was his newspaper's so-called father, then Lee came to assume a role as the publisher's own "mother." In part this characterization was an extension of Lee's famed benevolence, a trait that saw her home given the nickname of "Wayfarer's Rest" and lauded as a "mecca" for those in need.[48] However, Lee certainly appears to have treated Abbott like a surrogate son after he moved into 3159 State Street. Abbott biographer Roi Ottley writes that beyond providing the publisher with an office space and ample encouragement, Lee "fed Abbott, frequently supplied him with carfare, [and] often patched his shabby clothes."[49] Retrospective accounts of the newspaper's early years asserted that "when the sun failed in its effort to cast cheer and warmth on the dreary world, it was 'Mother' Lee who had a kind word and a steaming bowl for editor Abbott."[50] Somewhat awkwardly, Lee was also characterized as the "Mother of the *Defender*," simultaneously inhabiting roles as Abbott's surrogate parent and his de facto partner in the "birth" of his newspaper.

Oedipality aside, Lee continued to play an important supporting role as the *Defender* acquired new readers and contributors. One of the newspaper's first regular staffers was Fay Young, a waiter on the Chicago and North Western Railway who earned Abbott's favor by bringing discarded newspapers to the *Defender*'s headquarters after his shifts. Soon, Lee's kitchen table was attracting an ever-increasing number of supporters, who lent their (largely free) labor and expertise to Abbott's fledgling newspaper.[51] In lieu of payment, Young and other *Defender* scribes were rewarded with Lee's hospitality. Young recalled, "We swiped her cookies, used her kitchen . . . [and] cooked lunch on her stove." Echoing Abbott's own characterization of the *Defender*'s matriarch, his editor purported that "we looked up on her as our MOTHER, and of course, felt that her home was ours." Later additions such as Lucius Harper, who would go on to serve as the newspaper's executive editor, arrived at its offices to find Abbott "in bathrobe and slippers" and Lee "in the kitchen cooking." After Lee's death in 1926, Abbott reiterated her role as a "golden-starred mother" who gently nursed the *Defender* "from a tiny infant into the gigantic masterpiece it is today."[52]

Lee's mythical status as the *Defender*'s "mother" was part of a well-intentioned effort by Abbott to celebrate her role in the newspaper's development. As the landlady who fed and clothed him, and as the homemaker who provided residence for both publisher and publication, Lee certainly appeared to play the part of the supportive mother and doting wife, a "womanly" role that helped to reinforce Abbott's own positionality as a race man. By so clearly defining Lee's role in the *Defender*'s development through this lens, the newspaper positioned 3159 State Street as the unification of two overlapping but distinct sites: a "commercial" space embodied by Abbott's publishing ambitions and a "domestic" space dominated by Lee herself. Yet this gendered lens understates the breadth of Lee's contributions as a businessperson and civic leader. As census records show, Lee's business experience, through her role as a landlady, predate the *Defender*'s formation. Similarly, her social and economic capital were just as important to the *Defender*'s early development as her words of encouragement and culinary exploits.

From this perspective, Lee's patronage can be read as a calculated business gamble, one that positioned her as the *Defender*'s de facto business manager as well as its matriarch. This reading acknowledges the broader ways African American women navigated the intersections of domestic and commercial space and the formal and informal economies of Black urban life, and their critical role in the development of Black business and print interests, even if such contributions were often minimized within a heroic narrative of Black male exceptionalism and by a preoccupation with the achievements of race men such as Abbott. Indeed, given Lee's proximity to the *Defender*'s makeshift newsroom and her demonstrable influence over the newspaper's founder, we may push this reasoning one step further to position Lee as a *publisher* of sorts. In her obituary the *Defender* noted that Lee was "a great teacher" to many of the newspaper's early staffers, and it is not hard to imagine how her advice stretched from "lessons in human kindness" to questions of content. In turn, Abbott's own paeans to "Mother" Lee offered glimpses of her potential editorial influence: "Many today who occupy prominent niches in the fourth estate owe their successes to . . . 'Mother' Lee."[53]

The Wolf Is at Each Door

Familial atmosphere notwithstanding, the ad hoc nature of the *Defender*'s headquarters was emblematic of the broader challenges facing Abbott as he attempted to find his place within the world of Chicago's Black press. While historian Kim Gallon suggests that Chicago "did not host enough African Americans to support a thriving black press" before the early twentieth century, this sentiment arguably downplays the ferocity of competition between the city's early Black newspapers.[54] Upon its relocation from Salt Lake City to the shores of Lake Michigan in 1899, the *Broad Ax* noted that it was entering into a "very dangerous and perilous sea of journalism."[55] By the time Abbott decided to set sail, these waters included the Chicago-based *Conservator*, *Broad Ax*, *Illinois Idea*, *Appeal*, *Leader*, and *Reflector*, alongside a host of smaller publications and out-of-town periodicals.[56] This scene was indicative of an American media landscape that had been transformed by the democratization and commercialization of the news during the last third of the nineteenth century. In 1870 there were around six thousand newspapers in the country. By the beginning of the twentieth century, this number had rocketed to more than twenty-two thousand.[57]

The challenges facing Abbott were not simply of competition but also of class and capital. By attempting to cast the *Defender* as a commercially minded and politically independent institution, the publisher could not rely on the patronage of prominent Black leaders like Booker T. Washington, the head of the Tuskegee Institute in Alabama and perhaps the nation's most recognizable Black spokesperson, who briefly subsidized the *Chicago Leader*. Nor could he depend on the financial support of Black religious or fraternal organizations which had proved vital to the success of many nineteenth century Black newspapers.[58] Furthermore, whereas the professional and social standing and institutional connections of well-heeled publishers like the *Conservator*'s Ferdinand Lee Barnett allowed them to offset operational expenses, Abbott began his enterprise with little more than the clothes on his back. This economic precarity was emphasized by the *Defender*'s "dark" and "dingy" interiors, which paled alongside the "elegant quarters" of rival publications like the *Appeal*.[59] We can picture the chaotic scene in Lee's home, where Abbott and his small band of allies attempted to churn out copy amid bubbling pots and pans and the comings and goings of other lodgers and Lee's society friends. Further distraction arrived in the form of the Gale Piano Company, which moved into the first-floor offices of 3159 State Street.[60] The *Defender*'s living arrangements did little to inspire confidence in its future, with the paper noting that "the colored newspaper outlook in Chicago is something fierce . . . the wolf is at each door."[61]

As if to counteract the peripherality of his publication and the obscurity of its offices, Abbott sought to make himself a visible feature of the South Side's physical terrain. During the newspaper's early years, Ottley writes, the publisher was "his own newsboy."[62] Abbott pounded the streets daily, personally delivering the newspaper to customers "in State street saloons, Dearborn street churches and Federal street homes."[63] Although the city's trolley car service passed directly outside 3159 State Street, Abbott's meager finances meant he shunned public transport, save for his weekly trip to and from the printing press. As a result, the *Defender*'s initial circulation was in part limited by the distance that Abbott was able to walk from its offices. Before long, the publisher's daily rounds became something akin to a comedic ritual for many residents, who "stood by and scoffed" as he walked the streets. Imposed rather than chosen, Abbott's routine nevertheless helped to cement his and the *Defender*'s place within the daily lives of many Black Chicagoans, and such perseverance demonstrated his awareness of the intimate relationship between public visibility, journalistic place-making, and editorial prestige.[64] As historian David Henkin notes, "Newspapers were not simply simulacra of primary urban experience or abstract representations of the real spatial contours of the city. . . . They had a palpable material presence in the streets" that, if employed effectively, could be of significant strategic benefit.[65]

While 3159 State Street was far from an optimal working environment, the location proved to be useful in other ways, both to Abbott, in providing a spatial defense of his newspaper's relevance, and to us, in providing an instructive example of the city's shifting racial and media geographies. Many of the city's early Black newspapers had maintained downtown offices, including the *Conservator*, which began publication out of offices at 194 Clark Street before moving to 279 Clark Street, and the *Appeal*, which established offices at 180 Clark Street and subsequently moved to 325 Dearborn Street.[66] This clustering of Chicago's early Black print concerns offered both practical and strategic advantages, allowing journalists to cross-reference stories and providing the opportunity for competitive oversight. Concurrently, the location of Chicago's early Black newspaper offices, as well as their appearance on the city's downtown newsstands next to other Black periodicals, such as the *Indianapolis Freeman* and the *Cleveland Gazette*, reflected the (relatively) integrated nature of the city's small African American population during the last third of the nineteenth century.[67]

However, white resistance to continued Black in-migration prompted a hardening of the color line and the development of distinct Black enclaves around the city. By 1900 more than a quarter of Black Chicagoans lived in precincts that were over 50 percent African American, including a community in the Thirteenth Ward along West Lake Street and the "Eighteenth Ward Negroes" on the Near West Side.[68] The most notable of these enclaves stretched south from Twenty-Second Street along Dearborn and State, which by the turn of the twentieth century had become home to many of Chicago's most important Black institutions. This included congregations such as the Bethel AME Church, on the corner of Thirtieth Street and Dearborn, and Quinn Chapel, which moved into an impressive new structure designed by noted church architect Henry Starbuck at 2401 Wabash Avenue in 1892.[69] Other prominent landmarks included Provident Hospital, the city's first Black hospital, which opened its doors at Twenty-Ninth and Dearborn Street in 1891. Established by pioneering Black surgeon Daniel Hale Williams, Provident quickly became an important community anchor and a source of no little pride for Black Chicagoans.[70]

As Black Chicago moved, so did its papers. This began with some of the city's most venerable Black publications, as the *Conservator* shifted its base of operations from downtown to 2952 State Street and then to 3220 State Street several years later.[71] The offices of newer publications such as the *Reflector*, based at 2931 State Street, and the *Leader*, housed at 3245 State Street, followed suit.[72] Other sites included Edwin Faulkner's Afro-American news office at 3104 State Street, which by the *Defender*'s debut in 1905 was reported to sell more Black periodicals "than all of the other news dealers in Chicago combined."[73] To be sure, the *Defender*'s headquarters lacked the polish or political connections of the *Conservator*'s first State Street address, which also housed the Colored Democratic League, the "only Negro political headquarters in Chicago."[74] However, just as the *Defender*'s presence on the shelves of Faulkner's Afro-American news office alongside publications such as the *Conservator*, *Broad Ax*, and *Illinois Idea* helped to position it as a peer of more-established Black newspapers, so too did its spatial proximity to the buildings of other Black print concerns bolster Abbott's desire for the *Defender* to be taken seriously as a voice for the Black community.[75] From a different perspective, this cluster of offices marked the beginnings of what Carl Sandburg later described as a Black "newspaper row" along State Street, a geographically concentrated network of Black media outlets that became a mighty "propaganda machine" for millions of readers within and beyond Chicago.[76]

Along the Stroll

Perhaps most importantly, the *Defender*'s location at 3159 State Street positioned it close to the heart of the South Side's emergent Black business and commercial district. As white anxieties contributed to the enactment of racist housing covenants and zoning restrictions, the population density of Chicago's Black enclaves increased. By the turn of the twentieth century, the "Dearborn Street Corridor" had been prescribed a different name by the city's white media outlets, now being referred to as the "Black Belt," which conjured images of overcrowded tenement buildings and other racialized signifiers of urban pathology. It is certainly true that segregation and white racism funneled Black residents into some of the city's most dilapidated and congested neighborhoods. Conversely, it spurred the creation of new businesses and social organizations, inadvertently helping to create one of Black Chicago's most visible "corridors of opportunity and success."[77] The centerpiece of this corridor was the Stroll, a section of State Street that by the early 1910s stretched from around Twenty-Second Street to Thirty-Ninth Street. Here one could find a dizzying array of race enterprises, from theaters and restaurants to haunts considered less respectable, such as dance halls, saloons, and brothels. It was, as Davarian Baldwin attests, "the spatial articulation of New Negro intellectual life within the black metropolis vision."[78]

Abbott quickly recognized the Stroll's importance to the urban geography of Black Chicago. This began on the page, with literary scholar Elizabeth Schlabach contending that, thanks largely to the efforts of the *Defender*, the Stroll quickly became "the best-known street in African America," matched only by the legendary thoroughfares of Seventh and Lenox Avenues in Harlem.[79] In contrast to outlets such as the *Broad Ax*, which largely shunned entertainment news, the *Defender* championed the Stroll as the center of Black cultural and intellectual life, a "Mecca for Pleasure" that could be enjoyed by visitors of all class and racial backgrounds.[80] In addition to being spotlighted in regular stories on individual leisure spots and attractions along the Stroll, the thoroughfare featured prominently in *Defender* columns such as "Rambling About Chicago."[81] Later features included Columbus Bragg's "On and Off the Stroll," a column that was nominally focused on the district's theater activities but offered colorful updates on its many notable characters and institutions. Through such content, the *Defender* promoted the Stroll as a key site of community activism, social interaction, and Black pleasure.

At the same time, the *Defender* demonstrated a keen understanding of its role as a literary map that helped to both populate and police the geographical parameters of the Stroll and, by extension, the African American city. Accordingly, the *Defender*'s columns became a canvas on which to debate what Baldwin describes as "the space and meaning of the Stroll . . . a battleground over the three basic images of black primitivism, racial respectability, and leisure-based labor."[82] In some aspects of its editorial content, the *Defender* attempted to refute criticisms of the Stroll by white dailies and other Black newspapers as a hotspot for vice; its emphasis on "legitimate" Black consumer practices and marketplace autonomy helped to "re-map the Stroll . . . with alternate interpretations of enterprise, race pride, and respectability."[83] Concomitantly, the *Defender*'s pages frequently alluded to the district's more salacious forms of hospitality; for example, Cynthia Blair maintains that the State Street Corridor became a popular space for Black sex workers who strategically chose the location "as a way to profit from the lively traffic of amusement-seeking men."[84] Through such content, the *Defender* provided a compelling example of Black journalism as spatial practice and of the broader role of American journalists as cartographers and map-makers "who forge geographies of news."[85]

These editorial geographies were further complicated by the newspaper's advertising. Like the vast majority of Black periodicals during the early twentieth century, the *Defender* was unable to attract advertising from national outlets. Consequently, the bulk of its advertising content carried a distinctly local flavor and mapped out distinctly local concerns.[86] In some ways, such material helped to maintain and extend its efforts to uplift the South Side, as advertisements for "respectable" enterprises offered evidence of the neighborhood's civic potential. Geographer Phillip Gordon Mackintosh points out that advertising provided its own form of "social geographic information," with readers relying on newspapers to help identify "trustworthy fellow citizen-merchants" and better connect them to "both the city and city-system of commodities."[87] However, commercial demands often overruled editorial idealism, with large sections of advertising content promoting "undesirable" products or businesses.[88] Accordingly, the *Defender*'s advertising helped to construct "a new kind of city landscape," one that did not necessarily align with its expressed philosophical ambitions.[89]

Such contestations reflected not only the *Defender*'s complex navigation of editorial and commercial space but also its dual identity as an outlet for literary and visual representations *of* the Stroll and its physical residency *on* the Stroll. The newspaper's offices at 3159 State Street were just a few minutes away from cultural landmarks such as the Pekin Theatre on the corner of Twenty-Seventh and State Street, and the Dreamland Café at 3520 State Street, a "new and magnificent hall" that opened in 1914 and featured an eight-hundred-capacity dance floor.[90] Other, less reputable hotspots included the Elite Café at 3030 State Street and Hugh Hoskins's Iowa Club saloon at 3161 State Street, which gained a reputation as one of "the principal gambling places in the district."[91] At times the *Defender*'s staff appeared to embrace the newspaper's role as a battleground over "the space and meaning of the Stroll" a little too literally; indeed, Ottley reports that Abbott outlawed gambling at 3159 State Street after returning to the office late one evening to find his colleagues "down on their knees shooting craps."[92]

As the *Defender*'s popularity grew, Abbott found new ways of taking advantage of the Stroll's "lively traffic" to enhance the visibility of both his newspaper and its offices, chief among them a growing band of young helpers. At the end of every week, dozens of schoolchildren filtered into 3159 State Street before being expelled in every direction with copies of the *Defender* in hand, dramatically expanding the sphere of influence established by Abbott's earlier slogs through "the snow, slush and mud; selling the newspaper to a reluctant, doubting audience."[93] With white newsstand operators often unwilling to stock Black papers, the *Defender's* newsboys formed a vital local distribution network that helped to increase the newspaper's public visibility and drive its circulation up.[94] Phil Jones, the paper's first newsboy, proved "particularly adept at getting the paper to newsstands [and] recruiting newsboys."[95] Conscious of their value, Abbott aggressively courted prospective new recruits with the promise of "big money" and an editorial profile if they succeeded in selling one hundred copies.[96]

Other promotional and distribution strategies included the *Defender's* delivery wagon service, a fleet of horse-drawn carriages that prominently displayed the address of its State Street offices on their exterior as they moved along and beyond the Stroll. The *Defender* championed its wagon service as the only one of its kind among the nation's Black press and regularly printed wagon itineraries so that readers could track their progress through the city. Along with the newspaper's advertising and editorial content, the restaurants, shop fronts, barbershops, and news depots listed in the *Defender's* weekly wagon detail provided another way of mapping the South Side's business and commercial district.[97] Before long the service had been upgraded from horse-drawn carriages to automobiles, with the newspaper inviting readers to "watch them as they dash through the city Friday evening and Saturday."[98] Regardless of their choice of horsepower, the wagons' inevitable return to 3159 State Street reinforced the site's growing prominence within the geographies of Black urban life that were mapped and remapped across the *Defender's* own pages.

Indeed, if judging by the *Defender's* content, it would appear that every road in Black Chicago led to the intersection of Thirty-First and State Street, just a few meters away from its own offices. It was to this location that "congenial souls in all walks of life" were reportedly drawn for social interaction and civic debate, like "a bag of shot drawn to a powerful magnet."[99] Capitalizing on its closeness to this "festival center around which the colored population of Chicago revolve," the *Defender* connected the importance of Thirty-First and State Street as a public square, and the closeness of its headquarters to this site, to its own communicative value as

Newsboy selling the *Chicago Defender*. (Jack Delano /
Office of War Information, Library of Congress Prints
and Photographs Division)

a shaper of Black urban life.[100] The *Defender* implored its readers to "call in
and see us—your interests are naturally ours, for we represent the people."
Of course, such invitations were not without practical benefit. Like other
Black publications, budget restraints meant the *Defender* relied heavily on
citizen journalists and the informational networks of everyday Black folk.[101]
Accordingly, when the *Defender* asked its readers to "call in and see us," it
was also a plea for audience participation in its news-making practice. By
making its "unpretentious quarters" as accessible as the streets of the Stroll,
Abbott consciously sought to embed the *Defender* within the city's Black
public sphere and to emphasize its role as a civic institution. "COME IN,"
the newspaper declared. 'The *Chicago Defender* is the people's paper and its
office this year will be the meeting place of all the people."[102]

The South in Chicago

By embracing its location, the *Defender*'s headquarters began to assume a greater role in the South Side's cultural and political geography. In the process, it transitioned from a space from which to catalog the Stroll's various landmarks to a public landmark in its own right. The most visible manifestation of this transition came through the arrival of Black celebrities at 3159 State Street, with office sojourns by notables like heavyweight boxing champion Jack Johnson becoming front-page news. Johnson had relocated from New York to Chicago a few years after the *Defender* began publication, purchasing a home at 3344 Wabash Avenue, and the newspaper celebrated his arrival as further evidence of the South Side's growing notoriety.[103] Johnson was happy to reciprocate this good feeling, visiting the *Defender*'s offices in 1910 to purchase a yearly subscription, where he praised the newspaper as a "public organ . . . ever ready to defend those oppressed."[104] Several years later the *Defender* enthusiastically welcomed the opening of Johnson's Café de Champion at 41 West Thirty-First Street, mere yards away from its offices. Other prominent visitors included Booker T. Washington, the famed "wizard of Tuskegee," who dropped in for a tour while in Chicago to visit his son.[105]

Such high points of excitement added color to the building's more quotidian role within the daily patterns of Black Chicagoan life, as the sporadic visitors of the newspaper's early years became a steady flow of traffic. Taking note of Abbott's exhortations, community members came "rushing into the *Defender* office" to relay information about personal achievements, family bereavements, and other local talking points.[106] Aside from its weekly troupe of newsboys, perhaps the most important regular visitors were the Pullman porters, who became a vital part of Abbott's efforts to gain readers outside of Chicagoland. Abbott had long admired the porters as upstanding members of the Black professional class, and the *Defender*'s offices became a popular outpost for railway employees bringing news from far-flung places.[107] By convincing porters to help distribute the paper on their sojourns outside of the Midwest, Abbott created the groundwork for the *Defender*'s emergence as a truly national publication and a militant voice for disenfranchised African American communities in the Jim Crow South. Another pool of recruits came from the ranks of "peripatetic vaudevillians," who dutifully reported to the *Defender*'s offices before setting out to tour the country on the Chitlin' Circuit.[108]

Such partnerships were not without risk. The Black press's role in confronting racial discrimination and anti-Black violence carried potentially serious consequences for collaborators working or living below the Mason-Dixon Line, and Black editors ran the risk of white reprisal if they chose to print the "wrong" kind of news.[109] Many white Southerners understood coverage of anti-Black violence as an attack on white communities, "not merely for the way it affected black readers but also for what it said about whites."[110] From this perspective, the "logical" white response to the efforts of Black newspapers to document racial oppression across the South was a reactionary attempt to restrict circulation, intimidate local distributors, and threaten Black editors and their places of work. The enduring threat of white supremacist violence led to at least two *Defender* distributors being killed and countless more run out of town. When whites could not direct their "justice" toward individual Black publishers or newspaper distributors, their attention turned toward Black media buildings, leading to arson and other forms of property destruction.[111]

The relative security of the *Defender*'s home location allowed the newspaper to speak out forcefully against white supremacy and anti-Black violence. However, as its influence in the South grew, white efforts to seek retaliation spread outside of the region and toward Chicago. In November 1911 the *Defender* printed a front-page article written by an unnamed correspondent that reported on a developing criminal case in the small rural town of Washington in northeast Georgia. After a local white planter named J. B. Hollenshead raped a Black woman who was in his store, the woman's husband, A. B. Walker, retaliated by shooting and killing her assailant.[112] Applauding Walker's willingness to defend his partner by gunning Hollenshead down "like the dog he was," as well as his abilities to escape a mob of would-be lynchers, the *Defender* used the incident as an opportunity to attack the well-worn myth of Black female hypersexuality by contending that "the majority of the white males of the south revel in the intimacy of our women."[113]

When incensed local whites received news of the *Defender*'s coverage, they hired the services of two Pinkerton agents, who traveled to Chicago to try to find whoever had approved the article's publication. The agents allegedly forced their way into 3159 State Street, where they "confronted Robert Abbott in the kitchen and threatened to haul the editor back to Georgia" if he refused to divulge the name of his correspondent. Abbott was able to stall the agents while a messenger boy frantically searched for reinforcements.

Help finally arrived in the shape of Edward Wright, an influential Black attorney and political activist, and George Cleveland Hall, the chief surgeon at Provident Hospital and the head of the Chicago Urban League.[114] Both men were known for their uncompromising demeanors, most notably Hall, who had developed a reputation as a "loutish and even physically belligerent" character based largely on a rancorous personal rivalry with fellow Black physician Daniel Hale Williams.[115] Abbott put this reputation to good use, gleefully recalling later that Wright and Hall "ran the Georgia 'gentlemen' out of the *Defender* office and finally out of Chicago."[116]

On another occasion, after the newspaper had published an unflattering editorial about a Southern judge, a "huge, red-faced white man wearing a wide-brim Stetson" and going by the name of Sheriff Moon strong-armed his way into Abbott's office and demanded to see the publisher. The quick-thinking Abbott informed the intruder that he was not the publisher but that the man he sought would be available if Moon returned later that same day. Once again Abbott turned to Hall, and when Moon returned and served the physician, instead of the publisher, with an arrest warrant, Hall dramatically tore the document to shreds and threw it into the trash, declaring, "This is Illinois. . . . You can't get away with that in this town!"[117] While likely embellished, such stories of the defense of Abbott's publishing offices (and, by extension, Mother Lee's abode) helped position 3159 State Street as a proxy site for the newspaper's own role as "a defender of the race" and reinforced its status as about a family concern and community institution, one that was to be protected at all costs.[118]

The close-knit relationship between the *Defender*'s early staffers, compounded by the intimacy of its makeshift headquarters, meant that while victories against white infringement were widely celebrated, losses were keenly felt and collectively mourned. Among the most significant during the *Defender*'s formative years was the death of managing editor J. Hockley Smiley in 1915. Black press historian William Jordan identifies Smiley's arrival five years earlier as "perhaps the most important step in the *Defender*'s rise," as the editor was responsible for overseeing key updates to the newspaper's design and content.[119] A flamboyant character both on and off the page—Allan Spear suggests that "the hard-drinking [and] foppish Smiley made up in imagination what he lacked in newspaper experience"—the editor helped to separate the *Defender* from the crowded ranks of Chicago's Black press and laid the groundwork for its transformation from "a run-of-the-mill black weekly into the 'National Journal of the Race.'"[120] In tribute the *Defender* printed a cartoon picturing Smiley's empty desk at 3159 State Street, signaling how the loss of his oversized personality would be felt spatially as well as editorially.[121]

Building the Race

Although Smiley would not live to see the *Defender's* golden years, his role in transforming the newspaper's content contributed to a massive boom in circulation during its third lustrum. At the time of his death, the *Defender's* weekly paid readership was less than twenty thousand. By 1920 its audience had grown by more than a factor of ten.[122] Much of this growth was driven by the newspaper's popularity outside of Chicago, where, despite continued white suppression, thousands of Black readers were consuming the periodical every week. Coverage of the Stroll and advertisements for jazz clubs and movie theaters excited and beguiled in equal measure; one Mississippian reader informed the *Defender's* editors that State Street appeared to be "heaven itself."[123] Concurrently, the newspaper's lurid accounts of white terrorism hardened the resolve of many African Americans to pursue new futures outside of the South.[124] This resolve aligned with demands for Black labor in the industrial heartland of the Northeast and Midwest, demands heightened by the outbreak of World War I. By the winter of 1916, close to a quarter of a million African Americans had left the region, prompting a spate of handwringing from Southern whites who feared the loss of an underpaid and exploited Black workforce.

While the *Defender* initially discouraged large-scale migration, it was soon championing the flight of Southern Black migrants as a "Second Emancipation."[125] In 1917 the newspaper launched a "Great Northern Drive," imploring one million African Americans to abandon the South for personal and economic security. To many, Abbott emerged as the movement's prophet; historian Florette Henri characterizes the publisher as a "black Joshua" determined to lead his people north.[126] For the scores of migrants arriving in Chicago every week, the *Defender* was a crucial guide—signposting key local addresses, highlighting important social institutions, and helping to reconcile the imagined Chicago mapped out on its pages with the real city that greeted newcomers.[127] In turn, the newspaper reported that, upon arrival, many African Americans made a beeline for its State Street offices, a pragmatic decision guided by the newspaper's importance as an indigenous information source but also a symbolic gesture reflecting its pivotal role in guiding their path north.[128]

Abbott reveled in the *Defender*'s newfound visibility, but the newspaper's reputation as a militant outlet, coupled with America's entry into World War I, placed the newspaper under a heightened level of scrutiny. Federal efforts to crack down on wartime dissent, enshrined through the Espionage Act of 1917 and the Sedition Act of 1918, provided immense power for government agencies to police radicals, immigrants, and ethnic communities under the broad charge of "disloyal, profane, scurrilous, or abusive language."[129] In his 2002 study *Investigate Everything*, historian Theodore Kornweibel extensively details widespread federal surveillance of the *Defender* beginning in 1916, when a white reporter for the *New Orleans Times-Picayune* passed on his concerns about the paper to the Justice Department's Bureau of Investigation. By the following summer, multiple federal agencies were keeping tabs on the *Defender*'s content and its "disturbing" influence across the South. Less than a week after America's entry into World War I, bureau director Alexander Bruce Bielaski instructed his Chicago office to begin a formal investigation of Abbott's paper.[130]

If the *Defender*'s headquarters served as a beacon of hope for Southern Black migrants, then the building would come to play a very different role in warding off accusations of impropriety from federal investigators. When summoned for an interview with federal agent J. E. Hawkins at the bureau's Chicago office, Abbott presented his paper as a conservative emblem of American entrepreneurship, relaying the story of "how he had begun the newspaper on his landlady's kitchen table with only a quarter."[131] After the Military Intelligence Corps had taken up the case, a representative was dispatched to 3159 State Street, delivering a thinly veiled threat to Abbott that the "eye of the government" was fixed squarely on his paper.[132] In a lengthy written response, the publisher reiterated the tale of its offices as evidence of the *Defender*'s uniquely American backstory before noting that money set aside for the purchase of a new press and building had instead been pledged to the Liberty Loan drive. Thus he was able to sell the federal government on a decidedly different building history, reconfiguring his offices as an authentically American tale of bootstrap entrepreneurship and evidence of the *Defender*'s commitment to national unity.[133]

While Abbott's riposte underscored the multivalent performativity of 3159 State Street, he was telling the truth about his plans for a new building.

As the *Defender*'s size and circulation soared during the war years, space became a pressing concern. A flurry of new employees placed the already overcrowded interiors of the newspaper's offices under increasing strain, and many staffers were forced to write elsewhere. This included theater critic Tony Langston, who maintained desk space in a local music store, and former *Chicago Leader* editor W. Allison Sweeney, who, in keeping with his role as the *Defender*'s war correspondent, produced his copy from a bunker-like basement office on Vernon Avenue.[134] The creation of new editorial and administrative departments exacerbated matters, including a complaints department, which, with no little sense of irony, was primarily concerned with the enduring problem of substandard housing.[135] On occasion, contributors such as Lucius Harper found themselves working from "an old weather-beaten desk that had been discarded on the back porch."[136]

Such anecdotes reveal the disparities between the *Defender*'s self-professed status as the "world's greatest weekly" and its amateurish living arrangements. However, despite its obvious failings, Abbott appeared curiously reluctant to leave 3159 State Street, something that can be attributed to both superstition and a genuine affection for the newspaper's "birthplace."[137] Instead, he expanded internally: by the time Harper was hired as a reporter in 1916, Abbott had commandeered Lee's kitchen as his personal office, and her children's bedrooms were also claimed by the paper after they vacated the property.[138] In 1918 the publisher made his most significant move yet, presenting Henrietta Lee with the deed to her own home at 3312 Vernon Avenue, a little less than a mile east of the *Defender*'s offices along Thirty-First Street. A tasteful two-story brick and stone house designed by local architect W. H. Drake and constructed during the mid-1880s, the building went some way to acknowledging Lee's role in the *Defender*'s success.[139] After her relocation, the newspaper quickly took over the remainder of 3159 State Street, which became the formal offices of the newly chartered Robert S. Abbott Publishing Company.[140] Abbott temporarily remained Lee's lodger at Vernon Avenue before his marriage to Helen Morrison saw the couple move into an attractive brick bungalow at 4847 Champlain Avenue.[141]

Riots and After

As the creation of the *Defender*'s complaints department demonstrates, the newspaper's growing pains were indicative of broader housing concerns facing Chicago's African American residents. Black migrants arriving in the city continued to be funneled into segregated neighborhoods characterized by aging infrastructure and unsafe accommodations. The *Defender* asserted that the condition of many buildings on the South Side was in direct violation of city safety ordinances, with "tenement buildings without proper lights in the hallways, without safe elevators, without proper fire escapes, and in some cases with no fire escapes whatever [*sic*]."[142] By providing regular coverage of the struggle for better housing, and by implicitly linking this struggle to the idiosyncrasies of its own office space, the *Defender* helped to create a shared concern with its readers, further reinforcing its status as a community paper. By contrast, the city's white dailies detailed the development of Chicago's Black community with a mixture of fear and disdain, describing the neighborhood between Twenty-Second Street and Thirty-Ninth Street as "without a doubt . . . the foulest spot in Chicago."[143] As World War I raged abroad, Chicago's daily press waged their own war at home against the ongoing "negro invasion," seeing the expansion of the Black population as an unwelcome encroachment upon the white city.[144]

Such incendiary coverage stoked a violent backlash. Beginning in 1917 and continuing into the early 1920s, the South Side was rocked by an average of one "race bombing" every three weeks. The majority of these bombings occurred throughout the enclaves immediately below Forty-First Street, as Chicago's Black professional and business elite migrated southward to take advantage of the attractive vistas and various amusements of Washington Park.[145] However, residential and business properties were targeted wherever there was a significant Black presence.[146] Although most bombings were designed to merely intimidate, some had fatal consequences. In February 1919 a powerful explosion at 3365 Indiana Avenue claimed the life of Ernestine Ellis, a six-year-old Black girl sleeping in her grandmother's apartment on the second floor. The *Chicago Tribune* reported that the blast awakened people for blocks around, and it likely shook the window frames and residents of 3159 State Street, located just a few hundred yards northwest.[147] The *Defender*'s proximity to the incident, as well as its deadly consequences, prompted a sharp response, with the newspaper arguing that local police officers were complicit in the attack. The *Broad Ax* went one step further, denouncing the white perpetrators of such "brutal and fiendish acts" and saying they should be shot on sight.[148]

The bombing campaign was indicative of growing racial tensions on a local and national level during the war years, as the expansion of Black urban populations across the country reshaped labor markets and redrew racial and demographic boundaries. In cities such as East St. Louis, Illinois, white terrorism escalated to outright insurrection, with a 1917 uprising against the city's Black community leaving dozens dead and thousands homeless.[149] The East St. Louis massacre was a harbinger for what was to come, as postwar demobilization and the onset of an economic slump stretched social tensions to the breaking point. Upon his return from the European theater, the prevalence of racist violence prompted William Hayward, the commanding officer of the famed Black infantry division known as the Harlem Hellfighters, to bitterly declare that "in view of the sacrifices the negro soldiers made in this war to make the world safe for democracy, it might not be a bad idea to make the United States safe for democracy."[150] During the "Red Summer" of 1919, race riots engulfed dozens of cities across the country, marking the most intensive period of racial conflict since the Reconstruction era.

In Chicago, the scene of some of the nation's most destructive riots, the spark came on Sunday, July 27. After a group of young Black boys had unwittingly strayed across the invisible boundary that separated the waters of segregated beaches between Twenty-Sixth and Twenty-Ninth Street, they were pelted with rocks by onlooking whites. One boy named Eugene Williams was struck and went under. When his body was pulled from the lake, Black bathers demanded the arrest of the white man alleged to have thrown the fatal stone. Tensions between the police, African Americans, and a gathering crowd of white onlookers escalated, leading to gunfire. By the evening of July 27, white mobs had begun to roam the streets of Black neighborhoods, vandalizing property, assaulting pedestrians, and pulling passengers from streetcars. African Americans fought back, including some members of the Eighth Illinois National Guard, housed at 3533 Giles Street, the first armory in the country built for a Black military regiment. Violent clashes occurred across the city, with many of the worst confrontations concentrated within a ten-block stretch of State Street between Twenty-Ninth and Thirty-Ninth Streets. Over the following week, scores of lives were lost and property damage ran into the hundreds of thousands.[151]

As rioting escalated, the city's white press played a key role in exacerbating tensions and spreading misinformation. The Chicago Commission on Race Relations, an investigative committee established in the aftermath of the uprising, found that coverage in both the *Tribune* and the *Herald-Examiner* significantly overstated the number of white casualties and understated

National Guard during the 1919 Chicago Race Riots. (Jun Fujita negatives collection, Chicago History Museum)

the number of Black casualties. Similarly, Chicago's white newspapers were quick to label an incident at the Angelus apartment house at Thirty-Fifth Street and Wabash, a white-occupied building attacked by a large crowd of African Americans, as the catalyst for heightened unrest, rather than earlier violence in the Stock Yards district and west of Wentworth Avenue.[152] In doing so, they framed the riots as spreading outward from the Black Belt rather than encroaching upon it, evidence not of an African American enclave under siege but of Black criminality and social disorder spilling beyond its prescribed borders. This sentiment was reinforced by maps published in the *Tribune* and other white dailies that identified the Black Belt as "the center of the trouble."[153] The commission linked this coverage to the reluctance of white reporters to enter Black areas, as the coverage provided by the *Tribune* and other white dailies was composed primarily from the safety of their downtown headquarters.[154]

By contrast, Chicago's Black journalists found themselves and their offices at the center of a war zone. Lucius Harper narrowly avoided injury after being caught up in the Angelus incident, while *Broad Ax* editor Julius

Taylor personally intervened to help protect pedestrians on the corner of Thirty-Fifth and Indiana.[155] With violence concentrated in the area south of Twenty-Ninth Street, *Defender* office girl Genevieve Lee repeatedly braved the "gauntlet of this perilous firing line" to transport copy between 3159 State Street and the *Drover's Journal*, the white publishing company that now printed the *Defender*.[156] As Abbott and his editors soldiered on, truckloads of whites raced along the street outside, "firing indiscriminately at the people on the sidewalks."[157] In the nearby offices of the recently established *Chicago Whip*, contributor Chas Allen and driver F. W. Harsh decided to chance a run from its headquarters at 3457 State Street and its presses in a white neighborhood "far removed from the 'Black Belt.'" On the way to the printers, gunshots splintered the windshield of their automobile. On the return leg they "once more passed through a hail of bullets," with one shot tearing a hole in Allen's overcoat and another lodging itself in a stack of freshly printed papers.[158]

Despite such peril, the offices of the *Defender* and other Black publications emerged unscathed, even avoiding the temporary closures forced upon local Black saloons and athletic clubs by police chief John Garrity as part of efforts to calm the city during the weeks following the riots.[159] On a personal level Abbott even benefitted from the unrest, as his appointment to the city's Commission on Race Relations helped to further bolster his status as a leading spokesperson for the Black community.[160] However, the riots also brought other issues to a head—most notably, Abbott's dependency on the *Drover's Journal*.[161] The company was located at 836 Exchange Avenue in the Union Stock Yard—a key battleground during the riots—and its white workers, fearing potential retribution for printing a Black newspaper, were reluctant to honor their contract with Abbott. In Roi Ottley's retelling, "a nervous atmosphere pervaded the plant" upon the arrival of Abbott's staff to check galley copies and to make final alterations: "When the rioting broke out before the *Journal*'s door, no amount of persuasion could bring the men of the plant to continue working on a negro newspaper."[162]

With few viable alternatives, Abbott was forced to negotiate a short-term deal with the *Gary Tribune*, a daily newspaper located in northwest Indiana, around twenty-five miles south of the *Defender*'s offices. The ensuing delay meant that for perhaps the first time in the newspaper's history, its subscribers received their weekly edition a few days late.[163] Abbott's relationship with the *Drover's Journal* would be patched up, at least in the short term. However, the incident was a timely reminder that as long as the *Defender* relied on a white-owned printing company, it was beholden to the whims and prejudices of white America. Just as earlier Black publications such as the *Christian Recorder* had seen control over the built environment as a means of creating "some protection from the outside world," so too did Abbott understand that true editorial autonomy demanded full control over the means and spaces of production and distribution.[164] Motivated by this knowledge, Abbott redoubled his efforts to find a new home for the *Defender*, one that would minimize his reliance on external partners, allow for future expansion, and finally provide a space befitting the "world's greatest weekly."[165]

2

A Monument to Negro Enterprise

Shortly before the outbreak of the 1919 riots, Swedish American writer Carl Sandburg began a series for the *Chicago Daily News* focusing on the living and working conditions of the city's African American community.[1] In his 2011 study *Red Summer*, author Cameron McWhirter indicates that Sandburg was one of a select handful of white journalists to provide a measured account of the discrimination facing Black Chicagoans before the riots occurred, offering a largely sympathetic account of systemic overcrowding, stifled job opportunities, and white resentments that ran countercurrent to much of the daily press's reporting on the "race situation."[2] Unfortunately, the series' breadth was largely lost during the aftermath of the unrest, with the reporter bemoaning that "as usual everyone was more interested in the war than how it got loose."[3] Beyond simply laying out the conditions that precipitated the riots, Sandburg's articles offered an in-depth introduction to Chicago's vibrant Black community: underemployed and under duress but home to an embarrassment of Black cultural and political institutions.

As part of his series, Sandburg detailed the influence of a Black "newspaper row" stretching south along State Street. At the head of this row were the *Defender*'s offices, a fitting location for "the dean of the weekly newspaper group." By the early 1920s, other sites included the offices of established publications such as the *Broad Ax*, which had relocated from 5040 Armour Avenue to 4700 State Street during World War I, as well as emerging race enterprises such as the Associated Negro Press, housed at 3423 Indiana Avenue; the *Chicago Searchlight*, based at 3420 State Street; and the *Chicago Whip*, which moved from 3457 to 3420 State Street following the 1919 riots.[4] These assorted locations were far less visually impressive than sites such as the *Chicago Tribune*'s soaring gothic edifice on North Michigan Avenue, which opened its doors in July 1925.[5] Nevertheless, they were each cogs in a "propaganda machine" that played a major role in promoting racial consciousness and shaping Black public opinion, each a visual reminder that "the newspapers of the race are finally and forever on the map."[6]

The development of State Street's newspaper row was just one manifestation of an extraordinary Black commercial and political culture that had blossomed on the South Side during World War I and that continued to thrive after the 1919 riots. Chicago's Black population more than doubled between 1920 and 1930, boosting the fortunes of Black entrepreneurs like property mogul Jesse Binga, who at the peak of his powers "could lay claim to more footage on State Street . . . than any other man in the city," and providing a voting base for Black political leaders like Oscar DePriest, who in 1928 became the first African American elected to the House of Representatives since the nineteenth century.[7] Such achievements have led to descriptions of the 1920s as a "golden age" for the city's African American community, a moment when "black consciousness and the positive manifestations of racial solidarity reached their apex in black Chicago."[8] The *Defender* and other Black publications played a central role in this process, celebrating the emergence of Chicago's "new negroes" in ways that reiterated their own significance to African American readers.[9]

As the power of Chicago's Black press grew, its publishers dreamed of media buildings that would better embody their own success and the triumphant rise of Chicago's Black metropolis. This chapter focuses on three major additions to Black Chicago's skyline during this period, beginning with the *Defender*'s relocation from 3159 State Street to an impressive new headquarters at 3435 Indiana Avenue at the beginning of the 1920s, before turning to the media enterprises of Anthony Overton and their respective homes in the Overton Hygienic Building and the Chicago Bee Building on State Street, which were constructed later in the decade. As striking additions to and revisions of the South Side's built environment, these sites reflected both the shifting geography of Chicago's Black communities and the literary and literal role of Black periodicals in shaping the physical and metaphysical landscape of African American urban life. At the same time, public struggles over their visibility, reception, and representation reflected the efforts of Chicago's Black periodicals to demarcate their position within the city's Black literary terrain and to use the built environment as a "chosen instrument" in the battle for civic authority and racial uplift.[10]

A Temple for a Prophet

As the Red Summer of 1919 receded, Abbott pushed ahead with the *Defender*'s long-awaited relocation plans. His first move set the groundwork for an uncoupling from the *Drover's Journal*, as he made arrangements to purchase a high-speed Goss cylinder printing press. Wary of being discriminated against, Abbott used a middleman named Clarence Brown, a white foreman at the *Journal* with whom he was friendly, to inspect the machinery. Satisfied with Brown's feedback, Abbott immediately bought the press.[11] His next task was to locate a suitable building or lot that could both accommodate the newspaper's current needs and facilitate its anticipated future growth. During the late summer and autumn of 1919, Abbott combed the South Side in search of the ideal site for his new production facility. He finally agreed to a purchase contract on 3435 Indiana Avenue, a three-story, red-and-yellow-brick building owned by the Smith Bros. Storage and Warehouse Company that was situated a few blocks south and several streets east of the *Defender*'s existing location.[12]

The building had been designed during the late 1890s by Henry Newhouse, a Chicago native who had attended the Massachusetts Institute of Technology before establishing an architectural practice in Hyde Park, close to the University of Chicago campus.[13] Newhouse lent his talents to an eclectic mix of architectural projects, ranging from factory buildings and large-scale apartment hotels to picture houses such as the Howard Theatre, an ornate Neoclassical theater located in the North Side community of Rogers Park that was completed in 1917.[14] However, perhaps his most lasting contribution to the city's landscape came through a series of palatial residential properties on the South Side. This included 4726 Grand Boulevard, a thirty-two-room Chateauesque-style mansion with twin turrets and elaborate dormers that was constructed in 1903 for tailoring entrepreneur Simon L. Marks, and the similarly impressive 932 East Fifty-First Street, which was built in 1910 at the request of industrialist Jacob Franks.[15]

Many of the South Side buildings designed by Newhouse during the late nineteenth and early twentieth century were commissioned for or by members of German and Jewish immigrant communities, which dominated the areas outside of Black enclaves such as the Dearborn Street Corridor. This was similarly true of 3435 Indiana Avenue, better known as the Anshe Dorom synagogue, which was originally built to house the South Side Hebrew Congregation. Ground was broken on the project in March 1899 and the cornerstone was laid two months later.[16] By the time the building was formerly dedicated in October 1901, its ornate exterior, replete with Star of David stained-glass windows, decorative pilasters, and Hebrew inscriptions, had been completed. However, it would take several years for the congregation to finish the interior and pay off debts for the lot on which the synagogue was built. Local papers sporadically reported on continued fund-raising efforts, including an "Oriental Bazaar" held in the synagogue's vestry room in November 1902, an event billed as "a unique and exciting entertainment" designed to mimic the streets of Jerusalem.[17]

The transition of 3435 Indiana Avenue from Jewish to Black ownership (by way of a white-owned storage company) was emblematic of the South Side's broader demographic shifts during the first decades of the twentieth century. As growing numbers of Black migrants settled in the city, many of Chicago's Jews abandoned the South Side—first for neighborhoods such as Lawndale on the West Side and then for wealthier enclaves on the North Side or Lake Shore. This began with individual relocations, which saw the Marks mansion at 4726 Grand Boulevard transformed into "Elam House," a boardinghouse for single Black women owned by philanthropist Melissia Ann Elam.[18] Jewish civic and religious institutions quickly followed, leading to new roles for buildings like the one at 3140 Indiana Avenue. An attractive example of 1880s Queen Anne architecture, the three-story redbrick structure was commissioned by the Lakeside Club, a prominent Jewish social organization. By the end of World War I, it had become Unity Hall, the headquarters of the Peoples Movement Club and a center of local Black political activism.[19] Even more recognizable was the Kehilath Anshe Ma'ariv Synagogue at 3301 Indiana Avenue, constructed in 1890 and designed by famed Chicagoan architectural duo Louis Sullivan and Dankmar Adler. By the early 1920s, the synagogue had found a new host in the shape of the Pilgrim Baptist Church, an African American congregation whose legendary music director, Thomas Dorsey, achieved national recognition as the "father of gospel music."[20]

Its former lives as a synagogue and storage warehouse meant that 3435 Indiana Avenue required extensive modification, and Abbott initially leased the structure back to Smith Bros. as he made plans for its costly redevelopment.[21] Exterior changes included the removal of the building's dramatic sheet-metal cornice and several decorative pilasters, which allowed for new offices to be installed in the building's attic space and saw the dramatic front façade replaced with a more conventional storefront design. Internally, the front section of the building was redeveloped to house the *Defender*'s editorial and administrative departments, with the lower floor containing general offices; the circulation, advertising, and makeup departments; and Abbott's executive suite. Two-thirds of the second floor of the building were taken up by the synagogue's sanctuary, a lofty chamber that became the nerve center of the *Defender*'s editorial operations. The newsroom's back wall was partially glass, providing a window onto the composing room one

Home of the *Chicago Defender*. (*Simm's Blue Book and National Negro Business and Professional Directory*, New York Public Library Digital Collections)

floor below. To the rear, the building's auditorium became home to the *Defender*'s printing and linotype operations, including its new Goss printing press.[22]

While the building's dramatic renovation removed many vestiges of its former life, some original features remained, including Hebrew inscriptions on its façade and a stained-glass window that bathed its newsroom in multicolored light.[23] Over time, such idiosyncrasies became daily visual reminders of lingering structural and practical issues engendered by its previous usage. However, at the building's opening, they merely appeared to amplify the *Defender*'s own religiously infused justifications of its social and political importance. After all, what location could be better suited to help further embellish Abbott's reputation as a "prophet" and the *Defender*'s own role as a "beckoning instrument" leading thousands of Southern Black migrants toward the promised land of the urban North?[24] From this perspective, the spiritual significance of 3435 Indiana Avenue was not lost through the departure of its original congregation or its intermediary function as a storage warehouse; instead, it had been repurposed to suit the building's new role as a temple to Black print.

Our Path of Progress

This significance was not lost on many of the building's new congregation, who eagerly awaited news of the plant's formal opening. Finally, in April 1921, the *Defender* declared that it had moved into its new building and invited any and all interested parties to attend its public unveiling on May 6.[25] In addition to aggressively publicizing the building's opening through the *Defender*, Abbott sent invitations to some of the city's most prominent Black business and civic leaders, encouraging them to come out for the occasion. Such efforts maintained and expanded the *Defender*'s earlier efforts to position 3159 State Street as "the meeting place of all the people" and helped to cast the opening of its new headquarters as an important Black civic project inclusive of all community members: "We want you and your friends to be with us on this date that together we may fittingly mark the greatest milestone reached on our path of progress."[26] To accentuate just how far the paper had come over the preceding fifteen years, Abbott ensured that visitors to the new facility were greeted with an unusual sight upon entering the building's reception room: an exhibit of "the complete office equipment of the first *Defender*," something that amounted to little more than "a small folding table and a single chair."[27]

Beyond mere theatrics, such statements and installations reflected the centrality of the *Defender*'s new plant to its corporate history and editorial mission. As a concrete symbol of race pride and business acumen, the opening of 3435 Indiana Avenue embodied both Abbott's individual success as a race man and his publication's path of progress from Henrietta Lee's kitchen table to a position as one of the most widely read Black newspapers in the country. Taking note, contemporary critics such as Frederick Detweiler, writing in his 1922 study, *The Negro Press in the United States*, positioned the *Defender* and its building as a symbol for "the aspiration and enterprise of the race."[28] The newspaper's editors advanced this sentiment further while simultaneously leaning into the gendered representation of its previous offices. Fay Young declared that 3435 Indiana Avenue was a "print shop the like of which no colored man ever saw before or dreamed of owning." Here the role of Mother Lee was replaced by the publisher's actual mother, Flora Abbott, who traveled to Chicago from coastal Georgia for its formal opening, where she was given the honor of starting the building's presses.[29]

Mrs. Abbott was joined by thousands of visitors who began "filing under America's flag and the Defender's welcome which overhung the doors."[30] Not long removed from Abbott's run-ins with federal agents during World War I, some among the crowd that passed below the Stars and Stripes may have read its prominence as a somewhat cynical display. However, while the *Defender* remained a fierce critic of the nation's failings, the flag's visibility reflected Abbott's unwavering identification as an American patriot. Even as the *Defender* lambasted the entrenchment of Jim Crow and the persistence of racial discrimination, its publisher, like many of his readers, professed his desire to build a country where "the flag could fly over the free and the brave."[31] Abbott's enthusiastic flag-waving placed him on one side of a growing division within Black print culture during the early 1920s—between publications that courted American nationalism and the tone of outlets like Marcus Garvey's *Negro World* and the socialist *Messenger*, whose founders, A. Philip Randolph and Chandler Owen, famously declared in its inaugural issue that "patriotism has no appeal to us."[32]

Whereas Abbott took pride in displaying his nation's flag at the entrance to his newspaper plant, Garvey, the country's leading advocate of Black nationalism, dreamed of "a Negro flag in Africa."[33] Indeed, less than a year earlier, at the Universal Negro Improvement Association's first international conference in New York, Garvey had offered a Pan-African alternative to the American tricolor in the shape of the red, black, and green Black Liberation flag.[34] Since arriving in America in 1916, Garvey's call for Black separatism and a return to Africa had gathered significant support, drawing the ire of more moderate publishers such as Abbott, who believed that only full integration would help African Americans to scale "the walls of discrimination."[35] Abbott's use of the *Defender* to undermine Black nationalism prompted a furious Garvey to expand *Negro World*'s circulation in Chicago before visiting the city to deliver an address at the Eighth Infantry Armory, just a few streets from the *Defender*'s new building. However, as he took the stage, Garvey was arrested for illegal stock sales—based on evidence accrued by S. A. Brusseaux, a Black private detective in Abbott's employ.[36] Such subterfuge, along with his willingness to use the *Defender*'s building as a symbol of Black American exceptionalism, contributed to Abbott's rehabilitation among federal officials—from a supposed agitator to a ready collaborator "on all investigations pertaining to Negro radical activities."[37]

And yet, despite their ideological differences, Abbott remained appreciative of Garvey's efforts to highlight the diasporic connections between Black Americans and their racial kin overseas, something that would also be exhibited through the *Defender*'s new headquarters. As visitors poured into its reception room, they were greeted with two impressive artworks by African American muralist William Edouard Scott that towered above the *Defender*'s original office equipment.[38] A graduate from the Art Institute of Chicago, Scott had trained under pioneering Black painter Henry Ossawa Tanner in France before returning in 1914 to the United States, where he quickly established a reputation as one of the nation's leading African American artists.[39] Scott's impressionistic work regularly took inspiration from and sought to root the Black American experience in the history and culture of the African diaspora, and this inspiration was on ready display in the first of his murals for the *Defender*.[40] Located on the left as visitors entered the reception room, the mural depicted a "daughter of Ethiopia" holding a copy of the *Defender* in one hand and "the balance scales of the rights and wrongs of men before the oppressed of all lands and climes" in the other.[41]

If the first of Scott's murals emphasized the connections between African Americans and the Black diaspora, then the second reiterated the

Defender's quasi-religious role in helping to transport Black migrants from the agrarian South to the promise of urban modernity. At the forefront of the image, visitors could make out images of livestock and figures who served as symbols of a Southern way of life characterized by the Jim Crow system and, to greater or lesser degrees, by a continued connection to King Cotton. Toward the rear, onlookers could make out recognizable symbols of industrial and technological advancement such as the factory, the railway locomotive, ocean liner, and the airplane, which themselves were framed by that most modern of American inventions, the skyscraper. Behind all of these images loomed a facsimile of the *Defender* itself, a fitting tribute to the newspaper's oversized role in shaping the landscape of Black urban life. The connection was not lost on Black publications like the *Phoenix Tribune*, which described the *Defender*'s new headquarters as "unquestionably the biggest thing of its kind in the entire country . . . a real monument to sagacity and business daring."[42]

Building Defenderland

While Scott's artwork and the chair-and-table installation provided a visual reminder of the *Defender*'s role in "uplifting the race," the building's location reaffirmed the newspaper's connection to the South Side's Black community. Roi Ottley suggests that its purchase was influenced by Abbott's desire to fortify himself within the South Side, "perhaps as a defensive measure in case of [another] race riot."[43] Yet it is just as likely that Abbott's decision was shaped by his awareness of how the geographical boundaries of Black Chicago were shifting. As the city's Black population expanded, the heart of the Stroll migrated southward from the intersection of Thirty-First and State Street. In his *Autobiography of Black Chicago*, Dempsey Travis argues that by the early 1920s it was the corner of Thirty-Fifth and State that was now the epicenter for the "thousands of black Chicagoans who sought breathing space outside of their cubicle rooms and kitchenettes." Demonstrating his continued quest for visibility, Abbott could regularly be found there, "holding court on the corner of 35th and State with a big cigar in his mouth" mere yards from the entrance to his new headquarters.[44]

Abbott was far from the only Black businessman to sense this change, with the intersection of Thirty-Fifth and State becoming home to a new wave of Black commercial enterprises. A leading figure in this movement was Jesse Binga, who arguably did more than any other person to midwife the development of Black business in Chicago during the 1920s. Born in Detroit, Binga settled in Chicago around the time of the World's Columbian Exposition and later entered the real estate business, renting his first offices in a storefront at 3331 State Street during the late 1890s. Echoing the *Defender*'s humble origins story, Binga recalled that the premises consisted of little more than a desk, some chairs, and a "worn-out stove resting on two legs and a brick."[45] He compensated for his financial shortcomings with a keen business intuition and a domineering personality, attributes that helped him to evolve from "an itinerant street peddler into a powerful real estate mogul."[46] In 1908 he founded the Binga Bank at 3633 State Street, the first Black-owned and -directed bank in the North. The onset of World War I and the accompanying surge in Black migration further bolstered Binga's finances and notoriety; while the businessman was known to gouge tenants, he also invested heavily in real estate mortgages, allowing many African Americans to become home owners for the first time.[47]

Several months before the opening of the *Defender*'s Indiana Avenue headquarters, the Binga Bank was briefly closed and then reopened with a state charter. The *Broad Ax* applauded the occasion as "a history-making event among colored people residing in Chicago" and cataloged the thousands of patrons who lined up on the streets outside in order to "pour their money" into the enterprise.[48] The *Defender* was similarly enthusiastic about the bank's reopening, an unsurprising stance given that Abbott and Binga shared a close personal and professional relationship, and the newspaper became "a megaphone for Binga's success."[49] Buoyed by such support, Binga acquired a plot on the northwest corner of Thirty-Fifth and State Street, and in October 1924 the new Binga State Bank was officially opened on the site.[50] A three-story edifice reminiscent of a Greek temple, the bank's splendor even attracted the attention of white dailies, including the *Tribune*, who sent a reporter southward to inspect the new structure. They returned with breathless tales of "rich Ionic architecture" and "lofty reaches of marble and bronze," opulence that readers might "expect to find in the loop but not in 'the black belt.'"[51]

The incredulity of the *Tribune*'s reporter betrayed the continued marginalization of Chicago's African American community and the South Side's ascendant Black business and commercial district. This position was connected to a lack of knowledge about the city's Black press, which played a vital role in documenting the events and achievements of Black Chicagoans and their institutions. As Detweiler noted in his 1922 study, the diverse portraits of African American life contained in the *Defender* and other Black publications remained "virtually unknown to the white group."[52] As a result, it was difficult for many whites to visualize African American life and culture on the South Side beyond the spatially and conceptually restrictive parameters of the poverty-stricken "Black Belt." The term's pejorative racial connotations did not sit well with Binga, who complained that his bank's splendor was an example of, not an exception to, the South Side's booming business culture: "Most people don't realize it, but practically all our business institutions and our most substantial investments are located on or near 35th Street. Not less than $3,000,000 is invested by our people in commercial property in the area five blocks north and five blocks south of 35th Street between State and Cottage Grove."[53]

The continued failure of metropolitan white dailies in Chicago and other cities across the country to document African American life in any meaningful or representative way was particularly galling because such publications were an integral part of many Black urban dwellers' media diet. Kim Gallon notes that regardless of growing Black press power during the years following World War I, few African Americans saw publications such as the *Defender* as their sole source of news.[54] Instead, Black publications served a mainly supplemental role that helped to offset the racial myopia of white media coverage. In a 1947 analysis of the Black press for *Social Forces*, sociologist John Burma asserts that close to 90 percent of African Americans in the urban South read a local white paper, and it is possible that readership rates among Black Chicagoans during the 1920s were comparatively high. By devoting just a few column inches in every issue to coverage of "news concerning Negroes," publications such as the *Tribune* and the *Daily News* repeatedly demonstrated how little they cared about the desires or interests of Black readers.[55] Similarly, their continued description of the Black Belt as "the foulest spot in Chicago" helped to enforce the South Side's reputation as a racialized landscape of urban vice and social pathology.[56]

For the *Defender* it seemed clear that a new name was needed—one that celebrated the South Side's Black business district and emphasized the *Defender*'s position within it. For inspiration Abbott turned to the *Chicago Tribune*, whose offices served as the capital of what the newspaper had begun describing as "Tribune Land" during World War I.[57] The designation of "Tribune Land" nominally included Black South Siders and other African American enclaves around the city, just as the newspaper's audience extended to Black readers. However, the *Tribune*'s own coverage clearly positioned Chicago's Black communities outside the boundaries of "Tribune Land," just as the unveiling of the Tribune Tower in 1925 was presented as an architectural masterpiece to be enjoyed by the city's white residents and "the higher needs of a civilized community."[58] In response, Abbott set about creating "Defenderland," a name that historian Zoe Trodd asserts embodied "a South Side bound together in its identity by the newspaper."[59] By seeking to adopt this moniker, the publisher offered a counter-cartographic reading of Chicago's media culture and built environment, reasserting his understanding of the power of Black journalists as mapmakers and "symbolic workers who forge geographies of news," and reiterating the *Defender*'s role in making this "other Chicago" visible.[60]

Over time, "Tribune Land" would evolve into "Chicagoland," an area that the *Tribune* defined as encompassing "a 200-mile radius from Chicago, north, south, east, and west."[61] The term quickly entered the vocabulary of its readers and endures today as both an informal name for the city's metropolitan area and a literary reminder of how Chicago continues to dominate popular and literary representations of the Midwest.[62] By contrast, Enoch Waters writes that the *Defender*'s "obvious attempt to duplicate the *Tribune*'s designation," not to mention its hubristic overtones, made "Defenderland" a hard sell.[63] Despite this setback, Abbott's efforts to center 3435 Indiana Avenue within the cultural and political geography of Black Chicago proved significantly more successful, something acknowledged by local residents such as Dempsey Travis, as well as onlookers from further afield. In a 1929 article printed in *Opportunity*, a New York–based monthly journal published by the National Urban League, its editors invited readers to imagine themselves "in the hub of Negro activity in Chicago." Turning to the north, south, east or west, readers could see "the territory in which the Negro lives and thrives." *Opportunity* declared, "You are standing in the heart of the great, teeming Negro metropolis. . . . In other words, you are standing in the home office of the *Chicago Defender*."[64]

The Mouthpiece of 14 Million People

As *Opportunity*'s willingness to position the *Defender*'s plant as the heart of Black Chicago demonstrates, the newspaper's relocation not only helped to reaffirm its prominence within the city's emerging Black metropolis but also bolstered its national reputation. By 1920 the Commission on Race Relations estimated that around two-thirds of *Defender* readers lived outside of Chicago, and the newspaper contained significantly more "out-of-town" articles than its competitors.[65] By the time the *Defender* had entered its second year at 3435 Indiana Avenue, its weekly circulation had swollen to 223,550. When accounting for an estimated pass-on readership of five people, the newspaper claimed that each issue reached around 1.1 million readers, making the *Defender* the only Black periodical "that goes into every community in the United States."[66] Such self-aggrandizing rhetoric, and the content of the *Defender*'s own editorial pages, demonstrated the extent to which its focus and audience had expanded since its early days as a community paper.

The newspaper's Indiana Avenue plant was a testament to this expansion, and for readers located beyond Chicago and thus unable to visit the *Defender*'s building in person, Abbott vowed to bring it to them. To achieve this goal, the newspaper produced a series of illustrated brochures and informational pamphlets that were distributed to newsstand agents across the country. This literature, which "revealed some impressive facts and figures" about the *Defender*'s new plant, became a prominent part of subsequent subscription drives.[67] They featured detailed surveys of the building and photographic profiles of prominent *Defender* contributors. Abbott appeared behind the desk in the executive office "from which he directs the affairs of his great institution."[68] Photographs of locations such as the newsroom, library, and lobby were also included, along with north- and south-facing views of Indiana Avenue from the *Defender* headquarters. In addition to targeting individual readers and newsstand agents, information about the *Defender*'s facility was also sent to Black civic and educational institutions across the country. This included Abbott's alma mater, with office manager Phil Jones forwarding photographs of the plant to the Hampton Institute-accompanied by thanks "for any publicity you might give."[69]

Efforts to publicize the *Defender*'s plant stretched beyond printed copy to include audiovisual material; the newspaper commissioned a short educational film to showcase its offices. Offering a detailed tour of the plant's interior and close-up shots of the *Defender*'s various departments in action, the film promised to provide viewers with an intimate perspective on "the immense amount of detailed work required to get out an edition of a newspaper with a circulation extending not only throughout the

United States but most of the largest cities in Europe and Africa."[70] After an enthusiastic response to an initial screening at the Lincoln Theatre in Harlem, the *Defender* announced that the project would be distributed to movie houses across the country, allowing thousands of viewers the chance to "be taken step by step through the plant and see just how the 'World's Greatest Weekly' is made."[71] By the early 1930s, the film had even reached Abbott's hometown of Savannah, Georgia, where theatergoers were treated to images of the *Defender*'s headquarters as evidence of "a local boy who went away, started from scratch and made good."[72]

Such extraordinary efforts to render the building and its occupants visible—both through the *Defender*'s own pages and its various promotional endeavors—spoke to Abbott's grand ambitions for his newspaper and the centrality of its offices to this vision. If the precariousness of the newspaper's early years was symbolized by Mother Lee's kitchen table, and the newspaper's expansion throughout 3159 State Street during World War I mirrored its growing influence and circulation, then the move to Indiana Avenue provided the gateway to a "third period in the development of the *Defender*," one characterized by its national influence and orientation.[73] This ambition seemed vindicated by letters of congratulations "from dignitaries and noted Race leaders throughout the United States" as well as a steady stream of out-of-town visitors. Following a 1924 visit, a reporter for the *Topeka Plaindealer* declared that no Black person had truly been to Chicago "unless they have seen the *Chicago Defender* building, presses, and other equipment."[74] Such sentiments reiterated that the periodical was no longer a community paper housed in "unpretentious quarters on the second floor at 3159 State Street"; it was "the mouthpiece of 14 million people" with a headquarters to match.[75]

The role played by the *Defender*'s new facility in the newspaper's continued growth was not merely symbolic; according to Dewey Roscoe Jones, the relocation underpinned a major expansion program.[76] Improved facilities helped to streamline the newspaper's distribution and improve its overall size and production quality.[77] Control of its own printing press reduced the threat of third-party censure, allowing the publication to lean into the type of journalistic sensationalism and bombastic race rhetoric that had been pioneered by J. Hockley Smiley and that helped to drive newsstand circulation. Ownership of the plant and its printing presses cut operating costs by more than one thousand dollars per week and ensured that overhead was kept to a modest level, allowing Abbott to open more distribution outlets beyond Chicago and hire new editorial, administrative, and mechanical staff.[78] Within a year of its relocation, the *Defender* claimed that 3435 Indiana Avenue had become home to the "greatest galaxy of newspaper workers ever assembled" under the auspices of a Black periodical.[79]

On a personal level, the *Defender*'s relocation proved to be of enormous financial consequence for Abbott. The building's opening meant that "the flow of money into the newspaper [became] a torrent," and by the mid-1920s the publisher was drawing a personal salary of two thousand dollars per week, a dramatic transformation from his hardscrabble early years.[80] *Defender* biographer and Abbott's great-grandniece Myiti Sengstacke Rice suggests that this windfall made him one of the country's few African American millionaires.[81] With his coffers suddenly overflowing, the publisher looked for a home to match. He settled on a palatial mansion at 4742 South Parkway, which he purchased for twenty-four thousand dollars in 1926.[82] Built around the turn of the twentieth century, the building's severe gable roof, stone parapets, and limestone portico blended elements of Queen Anne and Neoclassical architectural style. Its lavish interiors, completed in "a style that made Negroes gape when they thronged the place during socials," solidified Abbott's status as a nationally renowned Black publisher and entrepreneur, while its address reflected how this standing was rooted in his connections to the South Side's Black community.[83]

As for the *Defender*, its own dual focus on local politics and national concerns would be most clearly encapsulated through an ambitious new publishing strategy. Shortly after the newspaper's relocation, Abbott purchased a second Goss printing press, which was installed in an adjacent building. The cost of the press was reported as one hundred thousand dollars, bringing the total value of the newspaper's printing plant to around half a million dollars.[84] More importantly, the combined presses allowed for the production of thirty-five thousand copies every hour, enabling Abbott to launch two distinct versions of the *Defender*: a city edition "suited to the peculiar needs of Chicago" and a national paper carrying "news of interest to people all over the world." It was the logical endpoint to the newspaper's simultaneous claims to be a local-oriented and nationally facing Black periodical and a development made possible by its new headquarters. The *Defender* declared that, built upon this "solid foundation," it had successfully become "a part of the average Negro's life," whether they lived on State Street or in southern Mississippi.[85]

Too Big to Pay Attention

However, for some of the *Defender's* competitors, the furor surrounding its new headquarters and increasingly national orientation provided evidence that the paper's focus had shifted away from Chicago's African American community. Such criticism overlapped with the emergence of a new wave of Black publications, many of which had their sights set on tapping into the *Defender's* local audience or even threatening its status as "the dean" of Chicago's Black press.[86] Among them were the *Chicago Enterprise*, a Republican Party organ founded in 1918 by Jacob Tipper and published out of 3116 State Street. By the end of the 1920s, the *Enterprise* had changed its name to the *World* and its weekly circulation had reached forty thousand.[87] Other publications included Fenton Johnson's *Favorite*, a monthly literary magazine based at 3518 State Street, which advertised itself to Black readers as "the only periodical fighting to make the world safe for you," and the *Searchlight*, a "newsy and clean publication" located at 3153 State Street and edited by influential local schoolteacher Willis Huggins.[88]

Undoubtedly the most eye-catching new publication was the *Chicago Whip*, a weekly paper founded in 1919 by local businessman William Linton and Joseph Bibb, a graduate of Yale Law School who later became the first African American appointed to the cabinet of an Illinois governor since Reconstruction.[89] Beginning just a few weeks before the outbreak of the Chicago race riots, the exploits of the *Whip's* staffers, who braved the bullets of white mobs to deliver the newspaper's copy to the printers, drew admiration, while its condemnation of white vigilantism prompted police officers to buy up newsstand copies lest its coverage incite further trouble.[90] Building on this early notoriety, the *Whip* quickly established itself as the most militant Black publication in the city, adopting an editorial approach that mimicked the sensational style popularized by the *Defender* while ramping up appeals to racial and economic radicalism.[91] Its propensity for slander was criticized by newspapers such as the *Broad Ax* but appeared to find a ready audience, with the *Whip* claiming a circulation of some sixty-five thousand by the end of its first year in print.[92]

The *Whip's* dramatic rise was rationalized in some quarters as a community response to the *Defender's* wavering focus. In an article for the *Indianapolis Freeman* published in September 1919 and reprinted in a subsequent issue of the *Whip*, Black journalist Sylvester Russell suggested that the *Defender*'s publication issues during the riots—a situation brought on by its dependence on the white-owned *Drover's Journal*—represented "an affront that cannot be erased." Furthermore, Russell argued that Black Chicagoans were dissatisfied with the *Defender*'s preoccupation with race conditions in other areas of the country, a tendency that ignored similar problems "right under the newspaper's nose."[93] Critically, the *Whip*'s circulation was overwhelmingly concentrated within Chicago, meaning that while the *Defender*'s total audience dwarfed that of its upstart rival, their respective influence within Chicago was more closely aligned. Stoking this competition further, Russell declared that "it is in the *Whip* that local interest is at present centered."[94]

Cognizant of the value that proximity to the community hotspot of Thirty-Fifth and State Street could provide their nascent publication, Bibb and his colleagues took pains to embed the *Whip* close to this location. The newspaper was initially published out of offices at 3613 State Street before settling at 3420 State Street.[95] Taking inspiration from Abbott's paper, the *Whip* used its "Society" page to print regular updates on visitors to its headquarters, whether they, like prominent West Side real estate agent Fred Johnson, came from other areas of the city, or, like Philadelphia resident George Goodwyn, were visiting from farther away.[96] Similarly, the *Whip* sought to mimic the legal and social welfare services provided by the *Defender* through its complaints department and similar initiatives, with the *Whip* imploring readers to write in or visit its offices in person if they were struggling with rent hikes or other housing problems.[97] The *Whip* was also quick to document its success in siphoning journalists away from the *Defender*'s plant and into its own "happy family" at 3420 State Street, with the arrival of *Defender* associate editor A. N. Fields one such cause for celebration.[98]

At the same time, the *Whip* took aim at the *Defender*'s editorial coverage in an attempt to drive a wedge between the paper and local Black residents. One recurrent area of critique was the *Defender*'s deference to respectability politics and its patronizing representation of working-class Black migrants. Even as the *Defender* continued to push Black migration, it assumed a prominent role in policing the behavior of new arrivals. Despite Abbott's own class and regional background, the *Defender* took aim at explicit markers of Southernness and working-class status. This included guidelines on demeanor and appearance, with the *Defender* even criticizing a South Side congregation that performed a baptism at the Twenty-Ninth Street Beach, a continuation of long established Black Southern folk traditions that used natural waterways for the ritual.[99] After one *Defender* editorial declared that "the offensive methods of the Newcomer will not be tolerated in the North," the *Whip* hit back, lambasting such prejudice as "absolutely devoid of judgement and diplomacy."[100]

These two forces—an understanding of the relationship between built environment and public standing, and a desire to critique the *Defender*'s editorial tone and coverage—would find a ready target after the unveiling of 3435 Indiana Avenue. At least initially, the *Whip* appeared impressed by the *Defender*'s new location, describing the building as "one of the monumental achievements of the age" and as "a distinctive credit to the owner and the class which he represents."[101] However, that soon changed, in large part due to concerns over the *Defender*'s apparent reluctance to address the prevalence of "vice in all its forms" along the streets of the South Side, a reluctance the *Whip* attributed to its competitor's national orientation and financial success. Describing Abbott's paper as "fat and insolent with prosperity," the *Whip* declared that the *Defender*'s emergence as "the most powerful and prosperous institution of its kind" meant it had become "too big to pay attention" to local concerns, with its new plant standing as "a mute witness" to extralegal activity and ongoing social problems.[102]

To accentuate this point, the *Whip* extensively documented incidents of vice that took place within the very shadow of the *Defender*'s new headquarters. During the years following the *Defender*'s relocation, the *Whip* estimated that there were close to two dozen brothels and gambling houses clustered along the 3400 block of Indiana Avenue. As the mighty presses in the *Defender* plant worked through the night, they printed "anything but a protest to the modern Sodom and Gomorrah under its very nose."[103] Such evocative descriptions cast doubts on the *Defender*'s ability to help migrants acclimate to their new surroundings, given that the very building "from which this mighty publication is issued rears . . . from a pool of slime." Perhaps more damagingly, they directly undermined the plant's effectiveness as a symbol of community pride and racial uplift. The *Whip* would go so far as to print a front-page image in December 1922 showing the *Defender*'s plant and a nearby gambling house at 3439 Indiana Avenue. The *Whip* declared that, ensconced in their ivory tower, the staff of the "world's greatest weekly" paid little mind to the "debauchery and shame" of its neighbors.[104]

A Monument to Negro Enterprise

With such sensational attacks on the *Defender*'s headquarters, Joseph Bibb and the *Whip* chose to go low in an effort to unseat Abbott's periodical. Other businessmen and publications chose to go high, utilizing architecture and the built environment not to undermine the *Defender*'s foundations but instead to emphasize the quality of their own enterprises. Among them was Anthony Overton, a cosmetics entrepreneur and the first African American to head a major business conglomerate. Born in Louisiana shortly before the end of the Civil War, Overton settled in Kansas City, Missouri, where he founded the Overton Hygienic Company in 1898. Thirteen years later Overton relocated to Chicago, establishing a base of operations in a two-story building at 5200 Wabash Avenue, several blocks west of Washington Park. Overton quickly became a leading voice within the South Side's Black business community, assuming the presidency of the Chicago Negro Business League and garnering praise as a public speaker. By 1915 the Overton Hygienic Company employed thirty-two people and had been capitalized at more than a quarter of a million dollars.[105]

The company's success provided Overton with the means to diversify his commercial interests, starting with the creation of the *Half-Century* magazine in 1916, which began publication at 3708 Wabash Avenue before being assimilated into Overton's main base of operations fifteen blocks south. In its first issue the magazine informed readers, "We are now living in a commercial era," and, as such, it would prioritize discussion of "the making and saving of money." More broadly, the *Half-Century* promised to chronicle "such doings of the race as may be of interest to [the] majority."[106] Like other Black Chicagoan periodicals, the *Half-Century* championed self-help, race pride, and Black business development, declaring itself to be "for Colored people, by Colored people, and containing only pictures of Colored people."[107] However, whereas publications such as the *Defender* and the *Whip* favored bold headlines and strident race rhetoric, the *Half-Century* took a more genteel position, informing readers that anybody "looking for a publication that propagates grievances . . . will have to look elsewhere."[108]

It is likely that Overton initially saw the *Half-Century* as little more than an advertising mechanism for his other commercial interests; writer Robert Weems suggests that the businessman shrewdly installed Katherine Williams as its owner and editor in order to "deflect charges of shameless self-promotion."[109] However, while Overton financed and ultimately controlled the enterprise, scholars Noliwe Rooks and Aria Halliday stress Williams's influence in guiding the *Half-Century* from its origins as "an informational guide for businessmen and homemakers" to a well-rounded and sophisticated literary magazine.[110] This shift can be traced through the magazine's content as the *Half-Century* became a popular outlet for Black women writers to publish short stories, poems, and other work. One regular contributor was Anita Scott Coleman, a Los Angeles–based schoolteacher and writer whose work forensically probed at the position of Black women in a sexist and racist society.[111] With a claimed circulation of seventy-five thousand per issue by the early 1920s, the *Half-Century* had cemented its status as an erudite and high-quality publication, its elegant visual design complemented by tasteful editorial and advertising features geared toward the social, sartorial, and political tastes of middle-class Black women.[112]

Just as Abbott reveled in his new offices and Binga boasted of owning "more footage on State Street . . . than any other man in the city," so too did Overton appear eager to leave his mark upon the South Side's physical terrain.[113] Accordingly, he made plans to vacate 5200 Wabash Avenue and move up—both professionally and geographically—toward the nexus of Chicago's Black business district. In 1921 *American Architect* informed its readers that Overton had secured a plot at Thirty-Sixth and State Street and was in the process of awarding a $350,000 contract for a mixed-use loft building.[114] Its designer was Z. Erol Smith, a young white architect who had settled in Chicago shortly before the outbreak of World War I.[115] Smith's penchant "for unusually elaborate and luxurious" designs quickly attracted attention, with projects like the Streeterville, a five-hundred-room hotel planned for the southwest corner of Chestnut Street and De Witt Place garnering widespread acclaim.[116] While Overton was likely familiar with Smith's work, proximity also may have precipitated their collaboration; the architect maintained a practice at 5501 Prairie Avenue, close to Overton's Wabash headquarters.

Initial plans for the building stretched to six stories, and renderings of the proposed structure were splashed across the *Half-Century*'s pages.[117] Spiraling construction costs meant that its height was capped at four stories, although, in anticipation of future growth, its elevator and mechanical shaft were built to the full height proposed in the original plans. Despite its downsizing, the building's striking exterior brickwork and terra-cotta glazing ensured that it was an attractive addition to the South Side's landscape.

The Overton Hygienic Building. (*Souvenir of Negro Progress: Chicago, 1779–1925*, New York Public Library Digital Collections)

A modern reinforced concrete frame meant it was "absolutely fireproof," while raised sections on the north and south corners gave its front façade a fortress-like appearance.[118] Crested patterning and untitled coats of arms added to this illusion and alluded to Smith's interest in the "good old days" of English style, something more clearly expressed through later mock-Tudor and Elizabethan-inspired apartment buildings. Such characteristics also provided an architectural language for the high-class sensibilities that the *Half-Century* articulated and that Overton's other enterprises embodied.[119]

Alongside the offices of the *Half-Century*, the building's residents included Victory Life, an Overton-controlled insurance company, whose first-floor offices were illuminated at night by "decorative light bulbs studding the terra-cotta string course above the storefronts."[120] Offices on the second floor were rented to members of Chicago's Black professional class, including Walter Bailey, the first Black architect to be licensed in the state of Illinois, who used the building as a base to work on plans for the National Pythias Temple, a towering eight-story yellow-brick edifice at 3737 State Street completed in 1928.[121] Perhaps the building's most prestigious resident was the Douglass National Bank, which relocated to 3619 State Street in 1923 after Overton gained control of the enterprise. The public response to its opening echoed that of the Binga Bank, with thousands lining up to tour its marble interiors, while publications such as the *Detroit Free Press* juxtaposed the bank's former residence in "an old two-story brick structure" with its elegant new quarters as evidence that Overton was "in the noonday of his business career."[122] From the commanding vantage point of 3619 State Street, Overton truly appeared to have become "the proverbial master of all he surveyed."[123]

The multifunctionality of the Overton building powerfully reiterates the intimate relationship between Black publishing and business enterprise in Chicago during the 1920s. Just as the editorial offices of the *Half-Century* and enterprises such as Victory Life Insurance sat side by side at 3619 State Street, these institutions also mutually benefited each other. Funds generated from the sale of Victory Life bonds helped to subsidize the *Half-Century*'s expansion, while in return the magazine provided Overton's disparate commercial ventures with valuable publicity. As the building's other tenants demonstrate, these intersections were not limited to Overton enterprises, with the building's usage by other Black periodicals further reinforcing the intimacy between commercial and literary ambition. This included the *Pittsburgh Courier*, which by the early 1920s had developed a large enough local audience to establish a regional office in Chicago. Originally based at 3451 Michigan Avenue, a stone's throw away from the *Defender*, the *Courier* quickly relocated into the Overton building, a more impressive location from which to expand its readership.[124]

This spatial convergence of publishing and business interests can also be traced through the development of the Associated Negro Press (ANP), a Black news service founded by Claude Barnett in 1919. Barnett had made his name in cosmetics through the Kashmir Chemical Company, an enterprise founded by dentist Theodore Mozee at 4709 State Street.[125] The success of Kashmir Chemical helped capitalize the ANP; according to Gerald Horne, the organization had secured subscriptions from around 350 Black newspapers within a year of its launch.[126] Initially housed in Barnett's advertising offices at 312 Clark Street, the ANP soon moved into the home of the Kashmir Chemical Company (renamed as the Nile Queen Corporation following a legal challenge), in a three-story, fifty-thousand-dollar structure at 3423 Indiana Avenue.[127] In addition to providing the ANP with more operational space, the location of Barnett's "new and elaborately appointed building" had the added benefit of more closely tying his news service to the South

Side's Black newspaper row, particularly the neighboring *Defender*, with whom Barnett and the ANP shared a close, if occasionally contentious, working relationship.[128]

As for the *Half-Century*, while the magazine was far from the Overton Hygienic Building's most illustrious tenant, its new offices provided a striking counterpoint to the *Defender*'s robust Indiana Avenue plant. Critically, whereas Abbott had chosen to redevelop a preexisting space, Overton was able to construct a building from the ground up, providing greater scope to link the architectural design of his building with the relative merits of his commercial endeavors. In its coverage of the building's unveiling, the *Half-Century* declared, "We have erected a monument, a building inside and outside that will stand as a memorial to Negro enterprise."[129] Based on circulation figures alone, the *Half-Century* was no match for the *Defender*'s popularity; however, its location in the Overton Hygienic Building reinforced its credentials as a successful publication that was for and by Black people. Similarly, through its attractive design and multifunctionality, Overton's new headquarters elegantly embodied the *Half-Century*'s role as a general interest magazine and an arbiter of African American taste, modernity, and middle-class respectability.

What the *Bee* (Building) Stands For

In 1925 Overton decided to retire the *Half-Century*. For nearly a decade the magazine had provided the businessman with a valuable advertising tool—first for his beauty products and later for his insurance and banking endeavors. Furthermore, under the steady hand of editor Katherine Williams, the *Half-Century* had evolved into a sophisticated and instructive organ of Black taste and cultural mores.[130] However, its circulation never threatened to seriously challenge the local influence of the *Defender*, while its monthly publication format and reputation as a "women-oriented" outlet made it difficult to cast itself as a legitimate alternative to Abbott's newspaper. In its place Overton unveiled a new weekly titled the *Chicago Bee*, which he believed could directly compete with the *Defender* for control of the city's Black press and, by extension, the attention and loyalty of its African American residents.[131]

Despite its format change, the *Bee* maintained some of the stylistic and editorial quirks that had helped to distinguish the *Half-Century* within

Chicago's increasingly congested Black literary terrain. One significant continuation, particularly when set against the heavily gendered parameters of American publishing writ large, was the *Bee's* reliance on a predominantly female workforce. Indeed, after the departure of founding editor Victor Gray to the *Baltimore Afro-American* in 1928, the newspaper was almost entirely staffed by women until its cancellation during the 1940s.[132] The *Bee's* commitment to "good, wholesome and authentic news" also helped to distinguish it from publications like the *Defender* and the *Whip*, as the *Bee* targeted readers alienated by the "stridency and sensationalism" of its competitors.[133] Legendary Black journalist Frank Marshall Davis, who moved to Chicago in 1927, recalled that the *Bee* harbored "enough sacred cows to stock a Texas ranch."[134] Taking up and expanding the *Half-Century's* discussion of urbanization and African American progress, the *Bee* presented a cosmopolitan yet carefully constructed vision of Black modernity to its audience. Tragically, the majority of the *Bee's* print run, including almost the entirety of its first fifteen years in print, has been lost to history.[135]

And yet one permanent reminder of the *Bee's* editorial philosophy and stylistic ambitions does endure. Eager to create a distinct home for his new weekly newspaper, Overton began to make plans for a custom-built publishing headquarters shortly after the *Bee's* inauguration. The businessman found a convenient location at 3647 State Street, half a block south of the increasingly crowded Overton Hygienic Building. To oversee the building's design, Overton renewed his relationship with Z. Erol Smith, who was tasked with creating a structure that would embody the *Bee's* commitment to high quality, class, and progressive thinking. In October 1929 the *Chicago Tribune* printed an architectural rendering of the *Bee's* prospective new home along with news that building contracts worth an estimated two hundred thousand dollars had been let for "modernistic bit for South State" that would house "a newspaper for colored folk."[136] Like its predecessor, the three-story building was designed as a mixed-used site. The *Bee* shared its first-floor offices with commercial storefront space, and apartments on the second and third floors, accessible through narrow street-facing doorways on the northern- and southernmost corners of the building.[137]

As the site gradually took shape, its striking exterior design attracted widespread attention. The façade of 3647 State Street was a dazzling array of terra-cotta tiles, with glossy black and gold tiling on the first floor complementing a pale green color scheme accented above by inset panels

Exterior of Chicago Bee Building. (Serhii Chrucky, Alamy Stock Photo)

featuring a range of Art Deco motifs. It is unclear whether the heavy use of terra-cotta or the gorgeous combination of geometric and floral designs was driven by Overton, Smith, or a third party such as Walter Bailey, whose National Pythian Temple featured hundreds of Egyptian revival panels fabricated by the Midland Terra Cotta Company.[138] The intricate designs on the Chicago Bee Building's façade were created by the Northwestern Terra Cotta Company, one of the nation's leading terra-cotta manufacturers. During the 1920s and into the 1930s, the company produced tiling for some of the city's most iconic buildings, including the Wrigley Building at 400 North Michigan Avenue and the Carbide and Carbon Building at 230 North Michigan Avenue.[139] Some motifs gestured toward the building's function, with gear-like patterns that "hinted at the mechanical printing press inside." More broadly, the building's lavish use of terra-cotta, striking color scheme, and bold mix of horizontal and transverse lines "created an impression of affluence and high style."[140]

Beyond impressing passing motorists and pedestrians, the *Bee* building provided a compelling visual counterpoint to the newspaper's upmarket editorial philosophy. In an interview with the *Tribune*, Smith made this point clear, emphasizing that "the paper's policy is to print only news which is fit to read." As Smith intimated, the building's clean lines and cultured motifs reflected the *Bee*'s proud status as "a clean newspaper that can go into any home," a welcome contrast to both the buildings and the pages of the city's other Black periodicals, which were more workmanlike and populated by "wildcat securities" and other questionable advertising.[141] Similarly, stories in the *Pittsburgh Courier* and other Black newspapers linked the construction of the *Bee* building to the newspaper's reputation as "a wonderful, busy and progressive institution." From this perspective, the *Bee*'s new headquarters offered a physical manifestation of the newspaper's five-plank editorial policy, a platform that included goals such as the "massing of Negro capital, wealth and resources" and an emphasis on increased Black educational attainment and political participation.[142]

Perhaps the most compelling example of the connection between the *Bee*'s editorial philosophy and architectural design can be found in the multivolume *Intercollegian Wonder Book*, published between 1927 and 1929. Also known as *The Negro in Chicago*, the *Wonder Book* was the brainchild of Frederic Robb, the enigmatic president of the Washington Intercollegiate Club housed at the Black YMCA at 3763 Wabash Avenue.[143] In 1926, while still a law student at Northwestern University, Robb determined that the club should produce "the largest and most elaborate Book ever published about the people of the great city of Chicago," which would document notable educational, entrepreneurial, and political interests and accomplishments within the community. The collaborative efforts of a diverse group of African American students, photographers, artists, and printers saw the first 232-page edition released the following year.[144] In his review of the first volume of *The Negro in Chicago*, Dewey Roscoe Jones described the book as a "masterpiece" and as a definitive reference book for Black life in the Windy City. Two years later a second and even more detailed volume was released, and *The Negro in Chicago*'s twin editions quickly became "legendary among local residents as guides to achievement, institutions and community life in Black Chicago."[145]

Included in the 1929 volume of *The Negro in Chicago* is a full-page feature on the *Bee* dominated by an architectural rendering of its yet-to-be-completed building at 3647 State Street. The bold design jumps from the page, alongside the heavily stylized lettering of the *Bee*'s title emblazoned across the top of the building's façade. Below this image we see a subheading titled "What the Bee Stands For," which reiterates the *Bee*'s emphasis on Black educational advancement, personal enlightenment, and business development. Equally as important is a second subheading, "What the Bee

Does Not Stand For," which confirms the *Bee*'s avoidance of questionable advertising and a sensational preoccupation with crime. When placed together, the building's rendering and the accompanying description of the *Bee*'s ambitions and exclusions offer a synergetic reading of its building design and editorial philosophy—not just a monument to "the promotion of Negro business" but the embodiment of "civic and racial improvement" and the goal of "good, wholesome and authentic news."[146] Such content helped to situate the *Bee* building as a more cultured vision of Black urban life—at once complementary to and in competition with the one promoted by the *Defender* and projected through its facility at 3435 Indiana Avenue.

From Monument to White Elephant?

If Overton's decision to construct the Overton Hygienic Building within sight of Thirty-Fifth and State Street during the early 1920s reiterated the intersection's centrality to the postwar development of Black Chicago, then the location of the Chicago Bee Building demonstrated his confidence in its future, even as an influx of capital threatened to shift the epicenter of Black business toward Forty-Seventh Street and South Parkway (formerly Grand Boulevard) during the second half of the 1920s.[147] The unveiling of the Regal Theater at 4719 South Parkway in 1928, part of a larger commercial complex that included the Savoy Ballroom and the South Center Department Store, was only the most prominent manifestation of this trend.[148] Overton's faith in the Thirty-Fifth Street Corridor was reinforced by Jesse Binga, who appeared even more committed to "putting all his financial empire building eggs into one geographic basket."[149] A few years after the opening of the Binga Bank, the entrepreneur unveiled plans to construct the Binga Arcade, a five-story mixed-use structure on the northwest corner of Thirty-Fifth and State that was completed in 1929, shortly after Overton broke ground on the *Bee* building.

However, other factors would intervene. Just two days after the *Chicago Tribune* had profiled the *Bee*'s "modernistic bit" on the South Side, the Wall Street Crash signaled the onset of the Great Depression. While the economic crisis impacted every area of society, Black Americans and Black business interests were disproportionately affected. As the "last hired and first fired," Black workers were among the first to be hit by pay cuts and redundancies; consequently, national Black unemployment rates peaked at around 50 percent, nearly three times the comparative unemployment rate for whites.[150] Shorn of their economic base, Black commercial districts in cities such as New York and Pittsburgh, which had thrived on the steady influx of Black migrants throughout the 1920s, were thrown into disarray. In Chicago, where a disproportionately high ratio of the city's Black community depended on industrial and manufacturing jobs, the impact was particularly acute. Within two years the South Side's Black population alone accounted for roughly 25 percent of the city's total relief cases.[151]

Despite the bleak economic outlook, Overton pushed ahead with the construction of the *Bee* building, and the site was finally completed in 1931. However, by the time of its opening, the *Bee* building appeared to mark not a proud continuation of the State Street Corridor's commercial ambition but the end of a golden age of Black business development and property investment on the South Side. Walking along the Stroll in August 1930, *Indianapolis Recorder* journalist Lee Jay Martin reported that the thoroughfare was now "a pitiful sight" characterized by "empty store rooms [and] automobiles parked on the sidewalk."[152] The *Defender* reported that the neighborhood had become overrun with beggars and that sites such as Unity Hall had been adapted into shelters for destitute men.[153] Among those to fall furthest was Jesse Binga, who had overreached in his pursuit of a real estate empire. By the summer of 1930, the Binga Bank was teetering, with a financial review indicating that the institution had an asset-to-liabilities deficit of more than five hundred thousand dollars. At the end of July a state auditor pasted a notice onto one of the bank's polished glass doors, declaring that the institution was "closed for examination and adjustment." Dispatches from the ANP reported that as news of the notice circulated, "a steady stream of stunned persons, stockholders and depositors, flowed to the closed little Doric temple of finance."[154] Two years later Binga went on trial for embezzlement, the first in a series of court appearances that would end with his imprisonment.[155]

While the Douglass National Bank survived the first wave of South Side foreclosures, it would soon be caught up in the economic chaos. The bank's problems were exacerbated by outstanding mortgages and bonds for both the construction of the Overton Hygienic Building and the Chicago Bee Building, which stressed its financial capacity. According to Robert Weems, by the early 1930s the Overton Hygienic Building in particular had become "a proverbial white elephant," tying funds to a single fixed-asset investment that could have been more productively invested elsewhere.[156] In 1932 the bank closed its doors and Overton was forced to vacate 3619 State Street, moving his remaining business enterprises into the recently completed Chicago Bee Building. From that location he was well placed to watch his "monument to negro thrift and industry" descend into a flophouse, with its stylish offices converted into tiny stalls and kitchenettes.[157] More broadly, the demise of the Binga State Bank and the Douglass National Bank, which at one point controlled a third of the nation's total Black bank resources, had a devastating impact on the State Street Corridor and precipitated the failure of dozens of smaller race enterprises.[158]

As Black businesses teetered across the South Side, Abbott and Overton struggled to reclaim their building narratives and reject critics who declared that their enterprises had emerged from a "pool of slime" or served as reminders of financial mismanagement. Instead, they stressed the value of the *Defender* plant and the *Bee* building as beacons of hope for Chicago's embattled Black communities. Concurrently, they framed their own relationships to these buildings in ways that emphasized their commonalities with, rather than their economic and social distance from, Chicago's Black proletariat. Despite deteriorating health, due to an ongoing battle against a chronic kidney ailment known as Bright's disease, Abbott continued to hold court in the lobby of 3435 Indiana Avenue when he was able. He particularly enjoyed meeting school groups, advising Black students to pursue work that benefited their communities and lecturing white youths on the "race issue."[159] As for Overton, the businessman had long cultivated a reputation as "a man of the people," and he leaned into this public image further during the Depression years, regularly walking the twenty blocks from his residence at Fifty-Fourth Street and Michigan Avenue to the *Bee* building at Thirty-Sixth and State.[160]

From Black Belt to Bronzeville

In the face of economic catastrophe, Chicago's Black publishers sought new ways to promote community cohesion, install civic pride, and offset the Depression's destructive impact. In keeping with its combative editorial approach, the *Whip* took aim at white-owned businesses that had laid off or refused to hire African American workers. The *Whip*'s "Don't Spend Your Money Where You Can't Work" campaign quickly gained traction and helped to lay the groundwork for similar Black consumer boycotts in cities such as Baltimore throughout the 1930s.[161] Following the incorporation of the Robert S. Abbott Publishing Company in 1918, the *Defender* had moved to formalize some of its more ad hoc charitable ventures through the Goodfellow Club. In collaboration with local businesses and philanthropists, the *Defender* staged events and fund-raising drives "for the poor and needy of Chicago."[162] Many of these efforts coalesced around holidays such as Thanksgiving and Christmas, with the newspaper's plant becoming the distribution center from which thousands of aid parcels were shipped out to "destitute families and individuals in dire need" throughout the city.[163]

Undoubtedly the *Defender*'s most ambitious public initiative was linked to its youth section and the character of "Bud Billiken," created by Lucius Harper in 1921 and embodied by one of the newspaper's junior correspondents. The first "Billiken" was newsboy Robert Watkins, who was assigned a corner desk at 3159 State Street where he composed columns after school.[164] The character quickly took on a life of its own, with dozens of "Billiken Clubs" established across the country and "Billiken visitors" becoming a regular feature at the *Defender*'s plant.[165] In November 1928 the *Defender* hosted "Bud's First Regal Party," which was attended by hundreds of Billiken Club members. Gathering at 3435 Indiana Avenue, the group marched south toward the newly opened Regal Theater at Forty-Seventh Street and South Parkway, where they were treated to a variety performance by local musicians and comedy acts.[166] In February 1930 the second Bud Billiken Parade saw thousands repeat this procession from 3435 Indiana Avenue to the Regal Theater.[167] The following year, the now annual Billiken Parade was moved to the summer and expanded to include a community picnic at Washington Park, where an estimated crowd of thirty-five thousand gathered to feast on free ice cream and lemonade.[168] By the mid-1930s, the Bud Billiken Parade and picnic had become one of the largest African American public gatherings in the nation.

The rapid expansion of the Billiken Parade in tandem with the onset of the Great Depression was far from coincidental. As Robert Bone and Richard Courage note, the event provided a "welcome distraction from the deepening gloom of the Depression."[169] Brian McCammack reiterates these sentiments, arguing that the *Defender*'s promotion of Bud Billiken Day came because "the Black Metropolis it had helped build up during the Great Migration years found itself in danger of being torn apart at the seams by widespread social and economic turmoil."[170] It is also revealing how the parade's route, particularly during its early years, served a function not dissimilar to the *Defender*'s earlier delivery wagons as it "publicly marked and then challenged the boundaries of an ever-expanding African American

South Side."[171] Beginning at the *Defender*'s headquarters and moving south toward the northwest corner of Washington Park, the procession reiterated the importance of 3435 Indiana Avenue as a gateway to Black Chicago, just as Southern migrants continued to use its offices as an entry point into the urban North.

At the same time, Chicago's Black periodicals pushed back against the neighborhood's continued denigration by the city's daily press. The onset of the Great Depression reinforced the inherent degeneracy of the Black Belt in the eyes of publications such as the *Chicago Tribune*, which described the region as part of a no-man's-land between city's "commercial core . . . and the residential periphery" that was "pocketed and blackened by slum districts."[172] In response to such characterizations, along with the continued neglect of its residents by Chicago's white political elite, the *Bee* launched a competition to anoint a "mayor" for the South Side's embattled Black residents. The brainchild of theater editor Jimmy Gentry, the position was a symbolic one intended to promote community pride and highlight the tremendous barriers that continued to inhibit Black engagement with the city's party politics. It was also an important example of democratic participation on the margins; Susan Herbst suggests that the "election" aimed to create a parallel political sphere in which South Side residents could elect a "nonpartisan mayor of their own community."[173]

Gentry implored the *Bee* to use the name "Bronzeville" in designating the imagined territory over which the successful mayoral candidate would govern. The term was one that had gained traction over the previous decade, most notably through its use in local Black beauty pageants such as "Miss Bronze America." While the label was primarily a reference to skin tone, it quickly assumed a broader cultural and political significance. If the "South Side" was a relatively neutral geographic descriptor, the "Black Belt" was an indicator of racialized pathology and "southern segregation moved north," and "Defenderland" was an attempt to align the fortunes of Black Chicago with the content of an individual paper, then "Bronzeville" became the name "most closely associated with racial achievement."[174] It was an attempt to reclaim ownership over the neighborhood's public representation and to create "a new name for a new feeling in the neighborhood," one that eloquently articulated a sense of pride and self-sufficiency.[175] At the same time, it appeared to encapsulate a more abstract vision for and expression of Black modernity, something that led to the term being used by African American urban communities across the country.

Despite Overton's support for the project, the *Bee*'s inaugural "Mayor of Bronzeville" competition in 1930 was largely unsuccessful. Two years later, however, when Gentry left the *Bee* for a comparable position at the *Defender*, he took his "Mayor of Bronzeville" concept with him.[176] With the help of *Defender* promotions manager Charles Browning and the newspaper's larger circulation, Gentry's idea quickly found greater visibility and a receptive audience. Within just a few short years, the competition had evolved into a major community event that was eagerly tracked through the *Defender*'s pages. A yearly board of directors, composed of "outstanding citizens" within the local community, was appointed to moderate the election, while posters and ballot boxes were set up in barbershops, drugstores, restaurants, and churches across the South Side. By 1935, when local mortician W. T. Brown was appointed as the Mayor of Bronzeville, the occasion was marked by a lavish "inaugural" ball at the Savoy Ballroom "in the presence of 4,000 enthusiastic Bronzeville citizens."[177]

The combined success of the Billiken Parade and the Mayor of Bronzeville competition helped to reassert the *Defender*'s role as Chicago's premier Black publishing institution and to recenter 3435 Indiana Avenue within the cultural and political geography of Black Chicago. Readers and local residents were invited to deposit their mayoral ballots in voting boxes at the *Defender*'s offices, while mail-in ballots and arrivals from polling booths from subsidiary locations threatened to overwhelm the *Defender*'s mailroom. The newspaper regularly printed photographs of prominent Black celebrities casting their votes at its headquarters, as well as images of the contest's judges and board of directors hard at work in the *Defender*'s offices.[178] Yet if 3435 Indiana Avenue emerged as the de facto home for the Mayor of Bronzeville, then it was the *Bee* building at 3647 State Street that arguably provided the most compelling physical articulation of the label's literary and imaginative potential. In different but complementary ways, these sites provided a reminder that, although the "golden decade" of Black Chicagoan business had ended, its media buildings were "finally and forever on the map."[179] Furthermore, through their usage, appearance, and public representation, these locations continued to supplement the efforts of their occupants—to give voice to Chicago's Black community and to give name and shape to the African American city.

3

A Building on a Front Street

Throughout the 1920s and into the early years of the Great Depression, Chicago's Black periodicals—through their content and their buildings—had sought to give voice to the city's Black communities and to give name and shape to the emerging Black metropolis. The opening of Chicago's second World's Fair, in 1933, provided another opportunity for publications like the *Defender* to center themselves within the city's Black cultural and political geography. Against the backdrop of ongoing economic turmoil, the modernist architecture and automated marvels of the Century of Progress International Exposition offered an optimistic vision of scientific and technological advancement.[1] Its organizers declared that the theme of progress extended to the question of race, with Robert Abbott among a number of prominent Black business leaders invited to join the fair's organizing committee.[2] However, like the 1893 World's Columbian Exposition, A Century of Progress continued to render Black people either invisible or represented through racist exhibits and "plantation shows" portraying an antebellum South filled with "happy slaves willing to do anything to please their masters."[3] Fair organizers ignored calls to hire African American architects such as Walter Bailey, and widespread discrimination of Black visitors drew widespread criticisms from civil rights organizations.[4] When planners offered an olive branch through a much vaunted "Negro Day" parade held in August 1933, the event was a financial and public relations disaster.[5]

In response, Black Chicagoan institutions sought to create counter-hegemonic spaces where fairgoers could experience more positive representations of Black life and culture. When organizers decided to reject Bailey's plans for a seventy-five-thousand-square-foot pavilion that would showcase Black achievement and create a "critical physical link to Bronzeville," Black artists and businessmen chose to make this link themselves.[6] At the National Pythian Temple on Thirty-Seventh Street, Bailey helped the African and American Negro Exhibit Society (AANES) create a historical display that offered a counternarrative to the misrepresentation and underrepresentation of Black life and culture within the official boundaries of the fair. Whereas the Black presence at the Century of Progress exposition was often treated as a novelty, the AANES exhibit provided a popular attraction that took Black achievements seriously.[7] Chicago's Black press was enthusiastically involved in such boosterism. In the build-up to the fair, the *Defender* launched a "Dress-Up Campaign" to help beautify Black neighborhoods.[8] Other initiatives such as open house events and walking tours served to showcase the best of Black Chicago, with the *Bee* building's glossy black and green terra-cotta tiles and ornate gold floral plaques drawing the attention of passing motorists and pedestrians alike.[9]

For the *Defender* in particular, the fair offered another chance to remind readers of its role in shaping Black Chicagoan life and the centrality of its headquarters to this project. After the exposition's grand opening, the newspaper reported that its offices were being overrun by out-of-town readers.[10] In response the *Defender* announced the appointment of a special guide to lead tours through the plant, "explaining in detail just how the World's Greatest Weekly is printed."[11] Scores of visitors took up this offer, ranging from Black college students from Tennessee and Baptist preachers from Rhode Island to Kansas physicians and Californian office workers.[12] The *Defender* also promoted its role in helping to keep visitors safe. "Will these thousands come to Chicago for education, employment and inspiration—many never in a large city like this before—and be "taken for a ride?" worried Nahum Daniel Brascher in an editorial printed shortly before the fair's opening. It was important that all visitors "know all the facts" and upon their arrival "go direct[ly] to reliable headquarters."[13] Just as it had helped earlier migrants navigate the complexities of Black urban life during the 1910s and 1920s, the *Defender* unveiled a public service bureau that would provide a range of services designed to maximize the visitor's fair experience.[14]

The *Defender*'s visibility during the World's Fair arguably culminated in the lead-up to the 1933 edition of the Bud Billiken Parade. As representatives from Billiken clubs across the country began to arrive in Chicago, the *Defender* implored its youthful readers to "come in to see us," reporting that "boys and girls from all sections of the country . . . are receiving a warm welcome from the entire *Chicago Defender* staff."[15] One week after the disaster of Negro Day, an estimated forty-five thousand onlookers flooded the streets of Bronzeville to participate in the now annual festivities.[16] Gathering at the *Defender*'s headquarters, parade participants were led on a procession along South Parkway toward Washington Park, where they settled in for an afternoon of picnicking, games, and musical entertainment. Writing in the *Defender*, youth correspondent Albert Barnett declared that from the size of the crowd, "you'da tho't the World's Fair had moved to 35th St.!" For young and old alike, a visit to 3435 Indiana Avenue or to other Black press offices was seen to represent a "pilgrimage of gratitude" in appreciation of the loyal services rendered by their inhabitants.[17]

We have no way of knowing for certain, but it is possible that among the many African Americans who lined the streets of the South Side during the 1933 Billiken Parade, or who chose to undertake a "pilgrimage of gratitude" to the *Defender*'s offices, was a Black teenager named John H. Johnson, who had recently arrived in Chicago with his mother, Gertrude. Johnson had been born in Arkansas City in 1918 in a shotgun house on the banks of the Mississippi River, and, like many other Black Southerners of his generation, had crafted images of Black life in the big city based on the content of the *Defender* and other Black newspapers that found their way down the rivers and railroads into states like Arkansas, Georgia, and Mississippi. He declared that Chicago was "what Mecca was to the Moslems [*sic*] and what Jerusalem was to the Jews: a place of magic and mirrors and dreams."[18] For Johnson, these dreams really did come true. Less than ten years after the 1933 World's Fair, his first magazine was among the top-selling Black periodicals in the country. And less than two decades after he first arrived in Chicago, Johnson had cemented a reputation as the nation's leading Black publisher, his flagship magazine, *Ebony*, had become the most economically successful publication in the history of Black journalism, and his enterprise was ensconced within "one of the most elegant office buildings in Black America."[19]

This chapter traces the development of the Johnson Publishing Company from Johnson's arrival in Chicago to his company's move into a new corporate headquarters at 1820 Michigan Avenue in 1949. Founded in a corner office at the Supreme Life building at 3501 South Parkway, Johnson's initial forays into print journalism provide an important reminder of the intimate connections between race and place, and can be situated within the broader cultural and political milieu of the Black Chicago Renaissance, a "dynamically prolific period of African American creativity in music, performance art, social science scholarship, and visual and literary artistic expression" which spanned the 1930s to the 1950s.[20] The company's early offices, and the people who worked within them, offer a window into the complex race and gender politics of mid-century publishing and ways in which these politics were negotiated and contested within and beyond the spatial constructs of the Black newsroom. Johnson's struggles to secure a larger headquarters highlight the continued impact of racial segregation in limiting Black business development and the physical movement of Black Chicagoans during and immediately following World War II. His eventual "victory" in this endeavor complemented the aspirational content of his publications and reinforced the role of media buildings as symbols of pride, protest, and the ability of African Americans to succeed against the odds.

Along the Streets of Bronzeville

The Johnsons entered a Black community undergoing a period of spatial and sociopolitical transition. During the first two decades of the twentieth century, housing below the boundary of Forty-Seventh Street had remained largely off limits to all but a small band of middle- and upper-class Black pioneers. However, the onset of the Great Migration saw Chicago's Black community more than double between 1920 and 1930, exerting enormous demands on residential housing that necessitated expansion. In 1920 the Black population of Grand Boulevard was 32 percent and in the adjacent community area of Washington Park, 15 percent. By 1930 these numbers had increased to 95 and 92 percent, respectively, a transition that led embittered white residents to suggest that the South Side's most popular green expanse should be renamed "Booker T. Washington Park."[21] Black in-migration slowed, but did not stop, after the economic crash, pushing the lower boundary of the Black Belt steadily south throughout the 1930s. At the same time, the emergence of new cultural hotspots such as the Regal Theater at 4719 South Parkway shifted the South Side's focal point away from Thirty-Fifth and State Street and toward the corner of Forty-Seventh Street and South Parkway.[22] In their landmark 1945 study, *Black Metropolis*, sociologists St. Clair Drake and Horace Cayton characterized this intersection as the new "center of the Black Belt," contending that "if you're trying to find a certain Negro in Chicago, stand on the corner of 47th and South Parkway long enough and you're bound to see him."[23]

The Johnsons' early experiences provide a personal insight into these shifting spatial and cultural boundaries, as well as how everyday Black Chicagoans struggled to survive during the Depression years. Upon their arrival at the Illinois Central Station on Twelfth Street and Michigan Avenue, the family roomed at a friend's house on East Forty-Fourth Street. Shortly thereafter they moved to 5610 Calumet Avenue before relocating into a four-room apartment at 5412 South Parkway with Johnson's half sister Beulah and stepfather, James Williams. To help make ends meet, the apartment's sole bedroom was rented out, so the adults slept in the dining room while Johnson took a couch in the living room. Such arrangements were all too common: a 1934 city census indicated that the average Black household in Chicago contained nearly seven people and that only a quarter of Black families had fewer than one person per room.[24] After Gertrude and Beulah lost their jobs in quick succession they were forced onto the welfare roll, with Johnson bitterly recalling the government food trucks that "would roar through the South Side, like invading convoys." When the trucks stopped in front of 5412 South Parkway, he pretended to live elsewhere or avoided the neighborhood altogether.[25]

Like many Black Chicagoans "who sought breathing space outside of their cubicle rooms and kitchenettes," Johnson chose to walk the streets of Bronzeville, savoring its cultural and commercial attractions and admiring its grand architecture.[26] The middle- and upper-class white and ethnic immigrant communities that had called neighborhoods such as Douglas and Grand Boulevard home during the late nineteenth and early twentieth centuries had departed; however, many of their residential and civic buildings remained. The result was a visual smorgasbord of dilapidated tenement buildings and crumbling shanties interspersed with stone mansions, imposing churches and elegant cafes and nightclubs.[27] Whereas the Mississippi had defined Johnson's early life in Arkansas City, it was the "concrete river" of South Parkway that dominated his formative years in the Windy City. If State Street had been synonymous with the Stroll during the 1910s and early 1920s, by the time Johnson arrived it appeared that "all roads of Black Chicago ran into South Parkway," a picture-book street lined with opulent dwellings and bifurcated by "a tree-lined oasis" that, at its widest, split five lanes of traffic in either direction.[28]

Johnson was hardly the first South Side resident to take inspiration from its landscape. Poet Gwendolyn Brooks, whose acclaimed 1945 collection, *A Street in Bronzeville*, was largely composed in a two-room kitchenette on East Sixty-Third Street, later contended, "If you wanted a poem, you had only to look out of a window."[29] Brooks was part of a group of Black artists, writers, and intellectuals who coalesced on the South Side during the 1930s and 1940s, contributing to a vibrant flowering of Black arts and letters that grew out of, but in some ways surpassed, the literary and conceptual ambitions of the Harlem Renaissance. Historian Darlene Clark Hine writes that prevailing economic conditions, coupled with Chicago's role as a major industrial center, infused the Black Chicago Renaissance with a unique, and often radical, working-class and internationalist perspective.[30] This was most famously personified by Richard Wright, who lived in Chicago for a decade and used the city as the backdrop for his best-selling 1940 novel, *Native Son*.[31] Robert Bone and Richard Courage enforce this sentiment, contending that the forces that underpinned Chicago's Black Renaissance were "decidedly antiromantic, frequently militant, and fundamentally documentary or realist in spirit."[32] Although its contributors shared disparate backgrounds and political affiliations, they found unity through the distinctive cultural and political terrain of the Black metropolis, with the South Side's streets and alleyways becoming the physical threads that bound the Renaissance together.[33]

Similarly, while the youthful naivety of Johnson and the hardened political sensibilities of writers like Wright were hardly comparable, their experiences of Black Chicago were rooted in and guided by its public and private institutions. Johnson's memories of the neighborhood are dominated by landmarks such as the Regal Theater at Forty-Seventh and South Parkway, the South Center Department Store at 421 East Forty-Seventh Street, and the lavish South Parkway mansion of *Defender* publisher Robert Abbott.[34] In turn, Renaissance writers such as Brooks, Arna Bontemps, and Margaret Walker leaned on Bronzeville's institutions to develop their craft and create new literary spaces. Chief among them was the South Side Writers Group, guided by Wright and comprised of around twenty Black writers, who met to break bread and critique one another's work. A recurrent meeting place was the Abraham Lincoln Center, located at 700 East Oakwood Boulevard on the boundary between the predominantly Black neighborhood of Douglas and the more racially mixed community of Oakland. Another was the South Side Community Arts Center, established at 3831 Michigan Avenue in 1940 with support from the Works Progress Administration's (WPA's) Federal Art Project.[35]

As literary scholar Leisl Olson notes, the efforts of Black Chicagoans to seek privacy in public spaces highlight not only the "different and overlapping spheres of public life in Bronzeville" but also the disparate ways in which Black residents drew on its institutions to retheorize the relationship between race and place.[36] Perhaps the site through which the experiences of Johnson and early contributors to Chicago's Black Renaissance most regularly overlapped was the George Cleveland Hall Branch of the Chicago Public Library at Forty-Eighth Street and Michigan Avenue. Described by the *Defender* as "the most beautiful in the city" following its opening in 1932, the library's design was inspired by Italian Renaissance architecture and composed of an octagonal rotunda surrounded by four main rooms.[37] Under the leadership of Vivian Harsh, the city's first Black branch manager, Hall quickly developed a national reputation for its Special Research Collection on African American life and culture.[38] Harsh was also responsible for starting a "Book Review and Lecture Forum," which introduced Bronzeville residents to the work of Wright, Brooks, and other major Renaissance writers. Johnson recalls the library as one of his favorite haunts and how as an ambitious young student he spent much time immersing himself in "the great classics of Black history and literature."[39]

The Supreme Sun

While Johnson's reading interests extended to works by Black writers and intellectuals such as W.E.B Du Bois and Langston Hughes, his literary exploits were primarily a project of gendered self-improvement. Upon his arrival in Chicago, Johnson had enrolled at Wendell Phillips High School at Thirty-Ninth Street and South Parkway before transferring to the new DuSable High School at 4934 Wabash Avenue, named in honor of the city's Black founder, Jean Baptiste DuSable.[40] Johnson's tattered clothes and thick country accent made him a target of mirth and provided a powerful incentive to "better" himself, leading to an obsession with the bootstrapping entrepreneurship of Black conservative business leaders like Booker T. Washington, as well as self-help books like Dale Carnegie's *How to Win Friends and Influence People*. Public speaking practice in the mirror at 5412 South Parkway eventually led to a position as class president and commencement speaker at his 1936 graduation. Shortly thereafter, at a luncheon hosted by the Chicago Urban League, Johnson met Harry Pace, the president of the Supreme Liberty Life Insurance Company. Impressed with Johnson's forthright attitude, Pace offered him a part-time job at Supreme Life to help finance his college education.[41]

Perhaps no sector of the South Side's business economy benefited more from Black migration during the first half of the twentieth century than its insurance companies. Black insurers were able to exploit the prejudices of white companies, who, where they did allow Black patronage, charged African Americans higher premiums than white customers.[42] Writing for the *Chicago Daily News* in 1927, Carroll Binder cited the presence of no less than seven major Black insurance companies in the city, including Anthony Overton's Victory Life Insurance Company at 3619 State Street, as evidence of its emergence as "one of the great business centers of the Negro race."[43] Among the most prominent was the Liberty Life Insurance Company, which was launched from 3515 Indiana Avenue in 1920 by Arkansas native Frank Gillespie.[44] The following year, the company signed a five-year lease for office space on the second floor of the Roosevelt State Bank located on the southeast corner of Thirty-Fifth Street and South Parkway. The two-story, Classical-style commercial building was designed by Albert Anis, a local white architect who was also responsible for the reconstruction of the Randolph-Franklin Building at 310 West Randolph Street. After relocating to Florida during the early 1930s, Anis gained widespread recognition for his contributions to the Miami Beach commercial district.[45]

Gillespie quickly built a staff of highly trained Black clerks and administrators headed by businessman W. Ellis Stewart and attorney Earl Dickerson. By the spring of 1923, the company had underwritten close to $3 million worth of insurance, demonstrating "the vast possibilities of a high-class life insurance company in the North, owned, operated by and for Negroes."[46] The following year, Liberty Life bought 3501 South Parkway from the Roosevelt State Bank and quickly expanded its offices throughout the property. The company's growth was so rapid that Liberty Life briefly considered replacing 3501 South Parkway with a custom-built "skyscraper

Supreme Liberty Life Insurance Company. (Curt Teich Postcard Archives, Newberry Library)

improvement" at the same location.[47] This ambition was shelved after Gillespie's death in 1925, although the company would expand by purchasing a row of townhouses to the south.[48] Shortly before the Wall Street Crash, Liberty Life merged with the Supreme Life and Casualty Company of Columbus, Ohio, as well as the Northeastern Life Insurance Company based in Newark, New Jersey, a move that nearly doubled its total assets, saw its name change to Supreme Liberty Life Insurance, and led to the installation of Harry Pace, the former head of Northeastern Life, as its new president.[49]

Pace was able to guide Supreme Life through the rocky early years of the Depression without suffering the losses endured by more precocious South Side businessmen such as Anthony Overton and Jesse Binga. By the mid-1930s, the company's prospects had stabilized, and as landmarks such as the Binga Bank and the Overton Hygienic Building slipped from the hands of Black owners, 3501 South Parkway became the new center for Black business along the Thirty-Fifth Street Corridor. When Johnson first walked into the Supreme Life Building in 1936, it was a throng of activity. For a young Black man who had been raised in rural poverty, the site of a vibrant Black professional class at work on the South Side, even in the midst of the Depression, was revelatory. Johnson declared, "I'd heard about

Black corporations, but I'd never examined one up close. Now, suddenly, I was surrounded by Black clerks, salesmen, and money managers. And just like that—click, click, click, click, CLICK!—Lights went on in my mind and my life."[50]

While Johnson's position at the company was intended to help subsidize his college tuition, he soon decided to forego formal education for the school of Supreme Life. Johnson initially served as a jack-of-all trades, working as an office boy and briefly as Pace's personal driver before being promoted to a role as an editorial assistant for the *Guardian*, the company's monthly newspaper. In addition to seeking Pace's counsel, Johnson turned to figures like Earl Dickerson, who had retained his position after the 1929 merger.[51] In a more abstract sense, just as Renaissance writers tapped into the South Side's institutional and spatial memory to present Bronzeville as "a distinctive place with a distinctive aesthetic for African American cultural production," so too did Johnson draw upon the institutional knowledge of Supreme Life as well as its broader function as a "symbol of the courage and vitality" of Chicago's Black community.[52] On some days it appeared that "all roads in Black Chicago led to Supreme" and that all of the community's major happenings were either "planned, organized, or financed by people who orbited around the Supreme Sun."[53]

An Unobtrusive Desk

It is fitting, then, that Supreme Life—and its building—provided Johnson with the necessary platform to embark upon his publishing career. By 1939 he had replaced Pace as the *Guardian*'s editor and was also entrusted with compiling a weekly news digest to keep Pace abreast of events related to Black life and cultural affairs.[54] After friends and family responded enthusiastically to the project, Johnson quickly surmised that the digest could be expanded and published commercially. His role at Supreme Life had offered a valuable education in Black print, and the company's address lists provided a pool of some twenty thousand potential subscribers. With a five-hundred-dollar loan taken out against his mother's furniture—a financial arrangement that echoed Robert Abbott's earlier dependency on Henrietta Lee and positioned Gertrude as an under-the-table investor— Johnson was able to print and mail thousands of letters to prospective readers. Thousands responded to his request for a two-dollar subscription advance, providing the necessary capital to move ahead with the endeavor. The Progress Printing Company on Thirty-Third Street and Halstead was responsible for producing the *Guardian*, and Johnson convinced the printers to take on an order for his nascent publication. Its name—*Negro Digest*—reflected Johnson's ambitions for it to become a Black version of the *Reader's Digest*, a general-interest magazine founded in Chappaqua, New York, by white publisher DeWitt Wallace and his wife, Lila, around two decades earlier. By the 1940s, the *Reader's Digest* was so popular that its sales were bested only by the Bible.[55]

Unable to afford his own editorial offices, Johnson set up shop on the second floor of 3501 South Parkway in Earl Dickerson's private law office and library. His relationship with Dickerson had grown stronger during the latter's successful 1939 aldermanic campaign and his unsuccessful bid to defeat incumbent William Dawson in the 1942 race for Illinois's First Congressional District.[56] Dickerson appeared to have little use for his offices in the Supreme Life Building, perhaps due to the proximity of his home address, a tasteful double-fronted townhouse located three blocks south at 3840 South Parkway and designed by Henry Newhouse, the same architect responsible for the *Defender*'s home at 3435 Indiana Avenue.[57] As the first issue of his magazine took shape, Johnson moved constantly between his office on the first floor of 3501 South Parkway, where he continued his day job as the *Guardian*'s editor, and Dickerson's second-floor offices, where he worked on the *Digest* after hours. Shortly before the first issue was released, Johnson was permitted to formally designate the space as his own. The publisher recalled that "a man came and painted letters on the frosty glass door—Negro Digest Publishing Company—and every letter was music to my soul."[58]

Through such recollections, Johnson reinforced the critical role played by Supreme Life in advancing his publishing ambitions and shaping his understanding of the communal and civic responsibility of Black businesses. Embracing a Washingtonian narrative of bootstraps entrepreneurialism, Johnson declared that Supreme Life "was *more* than a business. It was a statement, a petition, a demonstration and an argument."[59] As the physical extension of its occupant, 3501 South Parkway thus functioned as both a model for advancing the race and a performative space for Black professional excellence. In turn, just as Abbott's early efforts to establish the *Defender* at Henrietta Lee's kitchen table at 3159 State Street had bolstered its credentials as a community paper, the image of Johnson laboring after hours in the Supreme Life building suggested a publication that was rooted in and accountable to Chicago's Black communities. From this perspective, the *Digest* was destined to succeed not only because it was guided by a talented Black entrepreneur but also because it had been founded in a recognizably "Black" space.

However, other factors serve to complicate this representation of 3501 South Parkway and the *Digest*'s own origin story. The most notable was Ben Burns, a white Jewish editor who had worked for a series of communist newspapers throughout the 1930s before returning to his hometown of Chicago and entering the ranks of its Black press. This began at the *Defender*, where Burns was hired as its national editor by John Sengstacke, who had taken control of the paper when his uncle Robert Abbott died in 1940.[60] The historical significance of the *Defender*'s headquarters at 3435 Indiana Avenue was not lost on Burns, who dryly noted that "a Jew who had never attended *shul* would now spend most of my waking hours in a former synagogue." In his autobiography, *Nitty Gritty: A White Editor in Black Journalism*, the editor paints an entertaining, if likely embellished, picture of his efforts to navigate the racially charged geography of the *Defender*'s offices following his arrival. Although his influence over the *Defender*'s copy would rapidly increase, Burns endeavored to take up as little space as possible, beginning with his "unobtrusive desk in a far off second-floor corner where few visitors ever came."[61]

Burns encountered Johnson through their respective roles on Earl Dickerson's 1942 congressional campaign, as the pair met regularly in the attorney's library at 3501 South Parkway. While Johnson would later maintain that early issues of the *Digest* were largely crafted in this space, Burns offers a quite different version of events, contending that he undertook much of the editorial and makeup work at the kitchen table of his family home before taking the magazine's copy to be made up at the Progress Printing Company, located at 3325 South Halsted Street in the predominantly white neighborhood of Bridgeport, where it was pieced together by a mix of Polish and Lithuanian immigrants.[62] The return of the "kitchen table" trope provides a neat juxtaposition with the now institutionalized history of the *Defender*'s origins and offers another reminder of how fledgling Black publications were often forced to embrace the commercial potential of domestic space. However, Burns's account of the *Digest*'s early development also undercuts the performative role of recognizably "Black" spaces such as 3501 South Parkway in its creation.[63] These spatial contestations reflect the complexities of a "white presence" that historian Jonathan Scott Holloway suggests hung over the *Negro Digest* during its early years, something that can be traced through the editorial influence of Burns, the work of white contributors, and Johnson's ongoing efforts to court white readers.[64]

From Supreme Life to State Street

Johnson was far from the first Black publisher in Chicago who harbored aspirations to develop a general-interest Black magazine. Precursors included the *Half-Century*, based at the Overton Hygienic Building on State Street, and Fenton Johnson's *Favorite*, another inhabitant of Chicago's Black newspaper row, which was housed at 3518 State Street during the late 1910s and early 1920s. These organs were heavily marketed toward the Black middle class, and historians have characterized Johnson's *Favorite* as little more than a "vanity vehicle" for its publisher. Nevertheless, their limited success suggests that the magazine format held appeal for some Black Chicagoans during this period.[65] After the *Half-Century*'s cancellation in 1925, Robert Cole, the president of the Metropolitan Funeral System, funded the *Bronzeman*, a monthly publication marketed as "a popular magazine for all," which was published out of 418 East Forty-Seventh Street.[66] A comparable but more ambitious effort was *Abbott's Monthly*, edited by Lucius Harper and published out of the *Defender*'s Indiana Avenue plant. *Abbott's Monthly* offered readers an engaging mixture of fiction, poetry, and special interest stories until it was laid low by the economic ravages of the Depression.[67]

When compared to such endeavors, the *Digest*'s remit appeared unremarkable, its first issue promising to "summarize and condense the leading articles and comment on the Negro" into a single, easy-to-read periodical.[68] Yet in retrospect its launch can be understood as a watershed moment in Black print history. Adam Green submits that the magazine "was unlike any preceding it in black journalism," eschewing the traditional role of Black periodicals as a "fighting press" to instead present an eclectic and pluralistic model of race journalism.[69] In contrast to Black newspapers such as the *Pittsburgh Courier*, whose promotion of the "Double V" campaign during World War II—against racism at home as well as fascism abroad—led to government suppression, the *Digest*'s commitment to "the development of interracial understanding and the promotion of national unity" was applauded by federal agencies and helped to secure a generous wartime paper allowance.[70] Johnson correctly surmised that his magazine could satiate the diverse interests and demands of a Black community "that was desperate for news about itself that existed beyond what was printed in the weekly police blotter or crime column." True to this mission, early issues interspersed profiles of Black celebrities and entertainers, stories of overseas travel, and comedic short fiction with reports of medical research, political satire, and a variety of opinion pieces.[71]

Content aside, Johnson was also the beneficiary of circumstance, with the *Digest* well placed to take advantage of a resurgent wartime economy, an uptick in Black urbanization, and the rise of the so-called Negro market. While Black migration out of the South had slowed during the 1930s, it rebounded dramatically over the following two decades. In the 1940 census, Chicago's Black population was 277,731; by 1960 it had grown to 812,637.[72] Furthermore, Black migrants who ventured north as part of the first wave of the Great Migration century were largely sharecroppers and uneducated rural laborers. By contrast, migrants arriving in Chicago and other urban centers during and after World War II were more likely to have been residents of Southern cities, an already urbanized and ambitious class of people who were immediately receptive to Johnson's particular brand of racial uplift and middle-class consumerism. As historian James Hall articulates, the *Negro Digest*, as well as Johnson's subsequent publications, offered a compelling articulation of both "black consumer desire frustrated by Jim Crow *and* the aura of black success."[73]

If the "aura of Black success" was central to the *Digest*'s appeal, then this idea could be equally applied to its base of operations. In the months that followed the magazine's initial release, Johnson remained a full-time employee at Supreme Life, and the magazine's "offices" remained split between the Supreme Life Building at 3501 South Parkway and Ben Burn's kitchen table. However, Dickerson's quarters had the benefit of a separate entrance and therefore a separate street address at 3507 South Parkway, allowing Johnson to position his publication as an independent enterprise rather than as a Supreme Life subsidiary. This spatial inflation of the *Digest*'s stature was complemented by Johnson's use of Supreme Life colleagues to artificially boost his magazine's early circulation. The publisher provided funds for supporters to buy up newsstand copies that were then sold back to vendors, creating the illusion of demand and boosting the publication's material presence on the sidewalk.[74] If such sleight of hand helped to establish a local audience for the *Digest*, then innovative editorial features such as "If I Were a Negro," a series that invited sympathetic white liberals to imagine their own responses to the "race problem," provided "a model for a more national brand of race journalism."[75] Within months its circulation had reached fifty thousand, and a highly publicized contribution to "If I Were a Negro" by First Lady Eleanor Roosevelt saw this number double practically overnight.[76] In July 1943 the *Digest* printed an editorial anointing itself as "the biggest Negro magazine in the world, bar none."[77]

As the *Digest* expanded, Johnson sought to extend beyond the orbit of the "Supreme Sun." In late 1943 he paid the National News Company four thousand dollars for a modest storefront office at 5619 State Street, and the new address first appeared on the magazine's masthead in January 1944.[78] Keen to entrench himself as the face of the enterprise, Johnson positioned his desk up front by the plate-glass window.[79] The *Digest* shared the building with Beauty Star Cosmetics, a mail-order cosmetics firm established by Johnson as an alternative revenue stream.[80] The offices were close to the bustling east-to-west thoroughfare of Garfield Boulevard, which, by the early 1940s, boasted some of Chicago's most popular Black nightclubs and entertainment spots. Perhaps the most prominent was the Club DeLisa at 5521 State Street, a site that helped to launch the careers of entertainers such as Billy Eckstine.[81] Other notable locales included the delightfully named Rhumboogie Club at 343 East Garfield. Writing in 1944, *Pittsburgh Courier* journalist Wendell Smith reported that "everyone in Chicago, it seemed, tried to get into the Rhumboogie" on a Saturday night.[82]

With the *Digest* safely encamped in its own building, Johnson upgraded his domestic living arrangements by purchasing a three-story apartment at 6018 St. Lawrence Street, a stone's throw from the southern border of Washington Park.[83] Then he turned his attention toward an even more ambitious publishing endeavor. The *Digest* had provided a Black counterpoint to the *Reader's Digest*, and Johnson now recognized a gap in the market for a Black picture magazine. He carried ambitions for a Black equivalent to the New York–based *Life*, which had been relaunched as a weekly photo-editorial by Henry Luce in 1936, and its competitor *Look*, a glossy biweekly magazine edited by Mike Cowles, which began publication out of Des Moines, Iowa, the following year.[84] Expanding the *Digest*'s emphasis on Black success and tying it even closer to the tastes of the upwardly mobile urban Black consumer, Johnson envisioned a magazine that would "use photo-essays to showcase a high-functioning middle- and upper-class black world" and, in the process, break the color barrier in advertising.[85] In November 1945 the first issue of *Ebony* hit newsstands across the country, promising to "mirror the happier side of Negro life—the positive, everyday achievements from Harlem to Hollywood."[86]

Even when judged against the impressive benchmark set by the *Digest*, the public response to *Ebony* was extraordinary. Johnson admits to having been broadsided by the magazine's reception, one that rocketed it into "the top circulation brackets among Negro publications." Based on cash orders alone for its second issue, *Ebony*'s editors declared that it had already become "the biggest Negro magazine in the world in both size and circulation."[87] By the autumn of 1946, its monthly audience was reportedly "easing towards the half million mark."[88] Like *Negro Digest*, *Ebony* offered an eclectic range of stories discussing the complexity and diversity of Black life across the United States and, increasingly, the Black diaspora. However, its photo-editorial format provided a powerful visual counterpoint to its upbeat copy, producing what cultural critic Maren Stange describes as images of "iconic blackness articulated to equally naturalized and sanctioned symbols of class respectability, achievement, and American national identity."[89]

Looking for *Lebensraum*

The magazine's success prompted another relocation, with *Ebony* informing readers of its January 1946 issue that it had already "outgrown its diapers and will have to get a new home."[90] Less than six months after its first issue had appeared on newsstands, the magazine unveiled its new redbrick headquarters at 5125 Calumet Avenue, close to the northwest corner of Washington Park. Breezily described as "a big two-story affair with loads of room," the building became the new home for the company's editorial, circulation, and business departments, with the editorial department inhabiting the first floor and the latter departments sharing the second floor with the company's library.[91] Johnson also maintained his State Street offices as a warehousing and shipping facility.[92] By rationalizing the move as a way to "solve the housing crisis," *Ebony*'s editors reflected their attentiveness to local concerns, with many Black Chicagoans continuing to be siloed in overpriced and unsafe residential properties.[93] At the same time, the magazine's contention that the move would provide "more *lebensraum*," albeit a poorly chosen turn of phrase given its links to Nazi ideology, assumed a level of geopolitical knowledge befitting the image of its audience as an educated, cosmopolitan set.[94]

The Calumet Building was leased from and backed onto Parkway Community House at 5120 South Parkway. Built in 1899 to house the Chicago

Orphan Asylum, 5120 South Parkway was a dramatic redbrick structure, with two main wings buttressing a recessed section that housed the main entrance.[95] It was the centerpiece in a building complex that encompassed the better part of a city block, with the Negro Digest Publishing Company's new home among a series of interconnected "cottages" built behind 5120 South Parkway along with a school wing. Indeed, editor Ben Burns suggests

Parkway Community House. (Russell Lee / Office of War Information, Library of Congress Prints and Photographs Division)

that the company's new building was reminiscent of an educational institution, with "large high-ceilinged offices off long corridors [that] seemed like classrooms."[96] The site was developed by Shepley, Rutan, and Coolidge, a Massachusetts-based architectural firm perhaps best known for its work on the World's Congress Auxiliary Building, a grand Beaux Arts structure on Michigan Avenue constructed for the 1893 World's Fair that would subsequently become the home of the Art Institute of Chicago. The orphan asylum complex provided a cultured articulation of the Colonial Revival style, most notably seen through its main building, with its tasteful exterior complemented by pale yellow terra-cotta trim, pilaster clusters, and quoin-decorated archways.[97]

The shifting demographic composition of Washington Park during the decades following its completion, coupled with the development of social welfare agencies and changes in professional approaches to child care, led the orphan asylum to abandon its South Parkway complex in 1931 in favor of a much smaller building at 4911 Lake Park Avenue.[98] Nine years later the site was purchased by the Good Shepherd Church, a local Black congregation that aimed to redevelop it as a hub for Washington Park's African American community.[99] University of Chicago–based sociologist Horace Cayton was hired as the director of the Good Shepherd Community Center, although disagreements over its direction prompted a split from the church in 1942 and its renaming as Parkway Community House. By the time the Negro Digest Publishing Company moved into 5125 Calumet Avenue, Parkway Community House had become one of Black Chicago's most important institutions. For scholars like Lawrence Jackson, it was arguably "the major outreach center devoted to improving the social, educational, and recreational lives of Chicago's South Side blacks, . . . unmatched by any other black-run institution in North America for size and comprehensiveness."[100]

To a passing observer, Johnson's magazines, most notably *Ebony*, may not appear to have shared much common ground with the work of Cayton and his Parkway associates. The former championed middle-class consumerism and an embrace of democratic capitalism as an avenue to the "happier side of Negro life," while the latter represented a politically progressive community-based social welfare agency. However, both formed part of a spectrum of complex and often competing responses to the Black migratory experience. Among Parkway House's many celebrity supporters was novelist Richard Wright, who in a 1942 pamphlet titled "The Negro and the Parkway

Community House" declared it to be "the first institution equipped with scientific knowledge of the urban situation among Negroes to attempt to control, probe, and disseminate facts to the processes, meanings, causes and effects of urbanization."[101] In turn, Johnson's magazines sought to equip their audience with "a grammar for postmigration black existence, one matching new realities of urban challenge, societal complexity, and material change."[102]

The spatial connection between the Negro Digest Publishing Company and Parkway Community House provides another example of the "different and overlapping spheres of public life in Bronzeville" during the 1930s and 1940s, which were "also sites of creativity and artistic production."[103] In this regard, these physical sites, as well as the institutions they housed, became new threads in the cultural web of Chicago's Black Renaissance. During the center's formative years, its usage had been somewhat limited by the aspirations of Good Shepherd's middle-class congregation and leadership, who envisioned the site as a means to uplift poor and working-class African Americans. As historian Anne Meis Knupfer argues, Cayton's vision for the center's development was based on the participation of all members of Chicago's Black community, "including artists, intellectuals, labor unionists, and political groups." This was a concern for churchgoers, who feared that visits from leftist writers like Richard Wright would lead to "a reputation for being radical."[104] However, after its split from the church, Parkway Community House's literary and artistic programming significantly expanded, helping to position it as "a significant institution in the Chicago Black Renaissance."[105]

It is not hard to imagine employees of the Negro Digest Publishing Company slipping out on their lunch breaks to participate in writing groups or to view art and photograph exhibits. Perhaps staffers occasionally left work early to secure a good seat at one of Parkway House's well-attended lecture series or to savor public performances from prominent artists and intellectuals such as Paul Robeson and Marian Anderson.[106] Conversely, the building's proximity to Parkway House made it easier for visitors to swing by the offices of *Ebony* and *Negro Digest*, with writers such as Langston Hughes, Gwendolyn Brooks, Richard Wright, Frank London Brown, and Lorraine Hansberry all publishing, or seeking to publish, work in Johnson's magazines.[107] One of the company's most frequent collaborators was also one of its closest neighbors, as Cayton contributed articles to the *Digest* both before and after the company's move to 5125 Calumet Avenue.[108] At-testing to the strength of this connection, later accounts would incorrectly assert that Johnson Publishing "was founded in rooms in [the] back of Parkway."[109] Such intersections of place and literary production provide another reminder of Johnson's reliance on specific Black Chicagoan in-stitutions such as Supreme Life and Parkway Community House in the advancement of his publishing enterprise, as well as the intimate connec-tions between his magazines' content; their corporate headquarters; and the unique cultural, sociopolitical, and intellectual terrain of Chicago's Black metropolis.

On Space and Staff

And yet, despite these connections, it is likely that a good chunk of the ma-terial that appeared in Johnson's publications during this period continued to be edited outside of these spaces. Ben Burns says that while the Negro Digest Publishing Company relocated several times during the mid-1940s, "for all practical purposes, the editorial offices still remained my kitchen table."[110] By the time Johnson purchased 5619 State Street, Burns had moved to an apartment at 3725 Lake Park Avenue, a "lily-white" community sepa-rated from the South Side's Black neighborhoods by the unofficial barrier of Cottage Grove Avenue. And by the time that the company had relocated to Calumet Avenue, Burns had moved to an apartment at 4438 Jackson Bou-levard in West Garfield Park, more than forty minutes' drive northwest of *Ebony*'s offices and one of the many Chicago neighborhoods that remained heavily segregated due to a combination of street-level white resistance and racially discriminatory housing and lending practices. On occasions when Johnson visited to deliver typed proofs or discuss story ideas, his elegant style and gleaming automobile prompted curtain twitching from anxious white neighbors: "Who could this hulking black man in a big black Cadillac be, perhaps a gangster?"[111] Such incidents were indicative of the cognitive dissonance created for white racists upon seeing a Black body "out of place"—that is, removed from the spatial confines of the Black Belt and its connected visual signifiers of racialized inferiority. Novelist Margo Jefferson, whose family moved from Bronzeville to a predominantly white neighborhood during the 1940s, recalls her father being stopped by police officers on his way home from work—another case where the image of a well-dressed Black man in a white neighborhood could be rationalized only through an assumption of criminality.[112]

Burns's residence in a white West Side neighborhood certainly proved to be a source of misgiving: "Was I hypocritical in living 'white' while championing the Negro cause?"[113] When Johnson Publishing moved to 5125 Calumet Avenue, Burns did begin to spend more time in the company's editorial offices. However, this development merely raised different but equally thorny questions about his role and visibility within the Negro Digest Publishing Company. For his part, Burns appeared to navigate this transition through a problematic lens of autoethnography, writing that as he became acclimatized to his new surroundings, he "began to think and feel as a Negro, becoming as angry and bitter at moments as a racial zealot and also having to play the contrite Uncle Tom at times."[114] In a curious twist, the editor's swarthy complexion, combined with the racially charged backdrop of the company's offices, meant he was often assumed to be Black by association.[115] Adam Green suggests that Burns's visibility led to another form of cognitive dissonance, remarking, "The presence of an actual white person in such a thoroughly black-defined environment" proved difficult to reconcile for many guests.[116]

However, as visitors began to inspect the company's offices with increasing frequency, Johnson found himself having to answer difficult questions about the role of white contributors on his staff. After some readers charged that the outfit was "white owned and run by a group of paleface agitators," the publisher reprinted a statement of ownership in *Ebony* next to his own photograph to prove that he was the "brains and money behind the enterprise without strings attached."[117] White staffers during the early years included Kay Cremin, who took up a role as an associate editor for *Ebony*, and Mike Shea, a regular *Life* contributor, who quickly became one of *Ebony*'s most trusted freelancers.[118] Connections were often facilitated by Cayton, who introduced potential new contributors to Johnson's company. Among them was Wayne Miller, a gifted photographer who, after a chance meeting with Cayton and Burns at Parkway Community House, interspersed *Ebony* assignments with two consecutive Guggenheim Fellowships between 1946 and 1948. Exactly where to locate these staffers became a contentious issue, as Burns found himself sequestered "away from the vision of routine visitors," a move that echoed earlier efforts to minimize his presence at the *Defender*'s plant.[119]

Irrespective of Burns's continued influence over its direction, the rapid expansion of Johnson's publishing enterprise led to a wave of talented Black editors joining its payroll. One of the most significant early additions was Allan Morrison, who had established his journalistic reputation as the first Black correspondent for the U.S. military publication *Stars and Stripes* during World War II.[120] Described by Johnson as "a zealous New Yorker who believed civilization stopped at the Hudson River," Morrison did not take to Chicago, resigning from *Ebony* and returning to the East Coast after little more than a year to edit the Harlem-based *People's Voice*.[121] However, when Johnson opened a New York bureau, Morrison was rehired as *Ebony*'s New York editor and would remain with the publication up until his premature death in 1968.[122] Morrison was quickly joined by contributors such as Freda DeKnight, who became *Ebony*'s food editor, and Era Bell Thompson, a gifted writer who caught Johnson's eye following the publication of her 1946 autobiography *American Daughter*.[123]

This growing pool of staffers was primarily driven by *Ebony*'s unprecedented popularity. By 1947 the magazine had instituted an advertising guarantee of four hundred thousand readers per issue, prompting Johnson to shift his printing contract to the white-owned Hall Printing Company at 4600 West Diversey Avenue. Situated around eleven miles northwest of Johnson Publishing's home address, the Hall plant at 4600 West Diversey Avenue was reported to be the world's largest single printing plant.[124] Ironically, *Ebony*'s success threatened to be its undoing because its high production costs were not yet offset by comparative advertising revenues. In a rare moment of candor, the November 1947 edition of "Backstage," the magazine's regular "behind-the-scenes" feature, admitted that "there have been times when red ink threatened to wipe out the black on our ledgers."[125] However, a contract with the Zenith Radio Company helped Johnson secure a foothold in the lucrative white advertising market, and by February 1948 *Ebony* had expanded to sixty-eight pages per issue in order to accommodate advertising from companies such as Pepsi-Cola, Seagram's, and Remington-Rand.[126] These breakthroughs made it the first Black periodical to attract major corporate advertising and elevated Johnson to a position as one of the nation's most influential Black publishers and corporate spokespeople.[127] They also allowed its workforce to continue expanding; by the spring of 1948 the company had around one hundred full-time employees and thousands more independent distributors.[128]

Succeeding against the Odds

The seemingly inexorable growth of Johnson's publishing enterprise prompted him to reexamine his relationship with the South Side. As the first half of this chapter demonstrates, Bronzeville and its institutions played a critical role in nurturing the company's formation and early development, something reflected not only in its physical locations but also in the content of its publications. Furthermore, just as the *Defender*'s Indiana Avenue headquarters grounded its dual focus on local and national concerns, so too did the South Side offices of Johnson's magazines allow them to navigate these overlapping interests. As a result, *Ebony* and *Negro Digest* successfully laid claim to a "national brand of race journalism" while staying true to Black Chicago institutions and topics.[129] News of Black life across and beyond the United States remained interspersed with upbeat local interest stories like that of Clifford Blount, a World War II veteran who had built a successful sales business from a tiny stand on the South Side.[130] Through this process, Johnson's magazines were able to more persuasively advance their efforts to document "the Negro's everyday life on Main Street from coast to coast."[131]

Yet while his magazines continued to thrive and his efforts to entice white advertisers bore greater fruit, Johnson's attitudes toward the South Side appeared to shift. As Drake and Cayton note, despite its resurgence during the World War II era, Chicago's Black metropolis was still just the "Black Belt" to many white observers, a "dumping ground for vice, poor-quality merchandise, and inferior white city officials."[132] By the late 1940s, Johnson appeared to have taken such characterizations to heart, with the community that had been the source of such excitement during his teenage years now seen primarily as a site of constraint. Burns suggests that Johnson was desperate to "break out of the 'Black Belt,'" with the company's offices "no longer fitting Johnson's dreams of publishing glory." Johnson's own memoirs reinforce this sentiment: "What I really wanted was to move downtown. I was tired of working on back streets. State Street was a back street. Calumet Avenue was a back street. I wanted to work on a front street. I wanted to go first class."[133]

In 1949 Johnson decided to pursue this ambition further. He scoured the southern edge of Chicago's central Loop district, eventually finding a suitable location at 1820 Michigan Avenue. One of Chicago's great historic boulevards, the section of Michigan Avenue running south from Tenth Street initially rose to prominence as a prestigious residential neighborhood. The building Johnson had earmarked as his new corporate headquarters was close to a six-block stretch of Prairie Avenue and adjacent streets that had housed many of Chicago's business and political elite during the last decades of the nineteenth century. Known as "Millionaire's Row," this exclusive section included the homes of department store magnate Marshall Field, railroad entrepreneur George Pullman, and industrialist Philip Armour. Perhaps the most impressive residence was 1800 Prairie Avenue, located just a few hundred yards west of the intersection of Eighteenth Street and Michigan Avenue.[134] Designed by innovative young architect Henry Hobson Richardson for manufacturing magnate John Glessner, the building was a "revolutionary expression of the urban townhouse mansion."[135]

The building at 1820 Michigan Avenue had begun its life as a cultural center for Chicago's upper classes before being purchased by funeral director P. J. Hursen, who saw the three-story building as a perfect opportunity to expand his business. It was a prestigious site and former hotspot for the city's elite, and Hursen informed potential clients that the structure was "one of the most magnificent mansions ever built" along the Michigan Avenue Corridor.[136] In characteristically lucid advertising content placed in the *Chicago Tribune* after its purchase, the funeral director described 1820 Michigan Avenue as a "$100,000 palace, built in English Mansion style . . . [and] furnished in every detail in obedience to the demands of comfort, simple elegance and luxury."[137] For Hursen, whose success was carefully crafted around his reputation as a funeral provider of "extreme elegance," 1820 Michigan Avenue's "vaulted ceilings . . . [and] spacious interiors" offered a worthy complement to his company's funeral homes at 929 Belmont Avenue on the North Side and 2346 Madison Street on the West Side.[138] For Johnson the building's rich heritage and dramatic arched entranceway appeared to satisfy his dream of "an exceptional building that would suit *Ebony*'s vaunted status as the nation's foremost Black publication."[139]

However, the publisher's efforts to purchase the site quickly ran into difficulties. When Hursen discovered that Johnson was Black, he declared that the building was no longer for sale.[140] Beyond an exhibition of individual prejudice, this rejection was the latest example of white efforts to contain African American expansion outside the boundaries of the Black metropolis.

Understandably, much of the scholarship has focused on residential segregation, with redlining, restrictive housing covenants, discriminatory mortgage lending practices, and the efforts of neighborhood "improvement associations" all attempting to allay the encroachment of Black residents from Chicago's congested "Negro colony."[141] As Robin Bachin argues, these resentments highlight the "central role of territoriality and the racializing of urban space in determining white response to black settlement patterns."[142] However, it is important to note that discriminatory housing practices also impacted commercial property, stymieing the efforts of Black businessowners to establish a foothold in other areas of the city.

Unfazed by Hursen's racism, Johnson covertly plotted to secure the property. Colleagues suggested that he contact the NAACP and stage public demonstrations to raise awareness of the injustice, but Johnson believed that approach would scupper any chance he had of completing the deal.[143] Instead, he turned to the services of Louis Wilson, a white lawyer, and persuaded him to pose as a representative of an East Coast–based publishing company. After Wilson contacted Hursen and informed him of the alleged plans to open an office in Chicago, a sale price of fifty-two thousand dollars was quickly agreed upon. However, there was one condition: Wilson informed Hursen that the company had a Black janitor who would be living at the facility and whom they wanted to inspect the plant. Disguised in work overalls, Johnson was given a detailed tour of the building, including special attention to the boiler room where he would presumably be working. Johnson's final act of subterfuge involved changing his company's name from the Negro Digest Publishing Company to the more racially neutral designation of the Johnson Publishing Company to ensure the sale was completed smoothly. Satisfied that the space matched his "notions of a distinguished home for his expanding ventures," Johnson set about transforming it into "one of the most elegant office buildings in Black America."[144]

The tale of how Johnson was able to secure his new headquarters quickly became a key plank in his public representation as a shrewd business tactician and a tale he took no less enjoyment telling decades after the fact.[145] Beyond bolstering his individual reputation, Johnson's decision to disguise himself as the building's janitor took on a broader performative function by positioning him as a trickster, an enduring character in African American folklore. A key theme within Black trickster tales is the ability of the trickster to subvert racialized stereotypes or language, thus turning negative characteristics and social expectations into a positive outcome.[146] By disguising himself as a janitor, Johnson was able to weaponize white expectations of Black servitude to inspect 1820 Michigan Avenue without arousing suspicion—effectively flipping entrenched societal expectations of African Americans as unskilled domestics and iterant laborers to advance his own standing. It was a trope that would appear repeatedly in *Ebony* stories over subsequent years, with Black businessmen like manufacturer Charles Smith and bankers Joseph Morris and Bernard Garrett either mistaken for the help or donning janitorial garb "in order to inspect their financial interests."[147]

The effectiveness of Johnson's disguise was particularly resonant given his usual fastidiousness about personal appearance—something that had contributed to his earlier characterization as a "gangster" by scurrilous whites observing his visits to Burns's home on West Jackson Boulevard. The publisher's reputation for sartorial elegance was legendary; one former staffer recalled that he could not remember ever seeing Johnson "without either a vest or his suitcoat buttoned."[148] Similarly, this dapper appearance was on prominent display in profiles by local and national news outlets, with Johnson even appearing in full evening dress as part of a 1955 home photo shoot by the *Chicago Daily News*.[149] This context renders Johnson's decision to trade his glad rags for overalls even more powerful. It was also a decision that echoed the willingness of Robert Abbott to put the *Defender*'s early fortunes ahead of his own appearance when he had roved the streets of the South Side in an overcoat stuffed with newspaper and cardboard in his shoes. Johnson declared, "If I had to do it over again, I would. I stooped all the time to get what I wanted."[150]

Give-and-Take Affairs

In April 1949 the Johnson Publishing Company formally moved into 1820 Michigan Avenue. The funeral home's spacious reception rooms were converted into open-plan editorial spaces, its waiting rooms became executive offices, and its "sky-lighted, dust-proof showrooms" were transformed into administrative, mailing, promotional, and bookkeeping departments.[151] Exciting new facilities included a test kitchen for food editor Freda DeKnight, a specialist darkroom for the company's photographers, and "a complete library on the Negro, . . . one of the most extensive and thorough in the nation."[152] After renovations were completed, the company announced two separate open house events. The first was reserved for the city's press, and according to *Ebony*, "The folks from the newssheets and magazines went away pop-eyed." The second was an altogether more riotous affair thrown for Black celebrities and community leaders, who informed Johnson that the building was "one of the most elegant offices of any Negro business in the country." Whether white or Black, journalist or celebrity, the magazine reported that visitors couldn't miss its new headquarters, with an illuminated *Ebony* sign visible for more than a mile along Chicago's famed Michigan Avenue.[153]

Given that inviting the whole of its audience to an open house party was impossible, *Ebony* informed readers that "we'll be taking the liberty of coming into your home" instead.[154] In October 1949 the magazine made good on its promise by publishing a detailed photo guide that "puts our offices on display and shows how [the] magazine is brought to you."[155] The photographer tasked with shooting the company's "showpiece" headquarters was Stephen Deutch, a Hungarian immigrant whose sculptural training had a major influence over *Ebony*'s early visual style.[156] With grand ceremony, *Ebony* informed readers that the editorial provided the same tour that visitors had been treated to in person. Furthermore, the images of its new headquarters were interspersed with photos from the company's actual open house events. In providing readers with access to their own literary open house event *and* the building's real-world unveiling, *Ebony* sought to narrow the space between everyday Black readers and the Black elite, providing an aspirational and integrated vision of African American celebrity, class, and consumerism that reinforced the editorial messaging that lay at the heart of the magazine's mass appeal.

At the same time, the photo guide provided readers with a rare insight into the inner workings of a major Black publishing firm, one that positioned them as both valued customers and trusted confidantes. This was most evident through staged photographs of normally exclusive spaces, such as Johnson's executive suite, or potentially sensitive events, such as *Ebony*'s weekly editorial staff meetings. Described as "wide-open, give-and-take affairs with full freedom of discussion," images of the company's interracial and mixed-gender editorial staff clearly sought to make the private politics of the workplace legible for a wider audience, just as regular editorial features like "Backstage" endeavored to provide *Ebony*'s audience

Ebony magazine editorial meeting. (Stephen Deutch, Chicago History Museum)

with a glimpse into the behind-the-scenes workings of a major publishing company.[157] The perceived authenticity of such images had the additional benefit of reinforcing the company's reputation as a progressive and tight-knit publishing firm that provided equal opportunities to Black men and women who were talented enough to take them.

However, the experiences of editorial staff retold through archival papers and personal memoirs help to illuminate the spaces that often existed between this carefully crafted image of racial and gender harmony and the realities of life at Johnson Publishing. Ben Burns discovered that the contestations that had characterized his formative years at Johnson Publishing only continued after the company's relocation to 1820 Michigan Avenue. The editor's office, located on a mezzanine level overlooking the main editorial offices on the first floor, left him in the contentious position of "literally talking down to the staff like an overseer."[158] Some staffers found Burns's alleged status as a "race traitor" amusing, with *Ebony* contributor Kenneth Campbell posting an oversized notice on the company's bulletin board declaring, "Germany had Einstein, Britain had Shaw, But *Ebony* has the world's only white Mau Mau."[159] Others took aim at Burns and other white employees, such as photographer Bob Florian, who was in charge of running the company's darkroom. After Florian reportedly "evicted" Black photographers David Jackson and Isaac Sutton from the space, another bulletin board notice appeared accusing him of attempting "to make the darkroom lily-white." While such incidents were usually in good humor, they occasionally revealed deeper tensions over the continued role of whites in shaping the company's editorial and visual content.[160]

Similarly, the image of progressive gender politics exhibited through Deutch's photographs do not completely align with the experiences of Johnson Publishing's female staff. To be sure, the company provided an invaluable space for Black women, many of them routinely denied professional opportunities at white-owned businesses. Figures such as comptroller Mildred Clark and agency director Willie Burns, both of whom would later become vice presidents, were able to carve out rewarding administrative careers, while contributors such as food editor Freda DeKnight and librarian Doris Saunders were among the company's most influential and well-respected employees.[161] On the other hand, staffers like comanaging editor Era Bell Thompson often found themselves marginalized. After the move to 1820 Michigan Avenue, Thompson repeatedly complained to Johnson that she had been shut out of editorial meetings, asserting that "such unusual procedure certainly leaves a question in my mind as to my position here." For Thompson, such events were a reflection of her literary erasure, as she saw a pronounced lack of bylines with her name compared to those of male colleagues. The editor bitterly noted that despite claiming "more responsibility than any other member of the editorial staff, I am not even a full managing editor," a slight that led her to repeatedly threaten resignation.[162]

Thompson's experiences serve as a reminder that despite Johnson Publishing providing an important space for Black professional women, the company's female staffers were still beholden to the often-restrictive gender politics that characterized American professional and intellectual life at mid-century. As historian Kathleen Cairns attests, many professional American men, whether working within "the ivied walls of academe [or] little-strewn newsrooms . . . shared a mind-set and gender-coded language that served to keep women out of their fraternity."[163] The marginalization of female journalists, and of Black female journalists in particular, was the product of a hegemonic masculine culture that separated the newsroom into male "insiders" and female "outsiders," something that minimized Thompson's bylines and literally left her on the outside of editorial meetings. We can link these concerns to *Ebony*'s editorial content, with the magazine often neglecting the intellectual contributions of Black women and replicating problematic discourses around Black beauty and gender norms. The clearest example of such tensions can be seen on the magazine's covers, where portrait shots of Black male politicians, sports stars, and civic leaders contrasted with scantily clad, and overwhelmingly light-skinned, Black female models, an approach that historian Noliwe Rooks suggests was part of "a larger strategy to construct and market particular forms of African American female identity to African Americans and to white advertisers."[164]

More broadly, just as *Ebony*'s cover images and editorial content helped to reinforce gendered understandings of the social and political role inhabited by Black men and women, so too gender appeared to play a role in the division or demarcation of interior space within 1820 Michigan Avenue and, indeed, within newsrooms across the country. This can be seen through other sections of *Ebony*'s aforementioned photo essay, which provides the discerning reader with a spatial insight into the company's gendered hierarchies and power dynamics. In senior editorial spaces, largely the domain of men, built-in furniture, doors, and wooden panels offer exclusivity and privacy. By contrast, in spaces predominantly organized around or populated by women, such as the mailing and subscription departments, back-to-back desks and open-concept designs dominate.[165]

Perhaps the most clearly gendered space was Freda DeKnight's test kitchen, which at five thousand dollars, cost more than Johnson's first independent offices. Described as "a housewife's dream," the kitchen boasted a wide range of modern appliances, while the staff and guest dining rooms provided the food editor with plenty of opportunity to test recipes on fellow employees and "top-name celebrities."[166] By contrast, Johnson's lavish executive suite, resplendent with leather-covered furniture, heavy satin draperies, and an oversized desk, offered a gendered vision of Black professional achievement that reinforced his positionality as a race man. This sentiment was picked up by other magazines, such as *Business Week*, which gushed over the publisher's "1-inch-deep buff carpets, rust and green drapes, a huge bay window, and a massive white oak desk flanked by a bronze nude and a gold-painted Dictaphone."[167]

A Building on a Front Street

It is unlikely that many readers picked up or focused on such tensions, choosing instead to celebrate Deutch's images as a visual document of the company's continued success. Indeed, perhaps the most striking feature of *Ebony*'s photo essay was how it utilized the presumed "transparency" of the photographic medium to legitimate the company's role as a vehicle "for building and projecting the image of Black people in America," just as the magazine's broader use of images helped to reify Black experiences that were marginalized within the cultural and political mainstream.[168] As Maren Stange argues, *Ebony*'s editors used photographs "that would not only uphold familiar codes of journalistic objectivity but also detach images of blacks from their pervasive association with equally familiar cultural representations as spectacular and/or degraded Others."[169] This sentiment was articulated in much plainer terms by Johnson in his memoirs: "Black people wanted to see themselves in photographs. . . . We were going places we had never been before and doing things we'd never done before, and we wanted to see that."[170] From this perspective, the simple act of depicting its own offices allowed *Ebony* to chip away at the social and spatial limitations inscribed upon Black life by white people and media outlets.

In doing so, *Ebony* used its offices as an extension of its editorial efforts to normalize Black achievement, with the magazine endeavoring to present Black people as "everyday, common workingmen and professionals . . . neither winged angels . . . or problem children."[171] Yet at the same time, its photo essay provides another example of the magazine's continued efforts to create a visual language of "iconic blackness" that was rooted in classed notions of respectability, achievement, and national belonging.[172] The result was a representation of 1820 Michigan Avenue that was simultaneously quixotic and quotidian. It was a site where ordinary Black people did exceptional things, where employees carried out everyday tasks such as attend meetings, run switchboards, and order offices supplies, but did so in "one of the most elegant offices of any Negro business in the country."[173] Apart from an image of Johnson posing at his desk, staffers appeared oblivious to the camera, just as the Supreme Life employees "scurrying from office to office with stacks of papers and fat files" had been too busy to notice Johnson's gaze when he had entered 3501 South Parkway for the first time, more than a decade earlier.[174]

Of course, the occupants of 1820 Michigan Avenue *were* busy. John-son contended that "in the world today everything is moving along at a faster clip. There is more news and far less time to read it." Shortly after the company's relocation, it debuted *Tan Confessions*, designed to tap into the popularity of "true confessions" publications. In 1951 Johnson sus-pended *Negro Digest* and launched *Jet*, a "provocative little news weekly" that provided readers with a succinct, easy-to-read summary of Black life and culture. Local journalists were invited to the publication's unveiling at a swanky luncheon at 1820 Michigan Avenue, where they sipped cocktails and met with contributors like managing editor Edward Clayton.[175] *Hue*, a monthly outlet for Black gossip and celebrity, and *Copper Romance*, another confessional publication, followed.[176] These publications were matched by a flurry of new editorial appointments, with the promise of higher wages and exciting travel assignments tempting influential Black editors from across the country. Among them were Audrey Weaver, Vincent Tubbs, and Kenneth Carter, who were lured away from the *Afro-American*; Robert Johnson and Lerone Bennett Jr., who were poached from the *Atlanta Daily World*; Edgar Rouzeau, the editor of the *Oklahoma Eagle*; and Gerri Major, the longtime society editor of the *New York Amsterdam News*.[177] Just as the *Defender* had linked its move to Indiana Avenue with the creation of the "greatest galaxy of newspaper workers ever assembled," so too did *Ebony* suggest that 1820 Michigan Avenue generated its own physical pull. Several years after the relocation, Johnson proudly announced that "the best newspapermen in the business have gravitated to our Chicago offices."[178]

Perhaps inevitably, the addition of new publications and new staffers led to further building expansion. While 1820 Michigan Avenue had initially helped to alleviate a "bad case of growing pains," the company's continued growth meant that by 1953 its new headquarters was already close to ca-pacity. Johnson admitted, "Our growth has cramped us for space, and we have found expansion necessary once again."[179] The publisher purchased and remodeled an adjacent building, adding nearly thirty thousand square feet of office space.[180] The expanded plant was officially unveiled to read-ers through another visual tour, published in *Ebony*'s tenth-anniversary special.[181] To emphasize the company's insatiable expansion, a multipage spread included an image of employees lined up on the pavement outside its Michigan Avenue building, as if even the remodeled offices were not large enough to contain them. In a sense this impression was right, as dozens more employees were stationed in satellite offices in New York and Los Angeles, and a network of part-time stringers was needed to help fill the gaps in between.[182] For Chicago-based staffers, the move was physically "just a short trip—up the steps and through the arch into our new building next door." At the same time, "as an indication of the progress made by the company . . . the trip is enormous."[183]

Yet even as Johnson continued to bask in the glow of his company's impressive new corporate headquarters, readers may have balked at his apparent willingness to equate professional advancement with prime downtown real estate. The unique artistic and commercial culture of the South Side—a culture that had given rise to the Black Chicago Renaissance and facilitated the rise of hugely influential Black businesses like Supreme Life—had played a critical role in nurturing Johnson's magazines, whether through providing literal inspiration or literally housing his fledgling publications. However, his desire for a first-class and front street address appeared to be predicated on distancing himself from the Black metropolis and establishing closer geographical proximity to whiteness as coded through the city's central business district. As the following chapter demonstrates, such tensions would also come to bear at the *Chicago Defender* after the newspaper followed Johnson Publishing onto Michigan Avenue during the 1950s. In response, both outlets sought to reassert the significance of their buildings as key civic spaces, community hubs, and tourist sites for African Americans in Chicago, and for Black people within and beyond the United States.

4

A Meeting Place for
All the People

Among the many people in attendance at Johnson Publishing's open house events in 1949 was *Chicago Defender* publisher John Sengstacke. A nephew and protégé of Robert Abbott, Sengstacke had been groomed to succeed the newspaper's founder from a young age. Abbott helped to finance Sengstacke's education at the Hampton Institute—his own alma mater—and arranged valuable work experience at the *Defender* during Sengstacke's summer vacations.[1] In 1934 Sengstacke moved into Abbott's palatial South Parkway home and began a role in the *Defender*'s bookkeeping department. Six years later he assumed full control of the newspaper's operations following Abbott's death in February 1940 at the age of sixty-nine. After navigating a rocky first few years at the newspaper's helm, Sengstacke helped to widen the *Defender*'s sphere of influence and stabilize its finances. By the early 1950s, he had gone even further, adding "a chain of newspapers . . . that stretch[ed] from Memphis to New York City."[2] For Black leaders such as educator Mary McLeod Bethune, Sengstacke was a worthy heir to Abbott's empire, "carrying high the torch passed on to him by a distinguished sire."[3]

Pictured reviewing "business prospects" with *Ebony* publisher John H. Johnson in the magazine's coverage of its open house events, Sengstacke appeared suitably impressed with the company's new home.[4] However, his upbeat demeanor hid deeply rooted frustrations over the challenges he had faced in establishing control over the *Defender*'s newsroom and the continued deterioration of his own publishing plant. Within months of his attendance of Johnson's open house events, Sengstacke had begun to lobby for "the construction of a substantial *Chicago Defender* office and Community Building."[5] Beyond helping to distance himself from Abbott's long shadow and to solidify his own legacy as a successful Black publisher, Sengstacke saw the modernization of the *Defender*'s facilities as an important part of ensuring "a substantial and sound future" for the publication.[6] On the occasion of the *Defender*'s fiftieth anniversary, Sengstacke formally announced a million-dollar program for a new plant, presses, and other equipment. Several years later, the *Defender* completed its long-awaited move into a new headquarters at 2400 Michigan Avenue.

Just as the opening of the Johnson Publishing Building had been celebrated as a landmark moment in the company's rise, so too did Sengstacke believe that the *Defender*'s new plant would preserve its "position of leadership" and reputation as the "dean" of Chicago's Black newspaper group.[7] However, the respective relocations of Johnson Publishing and the *Defender* away from the heart of Chicago's Black metropolis raised difficult questions about their continued representation of, and relevance to, the city's African American community. In an attempt to mediate this transition, both enterprises championed their new offices as important civic centers for Black people within (and increasingly beyond) Chicago. Not just centripetal sites from which ideas, images, and information were distributed outward, these buildings became centrifugal sites that drew people and activity to them.[8] As exhibition spaces, social hubs, and tourist hotspots, 2400 Michigan Avenue and 1820 Michigan Avenue served as the gateway to Black Chicago, and Black America, for an eclectic cast of visitors. Through their new role as "a crossroads of the world," these buildings assumed cultural and political responsibilities that stretched far beyond their role as practical sites for the production of Black print. In the process, they expanded Robert Abbott's long-standing dream for Black media buildings to function as "the meeting place of all the people," providing a vibrant public square that complemented the Black public spheres curated by their inhabitants.[9]

A Changing of the Guard

Sengstacke's integration into the *Defender*'s workforce during the early 1930s was a lone bright spot for Abbott amid deepening economic malaise and deteriorating health. The Depression had pushed the newspaper to the brink of bankruptcy, while Abbott's ongoing battle with Bright's disease had left him largely bedridden.[10] Personal correspondence between the publisher and his nephew reveal the seriousness of the situation: "I am being bled on every hand in finances and I hope that you will do everything that you can to see that your *Defender* doesn't hit the bottom."[11] Abbott's desire to bring Sengstacke into the fold was likely influenced by growing suspicions about his workforce. During the 1920s, business manager Phil Jones and several senior staffers had been dismissed for embezzlement, and Black attorney Nathan McGill was just one member of Abbott's inner circle who used the publisher's failing health as an opportunity to enrich his own coffers.[12] When presented with hard evidence, Abbott fired McGill and handed effective control of the newspaper to Sengstacke, announcing via an all-department notice that his nephew was "not a spy or a so-called stool pigeon but an office manager with duties and responsibilities to perform."[13]

At just twenty-one years old and still adjusting to life in the urban North, Sengstacke suddenly found himself in control of a publication that seemed to be careering toward disaster. In addition to economic challenges and the health problems afflicting its publisher, the *Defender* found itself under attack for its use of white typesetters, composers, and press operators. Ethan Michaeli suggests that by the 1930s the *Defender*'s continued employment of white workers had become "a liability in the newspaper's ongoing competition with its peers," with the *Whip* and other Black publications criticizing the *Defender*'s willingness to employ whites at a time when Black unemployment rates were spiraling out of control.[14] The newspaper's use of the white-owned Charles Levy Circulating Company to handle its distribution was another point of contention.[15] Shortly after being appointed office manager, Sengstacke staged a symbolic lockout of the newspaper's white mechanical staff and replaced them with an all-Black team—a move that helped to quiet the *Defender*'s detractors and had the added benefit of reducing its payroll.

However, Sengstacke was initially able to do little about the newspaper's sliding circulation or the rise of rivals such as the *Pittsburgh Courier*.[16] Founded in 1907, the *Courier* was edited and governed by Robert Lee Vann, a prominent Black attorney and a graduate from the University of Pittsburgh. By the late 1920s, the newspaper's continued growth enabled Vann to construct a new headquarters at 2628 Centre Avenue in the Hill District, a neighborhood east of downtown that became the epicenter of Black life in Pittsburgh during the interwar period.[17] Its opening was the catalyst for a major circulation expansion, with the *Courier* supplanting the *Defender* as the nation's most popular Black periodical by the mid-1930s. Adding insult to injury, the *Courier* also opened a new Chicago bureau in the Ben Franklin store on Forty-Seventh Street, with its unveiling in 1939 attended by "hundreds of business and civic leaders."[18] The offices quickly became a popular meeting place, aided by public events designed "to boost Negro enterprises" such as an appearance by world speed-typing record holder Cortez Peters, with scores of curious pedestrians gathering outside the *Courier*'s bureau to watch Cortez "demonstrating his skill on a typewriter to the accompaniment of music."[19]

Despite such challenges, the *Defender*'s plant remained an exciting environment. In his 1987 autobiography, *American Diary*, legendary Black journalist Enoch Waters recounted his first experiences of 3435 Indiana Avenue after joining the *Defender* during the mid-1930s. A tour around the newsroom, which encompassed the majority of the building's second floor, immediately provided an insight into the *Defender*'s bustling internal politics. The private offices of staffers such as Lucius Harper, Frank Young, and Jay Jackson overlooked the domain of city editor Dewey Jones, who commanded a desk in the center of the room surrounded by more junior contributors, such as Dan Burley and Daniel Clay. Harper was a dynamic presence within the newsroom, "personally involved in every aspect of the editorial operation." Other gregarious personalities included society editor Rebecca Styles Taylor, a former secretary of the National Association of Colored Women. Waters recalls that Taylor held her own in the newsroom with a combination of caustic wit and the occasional nip "from the half pints of bourbon that were quietly circulated."[20] This characterization of Taylor as "one of the boys" reinforces Kathleen Cairns's assertion that "to breach the fortress walls of . . . the newsroom," women often had to rely on language and traits constructed as masculine in order "to turn gendered ideas back on themselves."[21]

The subversive, upstart spirit that had underpinned the *Defender*'s early years did not appear to have been diminished by its growth into a national organ. Waters relates that there "was always an undercurrent of humor and mischievousness in the *Defender*'s editorial office" that was often absent from other newsrooms he frequented. Despite continued economic

hardships, editors could always look forward to visits from Black entertainers or actors, accompanied, if they were lucky, by an impromptu performance.[22] When journalists from rival publications visited 3435 Indiana
Avenue, the cry would go up of "spy in the house"—at which point all
activity would cease, and copy and research notes would be dramatically
hidden. On one occasion Charley Loeb, a reporter for the *Cleveland Call
and Post*, decided to get in on the act, charging around the room taking
photographs and snatching papers from desks. In response, Waters recalls,
the *Defender*'s editorial office converged on Loeb in a mock assault: "With
all the hollering and shouting, pushing and tugging in progress, a stranger
coming into the newsroom would have thought a riot was taking place."[23]

Such amiable altercations were overshadowed by more serious ones after
Abbott's death in February 1940. At the next board meeting, Sengstacke
discovered that Abbott's second wife, Edna Denison, and attorney James
Cashin had conspired to remove him as publisher. However, they were unable to completely lock Sengstacke out of the *Defender*'s building, initiating
a fraught period that saw 3435 Indiana Avenue become the staging ground
for internecine conflict. Sengstacke dutifully came to work every day, with
his constant presence at the *Defender*'s offices welcomed by Abbott loyalists.
At the same time, Denison's lack of interest in the newspaper's operations
drew the ire of Cashin, who complained that she was too preoccupied with
shopping to attend business meetings at the *Defender*'s headquarters.[24] In
February 1942 Sengstacke descended on 3435 Indiana Avenue with his at-
torneys and brother Fred in tow, who was stationed outside the boardroom
with a revolver. With Cashin flipping his allegiances, Sengstacke dramatically ended Denison's tenure as the company's president. Denison's refusal
to accept her usurpation meant that "police were detailed to the plant at
3435 Indiana Avenue to prevent the seizure of any records."[25]

Even before Sengstacke had wrested back control of the *Defender*, America's entry into World War II had placed the Black press in the crosshairs
of the federal government. Driven by the *Pittsburgh Courier*'s "Double V"
campaign, the circulation of Black newspapers reached new highs. In response, the federal government threatened to use sedition laws to stifle
the voice of "radical" Black publishing institutions. While Attorney General
Francis Biddle's stance toward the *Defender* softened upon meeting with
Sengstacke at the Justice Department in June 1942, the threat of sedition charges were never fully lifted.[26] Persistent legal and labor disputes

continued to consume much of Sengstacke's time throughout the 1940s, most notably a prolonged standoff with the Chicago Typographical Union during the winter of 1947–48 that left the publisher scrambling to keep the *Defender* in production and led to the embarrassing spectacle of picketers marching outside the newspaper's plant.[27]

In response, Sengstacke sought to grow the *Defender* out of trouble through the creation of "the largest black-owned newspaper chain in American history."[28] This idea was born from structural changes within the Black press, which saw nationally circulating newspapers consolidate their influence through the creation of syndicates and subsidiary publications. Among the most successful was the Scott Newspaper Syndicate, a massive newspaper chain headed by the *Atlanta World*, and the *Afro-American*, which began local editions in Philadelphia, Washington, D.C., and Newark, New Jersey.[29] Sengstacke pursued a comparative strategy, beginning with the *Louisville Defender* and the *Michigan Chronicle*, which helped to generate valuable new advertising streams and put the massive printing presses at 3435 Indiana Avenue to work on days they otherwise would have remained idle.[30] By the early 1950s, Sengstacke's publishing empire, now organized under the label of Defender Publications, had become a "seven-paper family" that included publications such as the *Tri-State Defender* and the *New York Age*.[31] In tandem, Sengstacke revived Abbott's dormant concept of "Defenderland," not just as a name for a South Side "bound together in its identity by the newspaper" but for the larger physical and racial terrain covered by the *Defender* and its subsidiaries, which now represented "America's Number 1 Negro Market."[32]

A Substantial and Sound Future

Having established himself as a worthy heir to the *Defender*'s founder, Sengstacke looked to cement his own legacy. The newspaper's fiftieth anniversary provided a convenient opportunity to do so, with festivities centered on a "Citizens Tribute" to the *Defender* held at Chicago's Orchestra Hall. The event included a performance by gospel star Mahalia Jackson and a dramatic reading from local theater director Ann Helen Reuter, which depicted the *Defender*'s rise "from its humble start in a kitchen at 3159 State St., to its present position of world leadership."[33] To round out the evening, Sengstacke took to the stage to announce "one of the most ambitious programs in the history of Negro journalism": the introduction of a daily city edition of the *Defender*.[34] When the publication began in 1905, Chicago was home to less than forty thousand Black residents, just 2 percent of its total population. By its fiftieth anniversary, this number was approaching three-quarters of a million, close to 20 percent of the city's total population.[35] Beyond merely consolidating the *Defender*'s influence, Sengstacke explained, daily publication would allow the paper to better represent the full spectrum of Black Chicagoan life. When the ensuing applause had died down, the publisher unveiled the second phase of his program: a million-dollar building and reequipment project organized around the acquisition of "a new home office and plant."[36]

Plans to upgrade the *Defender*'s headquarters at 3435 Indiana Avenue had been a long-standing ambition, and the Johnson Publishing headquarters on Michigan Avenue provided fresh incentive to pursue this goal. Within months of attending Johnson Publishing's open house events, Sengstacke was lobbying influential Black Chicagoan leaders such as congressman William Dawson to support "the construction of a substantial *Chicago Defender* office and Community Building."[37] Another galvanizing factor may have been *One Tenth of a Nation*, a nationally syndicated documentary series about the Black community produced by American Newsreel. Whereas the *Defender* had earlier used film to showcase its offices, by the early 1950s its visual representation through *One Tenth of a Nation* was largely overshadowed by images of the Johnson Publishing plant, emphasized by narration informing viewers that Johnson's "luxurious editorial offices [were] eloquent testimony" to his company's success.[38] In the buildup to the *Defender*'s fiftieth anniversary, Sengstacke continued to stress the importance of a plant upgrade in creating "a substantial and sound future" for the publication.[39]

Upon its unveiling in 1921, the *Defender*'s Indiana Avenue headquarters had been championed as a "monument to sagacity and business daring."[40] However, over subsequent decades, as other Black newspapers updated their facilities, the *Defender* had fallen behind.[41] The building's functionality had been limited from the outset due to its former life as a synagogue, and, while Abbott had invested heavily in the site's adaptation, there was only so much that redevelopment could accomplish.[42] Photographs of the plant's newsroom in the 1940s, available through the Abbott-Sengstacke Family Papers at the Chicago Public Library and Getty Images, demonstrate the awkwardness of the space, with staff squeezed together amid trailing electrical leads and desks overflowing with paper and outdated office equipment. Much of the building was poorly ventilated and badly lit, while the vast expanses of glass on its street façade meant it was too cold in winter and too hot in summer. Such issues were further exacerbated by the *Defender*'s expansion into surrounding buildings, with the newspaper's headquarters in effect comprised of four separate sites rather than a single, unified plant.

While the release of the *Daily Defender*'s first issue in February 1956 was a cause for widespread celebration, Sengstacke was acutely aware of how the transition to daily publication would place even more strain on the newspaper's aging infrastructure.[43] In preparation for this transition, the paper's staff had swollen considerably, adding more bodies to the already congested confines of 3435 Indiana Avenue.[44] The plant's limitations were laid out in a report commissioned by Sengstacke to assess the newspaper's future prospects.[45] Based on audit reports, staff interviews, and other communications, the report singled out the *Defender*'s plant as a limiting factor for growth. This began with the building's machinery, as its main printing press was now more than three decades old. Stereotype and engraving equipment were also "in need of substantial replacements." Beyond such mechanical concerns, the plant's uneven expansion had created "a patchwork of inefficiency in layout and accommodations."[46] In marking the second anniversary of the *Daily Defender*, Sengstacke authored a frank assessment of the paper's challenges and maintained that a new press and a new home were "sorely needed."[47]

In his 1955 announcement at Chicago's Orchestra Hall, the publisher had promised that the *Defender*'s headquarters would be "specifically built and designed" for the newspaper's demands.[48] However, it quickly became clear that such plans were beyond the company's financial capabilities. Instead, Sengstacke had to make do with another renovation project. The publisher settled on a site at 2400 Michigan Avenue in Chicago's famed Motor Row District, one of the many "auto rows" that had sprung up across the nation during the early decades of the twentieth century.[49] In their efforts to entice potential customers, car manufacturers constructed ever more impressive "auto palaces," which adapted commercial architectural techniques to situate "the pursuit of modern commerce within a vocabulary of historicist architecture."[50] In Chicago the construction of buildings such as the Premier Auto Car Company Building at 2329 Michigan Avenue and the Cadillac showroom at 2301 Michigan Avenue prompted the *Tribune* to declare that no other American city possessed "such a magnificent collection of buildings devoted to the retailing of motor cars."[51]

The *Defender*'s new home, located on the southwest corner of Michigan Avenue and Twenty-Fourth Street, had been constructed in 1936 for the Illinois Automobile Club. Architect Philip Maher was originally hired in 1931 to design a property for the corner of Michigan Avenue and Erie Street on Chicago's Magnificent Mile. By the time the project relocated several miles south, it had transformed from a ten-story clubhouse into a Spanish Mission–style building. Comprised of three faces surrounding a central courtyard, the site's design also incorporated a striking four-story clock tower.[52] In addition to housing the automobile club's executive offices, the building included a swimming pool, handball courts, and "other club luxuries."[53] When the club filed for bankruptcy two decades later, the building was purchased by Community Neighbors Inc., a philanthropic organization that hoped to develop the site into a center for local charitable and civic groups.[54] However, Community Neighbors Inc. would soon be embroiled in its own legal battle, and bankruptcy hearings led to the building being once again put up for sale.

Sensing an opportunity, Sengstacke pounced. The price listed in the *Defender*'s corporate records was $150,000—an outlay that represented both a shrewd investment for "an architectural show piece," which the *Tribune* estimated would cost around $1 million to build from scratch, and a calculated gamble, considering the scope of renovations needed to transform the structure into a workable publishing plant.[55] Estimates for the redevelopment more than doubled the initial purchase cost, including a large chunk reserved for the removal of the building's basement swimming pool to make space for the company's new presses. Two lower floors would house its pressroom, composing, and stereotype departments. The editorial offices would be clustered on the building's first floor, with the automobile club's smoking lounge "retrofitted into a proper newsroom." The second floor would contain the newspaper's business, advertising, and circulation departments as well as Sengstacke's own executive offices, and the third floor would be predominantly reserved for conference and recreation rooms.[56] The redevelopment was directed by a team of architects from PACE Associates, including John W. Moutoussamy, a talented young Black designer who would go on to receive national attention for his role in designing a new corporate headquarters for Johnson Publishing at 820 Michigan Avenue.[57]

Chicago Daily Defender Building. (Albert Charabin, Chicago History Museum)

In early 1959 the *Defender* announced that the first stage of its big relocation had been completed and that the company's accounting, advertising,
circulation, and personnel departments were now safely ensconced in their
new home. The *Defender* marked the occasion with an article documenting staff reactions as they set up shop in the company's new building.[58] In
February 1960 the *Defender*'s editorial department followed suit, leaving
only mechanical staff at 3435 Indiana Avenue.[59] Several weeks later, South
Side residents were greeted by a procession of Linotype machines inching
slowly north from the *Defender*'s Indiana Avenue address toward their new
home at 2400 Michigan Avenue. Undeterred by inclement weather, the
firm tasked with the relocation of this vital equipment completed the job
in time, maintaining the newspaper's long-standing record of never having
missed an issue.[60] To celebrate, the *Defender* planned a weeklong series of
festivities, including a dedication ceremony, guided tours, and open house
events, while readers were treated to an in-depth photo tour of the plant
in the *Defender*'s fifty-fifth-anniversary issue.[61]

Location, Location, Location

Just as the move to 3435 Indiana Avenue had helped usher in a golden age for the *Defender* during the 1920s, Sengstacke hoped that the opening of 2400 Michigan Avenue would reestablish its position as the nation's leading Black newspaper, with a "modern plant . . . giving readers a more attractive publication."[62] More broadly, the *Defender*'s new building offered a powerful corrective to the narratives of Black press decline that had come to dominate mainstream American media outlets during the years following World War II. Such sentiments were on ready display in a 1955 survey of the Black press published in *Time*, which emphasized the challenges facing Black periodicals. The article contended that the majority of Black publishers had "been slow to learn that in an era of rapid progress toward full social, economic and political citizenship, the Negro is fast losing his interest in editorial policies largely based on racial protest." For *Time* and other mainstream media outlets, this decline was both embodied and exacerbated by the out-of-date and increasingly undermanned status of Black newspaper buildings as publishers began to lack the necessary capital "to modernize plants and beef up skimpy staffs."[63]

It is certainly true that the circulation of many Black newspapers had begun to decline by the late 1940s, a trend that Black press historian Patrick Washburn suggests quickly became "a stunning free fall."[64] However, claims that these declines were due to the Black populace losing interest in racial protest, particularly when set against the parallel rise of the postwar Black freedom struggle, were patently false. The *Defender* framed the introduction of its daily issue as a challenge to *Time*'s "low blow attack on the Negro press," while its new plant provided both a riposte to suggestions that Black periodicals were "falling behind" and a practical example of what a modern, forward-thinking Black newspaper plant might look like.[65] It was no coincidence that the theme of newness and technological sophistication was central to the paper's own coverage of its "ultra-modern" plant, which detailed "a $1,000,000 expansion program that has replaced everything old—from pins and pencils, to newspaper presses, from doorknobs to drapes to desks."[66]

Although Sengstacke never publicly admitted as much, the *Defender*'s relocation also provided a direct response to Johnson's purchase of 1820 Michigan Avenue. Sengstacke and Johnson retained a good personal and professional relationship, something the latter attributed to a mutual respect and their shared experiences as dark-skinned Southern migrants.[67] Nevertheless, they remained competitors in an often-cutthroat industry. During the early 1950s, against the backdrop of broader debates over the decline of Black newspapers and the ascendancy of Black consumer magazines, 1820 Michigan Avenue cast a figurative, if not literal, shadow over the *Defender*'s more dated plant at 3435 Indiana Avenue. From this perspective, the *Defender*'s move to Michigan Avenue provided a concrete reminder of the newspaper's importance as a voice for Chicago's Black communities and helped to spatially connect the newspaper's future to the vibrant representations of Black life found in Johnson's publications and embodied by the company's well-heeled headquarters.[68]

Concurrently, the *Defender*'s relocation appeared to confirm a significant shift in the geography of Chicago's Black press. During the early twentieth century, sites such as the Chicago Defender Building at 3435 Indiana Avenue and the Chicago Bee Building at 3647 State Street competed for primacy as "the heart of the great, teeming Negro metropolis," just as their inhabitants had battled to shape the South Side's real and imagined geography.[69] However, by the 1950s many former residents of Chicago's Black newspaper row had folded, including the *Broad Ax*, which ceased publication in 1931; the *Chicago Whip*, which closed its doors in the late 1930s; and the *Chicago Bee*, which ended circulation in 1946.[70] This decline was compounded by urban renewal projects such as Stateway Gardens, a public housing project constructed west of State Street between Thirty-Fifth and Thirty-Ninth Streets, that hollowed out the neighborhoods of Douglas and Grand Boulevard, the former center of the Black metropolis. Between 1950 and 1960 the Black population in these communities dropped by more than sixty-two thousand as African Americans flooded into Grand Crossing, Woodlawn, and other neighborhoods south of Washington Park.[71] This expansion also contributed to the decline of Chicago's Black Renaissance as "Bronzeville's moment of ascendancy . . . [was] undermined by the geographical dispersal of many of its creative artists and by social and demographic changes in Black Chicago."[72]

To some, the relocation of the *Defender* and Johnson Publishing represented a conscious uncoupling from the South Side, one that threatened to dislocate these landmark Black print institutions from the institutions and communities that had undergirded their success. For Johnson this sentiment was exacerbated by his open displeasure for the "back streets" of the

Black metropolis. The publisher had long faced criticism for his deference to white advertisers and his characterization of *Ebony* as a "Black version" of *Life*, something that positioned whiteness as both a societal and literary default and prompted scholars like E. Franklin Frazier to dismiss Johnson's publications as relevant only to readers desperate to win the approval of white society.[73] Johnson's apparent willingness to equate professional excellence with proximity to Chicago's predominantly white downtown business district compounded such critiques and cast doubt on his self-professed role as a race man.[74] The announcement of the *Defender*'s prospective relocation and the introduction of a daily edition at the 1955 anniversary gala raised similar tensions, with Sengstacke's contention that the newspaper would no longer "be limited in either our coverage or our distribution by reasons of race or color" suggesting a rebrand for the media mainstream.[75]

To casual observers such rhetoric could well have reinforced a sense that Chicago's two most visible Black publishing enterprises were beginning to distance themselves from the South Side. Conscious of such concerns, Johnson and Sengstacke sought to address them. As detailed in chapter 3, the racially charged politics surrounding the acquisition of 1820 Michigan Avenue helped Johnson to present the building's purchase as a victory for the race. As the story of Johnson's battle with Hursen spread, his new headquarters came to embody the broader efforts of Black Chicago to push back against housing segregation and municipal neglect. From this perspective the building's purchase was not simply a consequence of Johnson's desire for a "front street" location but a direct response to the racially prescribed boundaries of the Black metropolis. This framing situated Johnson and his company within a larger spectrum of Black spatial resistance that included the "block-busting" practices of Black property magnates and the efforts of middle-class Black pioneers to integrate predominantly white neighborhoods.[76]

More broadly, Chicago's Black press barons presented the spatial reorientation of their business practices and their relationship to the South Side as a logical outgrowth of their role as "a functional link" between the Black community and the white establishment.[77] Johnson enthusiastically embraced his reputation as a "Negro market" expert and leading Black business authority, describing himself as "a special ambassador to American Whites."[78] While Sengstacke was less publicly forthcoming, he worked behind the scenes to curry favor with Chicago's political and business elite, as well as the city's predominantly white police force.[79] Both publishers presented their Michigan Avenue headquarters as "perfectly situated at Bronzeville's northern border and within striking distance of the Loop"—a necessary midpoint between the city's white power structure and the core of its African American community.[80] At the same time, they intimated that the relocations created an intermediary space between the South Side and West Side neighborhoods such as North Lawndale and East Garfield Park, which saw significant postwar Black population increases.[81] This connection was reified by the *Defender* several years after its relocation, when the newspaper announced a significant expansion of its West Side offices at 2400 West Madison Street and the introduction of a West Side weekend edition that would be printed and distributed from its Michigan Avenue plant.[82]

Critically, the relocations provided Johnson and Sengstacke with an ideal public relations tool that they could employ to reinforce their commitment to Black communities within and beyond Chicago: their newly acquired buildings. While the geographical location of the Johnson Publishing and *Defender* plants may have shifted, their increased size and stature provided fresh opportunities to assume a range of civic and cultural responsibilities that extended well beyond their commercial function and day-to-day operation.[83] As "free spaces" located on the intersection of private enterprise and public sphere, 1820 and 2400 Michigan Avenue offered locations through which Black people could "acquire greater self-respect, strengthen their sense of dignity and independence, and work toward a heightened sense of communal and civic identity."[84] By embracing this potential, Chicago's Black media barons were able to transform their new buildings into key sites for the performance of corporate social responsibility and Black civic engagement.

A Unique Historical Gallery

For Johnson Publishing the move to 1820 Michigan Avenue enabled the company to more closely align itself with Chicago's Black public history movement. The city's rich tradition of Black history activism can be traced back to the nineteenth century, and as its African American population grew, so too did the demand for historical societies and organizations. In 1915 Chicago played host to the "Lincoln Jubilee," a three-week-long festival marking the fiftieth anniversary of emancipation. Among the exhibitors present was Black historian Carter G. Woodson, who three years earlier had become just the second African American to earn a doctorate from Harvard University.[85] On September 9, 1915, Woodson gathered a group of Black educators and community activists at the Wabash Avenue branch of Chicago's YMCA to establish the Association for the Study of Negro Life and History (ASNLH), the institutional heart of what Pero Dagbovie describes as the "early Black history movement." Expertly utilizing the reach of Black publications such as the *Pittsburgh Courier* and *New York Amsterdam News*, Woodson and other Black historians produced hundreds of syndicated columns to advance public awareness of the contributions made by Black people to the nation's development.[86]

During the 1920s and 1930s, Chicago's Black press became a vocal ally of the fledgling Black history movement, with Robert Abbott in particular throwing his "unstinted praise and support" behind the celebration of Negro History Week.[87] Other publishers attempted to launch Black history–themed periodicals, such as the short-lived *Up-Reach* magazine, an educational journal "devoted to the interests of negro teachers . . . and promoting the study and teaching of negro history," which was edited by Willis Huggins out of his home at 4345 Vincennes Avenue.[88] In turn, Chicago's Black media buildings played a growing role in the struggle for Black history education, with ASNLH agents like Lorenzo Greene becoming regular visitors at the offices of publications such as the *Defender* and the *Chicago Whip*.[89] After the reopening of its Chicago bureau, the *Pittsburgh Courier* made the most of the office's storefront design, as well as the high volume of passing foot traffic generated by its location in the Ben Franklin store, to stage modest Black history exhibitions and display material from J. A. Rogers's "Your History" series, a popular and widely syndicated Black history column that documented the accomplishments of forgotten Black heroes.

The efforts of Chicago's Black press to promote the African American past underpinned a range of local public history and Black heritage projects that flourished during and after World War II.[90] These efforts were organized around important community hubs such as the Hall Branch of Chicago Public Library at Forty-Eighth Street and Michigan Avenue, the Abraham Lincoln Center on East Oakwood Boulevard, and the South Side Community Arts Center at 3831 Michigan Avenue, which emerged as the "crown jewel"

           Chapter 4

Pittsburgh Courier offices, Chicago. (Russell Lee / Office of War Information, Library of Congress Prints and Photographs Division)

of Chicago's Black artistic community and a vital space for local activists following its opening in the early 1940s.[91] South Side schools with majority-Black student bodies also played a significant role in organizing and promoting local Black history activism, including DuSable High School, located at Wabash Avenue and Forty-Ninth Street, and Wendell Phillips High School, situated on the north side of East Pershing Road between Prairie Avenue and Giles Avenue. The creation of a permanent Black history museum on the South Side was another long-standing ambition for many activists, who organized under the banner of the National Negro Museum and Historical Foundation (NNMHF), and its successor, the African American Heritage Association (AAHA).

The tremendous response to projects like the SSCAC reflected a deep-rooted desire for more community arts and public history spaces on the South Side.[92] This desire was made more acute by the inadequacies of Chicago's leading downtown cultural institutions, with depictions of Black life and culture at sites such as the Art Institute of Chicago and the Field Museum perhaps most notable through their absence. However, the close connections between Black history activists, political radicals, and the Black left often stymied public history endeavors. Bill Mullen notes that upon the withdrawal of WPA funding from the SSCAC, the center's programming was "severely restricted and turned decidedly conservative in an attempt to maximize economic returns."[93] Artists were often forced to use their own homes as exhibition spaces; Margaret Burroughs and Bernard Goss, for example, rented an old mansion on South Parkway to use as an ad hoc gallery.[94] Similar sites included the United Packing Workers of America headquarters on Forty-Ninth Street and Wabash Avenue, which was used by the NNMHF to hold Black history exhibits.[95]

Building on the efforts of outlets like the *Courier* to encourage Black history engagement through installations at its storefront office, Johnson Publishing's relocation provided the company with an opportunity to advance this project further. In *Ebony*'s tour of 1820 Michigan Avenue, covered in its October 1949 issue, the magazine drew reader attention to its impressive reception room and noted that the space "will be used in [the] future for exhibitions of outstanding photography and art."[96] After a series of temporary exhibits and installations, *Ebony*'s editors used the magazine's tenth anniversary, in 1955, as an opportunity to unveil an ambitious new public history initiative, the *Ebony* "Hall of Fame," which promised to memorialize "distinguished American Negroes whose achievements have contributed to the progress of the Negro people."[97] The project was centered on the creation of a "unique historical gallery" that would become a permanent and publicly accessible feature. Readers were encouraged to visit the exhibition, which included "photographs, mementos and historical documents," as an alternative space for the celebration of Black history and culture.[98]

The first ten entrants into the Hall of Fame, including educator and civil rights activist Booker T. Washington, pioneering Black surgeon Daniel Hale Williams, and abolitionist leaders Sojourner Truth and Harriet Tubman, were chosen by the magazine's editors. *Ebony* informed its readers that subsequent entrants would be chosen by public ballot and that successful nominees would be announced every February to coincide with the celebration of Negro History Week.[99] The role of the public in curating the *Ebony* Hall of Fame helped to establish its credentials as a collaborative, community-driven project. The first reader-selected inductee was African American businesswoman and beauty pioneer Madame C. J. Walker, who received 60 percent of the public vote.[100] Subsequent nominations included sociologist and civil rights activist Charles Spurgeon Johnson, who had served as the first Black president of Fisk University, and Carter G. Woodson, the man who had "helped put the Negro back into the history books."[101] Each new entry was accompanied by an article in *Ebony* documenting the nominee's achievements and reminding readers to visit "the historical gallery housed in the home office of the Johnson Publishing Company."[102]

I do not mean to suggest that the *Ebony* Hall of Fame led to the Johnson Publishing headquarters being viewed as a Black cultural site comparable to institutions such as the SSCAC, whose ambitions far outstripped Johnson's relatively modest efforts to create a permanent space within his company's offices for the documentation and preservation of Black history. Nevertheless, coverage of the Hall of Fame in Johnson's magazines and other periodicals indicated that the project was enthusiastically received within the local community.[103] Its creation also reflected a growing engagement with Black history across Johnson Publishing as a whole. One aspect of this trend came through the use of Black history–themed material in the company's advertising and public education campaigns. Material from the *Ebony* Hall of Fame appeared in educational kits produced in collaboration with the Chicago Urban League, while the company also created a series of brochures informing potential subscribers of its role in "digging up" the Black past.[104] Within the company's magazines, this turn toward Black history can be traced through regular features such as *Jet*'s "This Week in Negro History," while at *Ebony* senior editor and in-house historian Lerone Bennett Jr. helped transform the publication into a leading outlet for popular Black history.[105]

In turn, the *Ebony* Hall of Fame spoke to the broader role of Chicago's Black periodicals in popularizing African American history during the years following World War II. The *Defender* and other veteran outlets, as well as Claude Barnett's Associated Negro Press, continued to promote Negro History Week, while influential editors such as Frank Marshall Davis became embedded within local Black history organizations.[106] Other Black history boosters included the *Chicago Crusader*, which had been founded in 1940 by labor activist Balm Leavelle and businessman Joseph Jackson. The *Crusader* was initially published out of the Ida B. Wells Housing Projects before moving to an office at 6429 South Parkway on the border between Woodlawn and Grand Crossing.[107] This role was recognized by the AAHA in 1958, with the organization presenting awards to Johnson, Sengstacke, Barnett, and Leavelle for their "significant contributions to the development and dissemination of Negro heritage and history."[108] These contributions helped lay the groundwork for the creation of more substantial Black historical institutions.[109] Six years after the introduction of the *Ebony* Hall of Fame, Margaret Burroughs and Charles Burroughs (her second husband) opened the revealingly titled Ebony Museum of Negro History and Art at 3806 Michigan Avenue, the first independent Black museum in the country.[110]

A Home for the Community

The *Defender* had no plans to develop a public arts space that would rival the *Ebony* Hall of Fame. However, Sengstacke was eager to build on the newspaper's long-standing role as a civic institution and, like Abbott before him, understood the role of its headquarters in this endeavor. Community Neighbors Inc., the previous occupants of 2400 Michigan Avenue, had intended for the location to become a hub "available to all civic, church, and community groups," and Sengstacke expanded this ambition.[111] Indeed, even before the *Defender* had completed its relocation to 2400 Michigan Avenue, Sengstacke had organized a tour of the building for hundreds of representatives from local Black fraternities, civic groups, and business organizations, which provided a behind-the-scenes look at how the *Defender*'s new facilities "will enable the newspaper to serve the community more efficiently."[112] This included a variety of function spaces suitable "for small group meetings and other affairs," as well as the building's courtyard, which Society editor Marion Campfield suggested would be "ideal for those summer weddings, parties, and ultra-social fetes."[113]

Undoubtedly the building's most attractive space, at least from the perspective of local community groups, was the "picturesque and delightfully adaptable Boulevard Room" located on the third floor. Following the *Defender*'s relocation, Campfield reported that the room was "fast becoming the popular spot for fashionable and fastidious social functions."[114] Its early patrons included the Chicago Music Association Branch of the National Association of Negro Musicians, which rented the Boulevard Room to stage its yearly review show, and the Real Estate Broker's Wives Club, which used the space as the location for its annual coffee benefit.[115] Among the numerous other local organizations that quickly made use of the new *Defender* plant were the Hammonette Social Club, which transformed the Boulevard Room into a "Fabulous Fashion Show"; the Chicago Idlewilders, a group of socialites linked by their enthusiasm for Idlewild, an idyllic Black resort town in Michigan that was a favorite haunt of the city's African American elite; and the Chicago Housewives Association, a twenty-five-hundred-strong Black women's organization founded in 1956 by Lovonia H. Brown, which briefly made the *Defender* plant its official headquarters [116]

As the names of such organizations suggest, many of the Boulevard Room's visitors were members of Chicago's cosmopolitan Black middle-class. While ostensibly oriented toward community improvement, such meetings often provided little more than an opportunity for Chicago's Black bourgeoisie to meet in comfort, with the splendor of the Boulevard Room complementing the "beautifully gowned and immaculately groomed" men and women who graced it.[117] However, groups that were more civic-minded also took advantage of the Boulevard Room to plan and carry out fund-raising efforts to benefit some of Black Chicago's less prosperous residents. McKinley House, a Chicago-based agency that provided support for underprivileged African American children and families, was just one social welfare group to use the Boulevard Room for its annual fund-raiser, while members of the local chapter of Zeta Phi Beta fraternity hosted events in the building as part of an ongoing collaboration with Chicago Defender Charities Inc., an initiative established during the 1940s and headed by Marjorie Stewart Joyner, which aimed to "improve the quality of life for African Americans through educational, cultural and social programs."[118]

In addition to being frequented by Black social and civic organizations, the *Defender* plant emerged as a popular location for more personal events. On the occasion of sports editor Lee Jenkins's twentieth wedding anniversary, more than a hundred "close friends and guests representing a cross-section of Windy City activities" converged on the Boulevard Room, where they were treated to an evening of dancing and a five-course banquet.[119] The Boulevard Room regularly hosted birthday parties, wedding receptions, and other similar functions, with guests complementing the location's "picturesque elegance" and expressing their satisfaction at the plant's excellent facilities and free parking lot. The *Defender* declared, "Whether it's the intimate one wants or the lavish and lush social function, the Boulevard Room of the magnificent Chicago Daily Defender at 2400 S. Michigan Ave. lends itself admirably."[120] Outdoor space was also an option—while a step down from the grand public plaza in front of the Chicago Daily News Building, 2400 Michigan Avenue still had "Defender Court," a space that, like the building's interiors, was presented as "impressive, inspiring, and in good taste."[121]

Such commentary promised Black patrons' access to a welcoming and inclusive space in a city where many public and private facilities continued to remain off-limits for African Americans. As scholars such as Arnold Hirsch note, the continued expansion of Chicago's Black population during the decades immediately following World War II led not to increased integration and a relaxation of the color line but instead resulted in the expansion and entrenchment of the "black ghetto."[122] Difficulties in finding suitable and safe locations for all manner of social functions were just one example of an extensive network of segregation in Chicago that persisted during the decades after World War II and included residential housing, business property, and recreational facilities. In 1957 a major riot broke out in Calumet Park when a large white mob attacked a Black mothers club that had reserved facilities for a picnic. Faced with such extreme hostility, the decision to host events at the *Defender* plant may well have been an easy decision for many patrons—one made all the more satisfying with the knowledge that the Illinois Automobile Club, the building's original occupant, had "formerly excluded Negroes."[123]

Perhaps more significantly, the *Defender*'s eagerness to broadcast the eclectic range of social events taking place at its new plant provided evidence of both the building's civic possibilities and its role as an extension of the newspaper's own considerable "services to the community and the nation."[124] From this perspective the *Defender*'s move north represented not a loosening of its relationship to Chicago's African American community but a renewing of this historic bond. The opening of its new offices offered exciting new spaces through which the full diversity of Black life and culture could be experienced and provided Black Chicagoans with new opportunities "to entertain, to gather in resplendent surroundings and to confer in comfort and charm."[125] From the city's fashionable set to concerns benefiting less fortunate African American residents, all manner of events and enterprises were welcomed. Thus, 2400 Michigan Avenue became "a signal point for the paper, and for the community which it made great."[126]

The Meeting Place of All the People

Beyond their specific roles as exhibition spaces or civic hubs, the Johnson Publishing and *Defender* buildings on Michigan Avenue were important Black public landmarks and symbols of community pride. Accordingly, after their respective openings, they quickly became popular tourist destinations for a wide variety of visitors. For the *Defender* this function built on the appeal of its previous home on Indiana Avenue and expanded Robert Abbott's long-standing ambition for its offices to be "the meeting place of all the people."[127] At Johnson Publishing, heavy coverage of its relocation to 1820 Michigan Avenue in 1949 contrasted with representations of its earlier offices. Although *Ebony* had invited readers to "drop by if you're ever in Chicago" upon its move to 5125 Calumet Avenue, the company's first three locations were rarely commented on within the pages of Johnson's magazines.[128] However, the company could hardly wait to put its Michigan Avenue offices "on display" and document the "flocks of visitors" who were drawn through its doors.[129]

Local school, church, and civic groups were among the most frequent visitors to the new Johnson Publishing and *Defender* buildings, with many such tours conducted in collaboration with the Chicago Urban League. Frayser Lane, the director of the league's public education department, bemoaned the fact that while many Black Chicagoans regarded the South Side as the most important area of the city, "to most other Chicagoans, the section is one they rarely see and little understand."[130] Recognizing their significance as symbols of Black success, Lane prioritized the inclusion of the *Defender* and Johnson Publishing plants as part of tours designed to provide an insight into Chicago's African American communities. Such visits were not limited to term time, with *Ebony* editor Ben Burns complaining that even during the school vacation his work continued to be disrupted by "entire classes of tots and teenagers."[131] Similarly, elementary and high school students visited the *Defender* plant year-round; some aspiring journalists were even invited to contribute to the newspaper's youth department.[132] Chicago's popularity as a convention center meant that organized tours were regularly held for visitors from further afield, ranging from members of Black professional organizations and fraternities to beauty pageant contestants.

Formal tours were only one means by which visitors arrived at the Johnson Publishing and *Defender* headquarters, with more spontaneous trips making up the bulk of sojourners. Following the opening of 2400 Michigan Avenue, the *Defender* reported that the building was quickly becoming a "must-see" for out-of-town visitors, who staged impromptu tours while in the city.[133] The Johnson Publishing plant appeared to carry an even greater draw. Four years after its move to 1820 Michigan Avenue the company had

Beauty pageant contestants at the Chicago Defender Building. (Abbott Sengstacke Family Papers / Getty Images)

allegedly received thousands of visitors "from every state in the union."[134] Heavy foot traffic reflected the enduring resonance of Black press buildings and was promoted further through regular editorial coverage. Encouraging local residents and out-of-town residents to frequent their buildings had obvious practical benefits with regard to news acquisition and redistribution, with the inflow of people providing the *Defender* and Johnson Publishing with greater access to communal knowledge, hot topics, and story ideas. At the same time, the constant influx of curious onlookers worked to craft a material, tangible center for the often-abstract processes of information gathering and media dissemination.[135]

Such in-migration also helped to complement claims that these outlets' editorial content and audiences constituted "a representative cross-section of black America."[136] As the coverage of building visits printed in the *Defender* and Johnson Publishing's magazines made clear, both parties understood their offices as not only "central site[s] in the urban cultural geography of communications" but as key entry points into Black America as well.[137] This was particularly true of *Ebony*, which explicitly linked the diversity of its guests with its editorial efforts to document "the whole spectrum of black life."[138] Through regular features such as "Backstage," the magazine kept readers updated on the eclectic cast of characters who poured into its Michigan Avenue plant.[139] This included a circus entertainer who "gave a demonstration of his fire-eating proclivities in the center of the lobby," a hypnotist who put Black actress Dorothy Dandridge to sleep in the conference room, and even a uranium salesman who "almost set up shop in the driveway." Through the front doors of 1820 Michigan Avenue "walked boxing champions, stage stars, Negro leaders, giants of industry, crowned heads and plain Joes and Janes. With equal ardor, we shake their hands."[140]

Perhaps the most intriguing dynamic to be reflected through the company's increased editorial coverage of its workplace related to its magazines' gender and sexual politics. As Laila Haidarali and Noliwe Rooks observe, the content of Johnson's magazines during the years leading up to and immediately following its relocation often provided a "spicy diet of sex and sensation" designed to attract the attention of newsstand readers, who comprised the majority of its early audience.[141] Similarly, the introduction of confessional magazines such as *Copper Romance* and *Tan Confessions* promised stories of "true love and exciting romance" to an eager audience.[142] At times such salacious tales appeared to make their way beyond the page and into the company's offices, where "Backstage" reported that "romance sometimes rears its lovely head." One tale relayed to *Ebony*'s audience involved a visiting tourist who became so enamored with one of the company's female employees that he "proposed to her on the very day they met." The unnamed staffer politely but firmly declined the offer, something *Ebony* reported to be a good thing, given that the man was subsequently found to have "a wife back home all the time."[143]

From a similar perspective, despite their preoccupation with respectability politics, Johnson's magazines were not averse to discussions of queer Black life, most notably through coverage of drag balls and female impersonators in cities such as Chicago, Detroit, and New York during the late 1940s and early 1950s. In a representative article from *Jet* in October 1952, the magazine contended that "nearly every big U.S. Negro community has—or has had—at least one nightclub where swishing, clean-shaven men dress in women's clothes and entertain cash customers." *Ebony* followed suit, regaling readers with tails of men who "don silks, satins and laces," who were "as style-conscious as the women of a social club" and who spent "months and hundreds of dollars readying wardrobes" for their debutante appearances.[144] Once again, this editorial coverage intermittently made the leap from newsprint to newsroom. On one occasion, "a tall, handsome young man minced through the office eliciting all sorts of 'Oh's' and 'Ah's from the female workers—until they learned that he had won first prize at the female impersonators ball."[145]

Such coverage rarely, if ever, amounted to an open acceptance of queer Black identities; in fact, the coverage provided by Johnson's magazines, as well as outlets such as the *Defender*, often suggested a profound ambivalence toward queer Black people on the part of the Black press. Concordantly, the appearance of a female impersonator at Johnson's headquarters appeared less an indicator of the site's potential as a safe space for nonheteronormative Black identities than another example of visiting "curiosities" that delighted and bedeviled its staff in equal measure. Nevertheless, such incidents and their editorial coverage point to "an open fascination with representations of homosexuality and drag within black communities which were rarely, if ever, evidenced in the mainstream press" during this period.[146] They also reinforced the connection between the buildings of Chicago's Black press and their claims to representative coverage. Just as publications such as *Ebony* and the *Defender* sought to mirror the diversity and complexity of African America, so too were their offices presented as a lively microcosm of the Black world, an extension of the "public square" function embodied in earlier decades by prominent South Side intersections such as Thirty-Fifth and State Street, where notions of Black respectability, identity, and community were constantly made and remade.

A Crossroads of the World

While most of the people who passed through the *Defender* and Johnson Publishing offices hailed from the continental United States, many came from further afield. For foreign students or journalists visiting Chicago on cultural exchanges or writing assignments, the Black press buildings on Michigan Avenue provided a popular attraction; *Ebony* reported that its headquarters was frequented by "students from Norway and Sweden, photographers from Germany and newspapermen from Damascus."[147] More broadly, the location of the *Defender* and Johnson Publishing plants appealed to curious international tourists as sites that offered a window into

Black Chicago life without having to stray too far from the city's downtown district or risk venturing into the "other Chicago" contained on the South Side.[148] Just a few years after the opening of its Michigan Avenue plant, *Ebony* announced that its headquarters had been visited by citizens of at least thirty foreign countries. By its tenth anniversary, the magazine declared that its publishing offices had become a "crossroads of the world" and that groups of overseas visitors were being "constantly escorted through the building."[149]

The growing number of international visitors to the Johnson Publishing headquarters reflected the increasingly global audience of the company's magazines. This was most clearly traceable through *Ebony*, which quickly gained a significant foreign circulation after its introduction in 1945. Beginning with just its second issue, the magazine regularly published letters from international readers who expressed "profound pleasure to learn that a Negro magazine such as *Ebony* has been presented to the world."[150] For foreign readers of all races, the periodical provided a valuable insight into the African American experience, one that was often difficult to attain through mainstream American periodicals. As food editor Freda DeKnight noted following a culinary tour of Europe during the early 1950s, "Native Europeans . . . depend upon *Ebony* to give them an honest, well-illustrated picture of Negro life in America."[151] Interest was highest within the Black diaspora, with readers in Africa and the Caribbean clamoring to get their hands on the publication. Returning from a 1956 trip to Liberia, Black sociologist St. Clair Drake called the Johnson Publishing offices to inform its staff that every copy "seemed to increase in value as it grew older and more dog-eared."[152]

Ebony's international popularity, as well as the appeal of the magazine's Chicago headquarters to foreign tourists, was linked to its growing coverage of Black life beyond the United States. As the magazine's editors boasted, visitors from "South Africa, Brazil, Liberia and other far-flung spots come not just because they have heard about our beautiful building but because they have been pleased and impressed with what they have read in our publications."[153] Era Bell Thompson, who would go on to become *Ebony*'s first international editor, was just one contributor who conducted extensive overseas research trips for articles and special series. In 1953 Thompson embarked on a four-month-long research trip through more than fifteen African nations, collecting a wealth of material for *Ebony* stories and for her book-length work, *Africa, Land of my Fathers*, which was published by Doubleday the following year.[154] Other Black Chicago publishing institutions also expanded their engagement with the Black diaspora, including Claude Barnett's Associated Negro Press (ANP), which consolidated its position as a Pan-African news network during the early Cold War. From its base of operations—which by the 1950s had moved to the Supreme Life Building at 3501 South Parkway—the ANP called for racial solidarity between Black Americans and their racial kin in Africa, the Caribbean, and other regions.[155]

Of particular interest to Black Chicago publishers was Haiti, owing in large part to its historical significance as an emancipated slave state and its close (albeit complex) modern relationship with the United States. After a decades-long occupation by U.S. military forces, the American government intervened to help install Élie Lescot as Haiti's president in 1941.[156] In one of its first major international stories, *Ebony* provided readers with an unfavorable profile of Lescot's authoritarian regime and a sympathetic portrayal of the Haitian resistance movement, just weeks before a military junta removed him from power and installed Dumarsais Estimé as his successor.[157] Eager to establish good relations with the prominent Black publishers, Estimé invited Johnson and Ben Burns, along with their respective partners and photographer Gordon Parks, to Haiti for two weeks in 1948 to sample the island's "wonderful character and the hospitality of the Haitian people."[158] Two years later Barnett would visit Haiti himself, where he accompanied Estimé on a day cruise on his presidential yacht.[159]

This warm feeling toward the Caribbean republic would endure following Estimé's usurpation in May 1950 by Paul Magloire, a member of the junta that had toppled Lescot four years earlier, with Johnson installing paintings from his Haiti trip in his executive office at 1820 Michigan Avenue. In time, Sengstacke became a valuable contact for the new president, flying to Haiti at the beginning of 1955 to confer with Magloire before returning to the United States with the president as he began a two-week diplomatic tour.[160] As part of a two-day stopover in Chicago, the Haitian president made time to visit the offices of Johnson Publishing and the *Defender*. In a show of international solidarity, Johnson arranged for his headquarters to be decorated with Haitian and U.S. flags and presented Magloire with a photographic gift book. In return, the Haitian president charmed his way through the company's offices by planting "gallant hand kiss[es]" on figures such as secretary Virginia Tibbs and the publisher's own mother, Gertrude Johnson.[161]

Another Black nation that caught the attention of Chicago's Black editors and publishers was Liberia. Barnett traveled to the West African state in 1947 in search of new correspondents and business opportunities, and Era Bell Thompson followed suit during the early 1950s. Upon her return, Thompson informed *Ebony*'s readers that "perhaps nowhere in Africa is the American Negro thought of with more friendliness and brotherly love than in Liberia. . . . The tiny Republic especially welcomes him, not only as a visitor but as an investor, a businessman and a citizen."[162] In the same issue, Liberian president William Tubman penned a "letter to the American Negro" calling for a revitalization of diasporic ties. In 1954 Thompson and Tubman were reunited at the Johnson Publishing headquarters in Chicago, during a U.S. diplomatic tour by the Liberian premier. A picture printed in *Ebony* to commemorate the visit shows Tubman patiently waiting as the editor signs a copy of her latest book.[163] Johnson would remain on familial terms with Tubman after his visit, sending birthday commemorations that included a signed photograph of the publisher taken at 1820 Michigan Avenue.[164] The *Defender* would also serve as a prominent booster of the West African republic after its move to Motor Row, holding multiple receptions in the Grand Boulevard Room to honor Liberian consul William Jones and holding tours of its plant for Jones and fellow Liberian diplomat R. Burlington King.[165]

To Emphasize the Seriousness of the Occasion

Even as Chicago's Black publishers welcomed dignitaries from independent Black nations such as Haiti and Liberia, their engagement with leaders from occupied Black countries in Africa and the Caribbean expanded as the decolonization movement swept across the third world. By the mid-1950s, Ghana had emerged as the front-runner for independence among the English-speaking African colonies, while Kwame Nkrumah, the enigmatic leader of the independence movement, who had lived and studied in America during the late 1930s and early 1940s, had become a source of fascination for many Black American journalists. In 1957 Barnett and Johnson accompanied Vice President Richard Nixon to witness firsthand Ghana's independence ceremony and the installation of Nkrumah as the nation's first prime minister, the focal point of an extensive goodwill tour that visited half a dozen African states. A personal highlight of the trip for Johnson occurred during the delegation's visit to Ethiopia, where the country's emperor, Haile Selassie, informed the publisher that he was an "avid reader" of *Ebony* and congratulated him for the job his magazines were doing "in letting the people of the world know about the progress of American Blacks."[166]

The following year, when Nkrumah made a triumphant return to the United States, the Black press played a major role in promoting his activities and documenting his rapport with Black enclaves across the country. *Jet* magazine featured Nkrumah on its cover and declared that his visit would "renew friendships among Negroes in [the] U.S."[167] Similarly, historian James Meriwether writes that anyone who picked up newspapers such as *Defender* and the *Pittsburgh Courier* "saw Nkrumah being embraced by the nation's elite," with the laudatory coverage of the prime minister's visit provided by the Black press helping to reshape Black American attitudes toward Africa.[168] When Nkrumah visited Chicago, his visit was overseen by a Civic Reception Committee headed by Claude Barnett, while a highlight of the trip came in the shape of a guided tour through the Johnson Publishing Building.[169] Reveling in his status as publisher and showman, Johnson led the Ghanaian leader through 1820 Michigan Avenue, proudly showing off the building's lavish furnishings and presenting Nkrumah with an album of photographs taken during his own trip to Ghana the previous year. Nkrumah appeared most impressed by the plant's modern technology, as evidenced by *Jet* informing readers that the prime minister "wanted to know all about [the] automatic office equipment" and was "fascinated as he watched an automatic typewriter tapping away without an operator."[170]

Other prominent African diplomats would visit Chicago over subsequent years as the pace of decolonization continued to quicken, with many frequenting the buildings of Chicago's leading Black periodicals. This included Guinean president Sékou Touré, who visited Chicago during a fifteen-day-long diplomatic tour in late 1959.[171] *Ebony* reported that Touré was left suitably impressed by the "size and amplitude" of the Johnson Publishing plant, and although *Jet* described the "stern-faced" Touré as "perhaps the most controversial figure to emerge from the political ferment of black African nationalism," this demeanor visibly thawed after Johnson presented him with a lifetime subscription to the magazine.[172] Nigerian ambassador

Julius Momo Udochi was another prominent visitor, touring the Johnson Publishing and *Defender* plants during a 1961 trip masterminded by Earl B. Dickerson.[173] Photographs in Dickerson's papers at the Chicago Public Library capture the diplomat enjoying a meal in the executive dining room at Johnson Publishing alongside employees such as Era Bell Thompson and Leroy Jeffries, before traveling a few minutes south to the *Defender* building at 2400 Michigan Avenue, where general manager Kenneth Wilson "escorted Udochi and his aides on a tour of the newspaper plant." A highlight of the trip came through a viewing of the plant's basement-level presses, where Udochi was reportedly "awed by the huge rolls of newsprint."[174]

Such visits demonstrated the awareness of Black diasporic leaders as to the influence of African American periodicals in shaping the Black public within and beyond the United States, and the importance of Chicago as a national, and increasingly global, Black print capital. The willingness of Nkrumah and other Black African and Caribbean leaders to collaborate with Black Chicagoan publications and visit their buildings was directly linked to their usefulness "in rallying international support" for the global Black freedom struggle. As historians such as James Campbell and Penny Von Eschen note, the coverage provided by outlets such as *Ebony* and the *Defender* helped to popularize knowledge of and sympathy for the anticolonial struggle, while Claude Barnett's Associated Negro Press made foreign news reporting accessible to smaller Black periodicals that lacked the capacity to report on international Black politics. Similarly, through establishing connections with Black activists and journalists across the diaspora, African American periodicals played a critical role in "marshalling the resources of important black middle-class and entrepreneurial institutions to create an international anticolonial discourse."[175]

It is little wonder, then, that many colonial states attempted to suppress the local circulation of Black American publications and impede the investigations of their journalists. South African writer Peter Abrahams informed *Ebony* that copies of the magazine had to be "smuggled in by merchant seamen and missionaries."[176] During her 1953 African sojourn, Thompson faced an escalating campaign of harassment from colonial officials who had "come to the conclusion that she and her magazine were a threat to colonial rule."[177] On a subsequent trip to South Africa with staff photographer G. Marshall Wilson in 1957, the pair were detained and interrogated by local police. Upon their return to Chicago, Thompson paraded throughout the company's office in prison garb "to emphasize the seriousness of the occasion."[178] Several years later, *Ebony*'s criticism of the apartheid regime reached a new level through a devastating expose of the 1960 Sharpeville Massacre authored by Lerone Bennett Jr. that was applauded by the magazine's readers for revealing the "tyrannical and cruel character" of the South African government.[179]

For Johnson, the arrival of Black diasporic diplomats and celebrities marked the logical endpoint of his ambition for the company's headquarters to serve as a "crossroads of the world." Watching Ghanaian prime minister Nkrumah inspect his office equipment or Gambian premier Sékou Touré sign the company's guest book must have been a surreal moment for the publisher. Less than two decades earlier he had been attempting to launch the *Negro Digest* from a corner office in the Supreme Life Building at 3501 South Parkway. Now he was welcoming some of the most famous leaders in the Black world into "one of the most elegant office buildings in Black America."[180] Similarly, the visitors who poured into the *Defender*'s new plant after its opening reflected Sengstacke's success in fully realizing Robert Abbott's dream of his plant becoming "the meeting place of all the people." Taking on a cultural and political significance that far outweighed their function as production spaces, Chicago's Black media buildings became "a recognized tourist attraction" and "a wonder of the Negro world."[181]

However, the convergence of visitors from home and abroad also cast a harsh spotlight on the ways in which African Americans were falling behind. During his visit to Ghana in 1957, a young African had jubilantly informed John Johnson, "We Africans have our freedom" before asking the question "When are you Negroes going to get yours?"[182] Two years later, in an impromptu speech given at the Johnson Publishing plant during his visit to Chicago, Sékou Touré championed the rise of an independent Africa and declared that soon "our 180 million people will be placed in a position to freely develop our own resources."[183] Even as editors like Era Bell Thompson returned from overseas with tales of the "winds of change" sweeping over Africa and across much of the third world, *Ebony* field reporters arrived back at 1820 Michigan Avenue with harrowing tales of racial violence and systemic discrimination across the American South.[184] As civil rights activism began to coalesce across the country, Chicago's Black publications, and their buildings, found themselves on the front lines of the struggle.

5

A House for the Struggle

On May 17, 1954, Johnson Publishing staffers waited with bated breath inside the company's Michigan Avenue headquarters. *Ebony* described a tense scene to its readers: "The whole office was alerted. Work ceased."[1] The reason for the disruption was a phone call from Washington, D.C., where a special correspondent was providing live updates from the Supreme Court's impending ruling in the case of *Brown v. Board of Education*, a landmark challenge to the constitutionality of racial segregation in public schools. As news of the court's verdict broke, the tension lifted: "It was not a hilarious reaction, no cheering or shouting, but within everyone present was a deep surge of joy." True to the building's reputation as a "crossroads of the world," at that very moment Black boxing champion Joe Louis walked in. "Tell me," Louis asked, in reference to the sitting governor of Georgia and one of the nation's most notorious segregationists, "did Herman Talmadge drop dead?" Secretary Marguerite Neal was tasked with typing up the decision, and *Ebony* marked the occasion by printing a photograph of Louis and several company staffers clustered around Neal's desk "to see with their own eyes the words that made 16 million Negroes free and happy."[2]

Five years later, after the *Chicago Defender* had completed the first phase of its move to 2400 Michigan Avenue, publisher John Sengstacke formally welcomed the newspaper's employees into their impressive new offices. Reflecting on the underlying editorial premise that continued to drive the

Defender's coverage—that "American race prejudice must be destroyed"—
Sengstacke thanked his staff for their role in making the move a resounding
success and reiterated the importance of the building's acquisition to the
Defender's broader expansion program. In speaking of the "bright future
that lies ahead for all of us," Sengstacke linked 2400 Michigan Avenue and
the introduction of the *Daily Defender* to the upward trajectory of both
Chicago's Black residents and the nation's African American community,
clearly framing the newspaper's relocation against the backdrop of the ongoing struggle for civil rights.[3]

This chapter explores the impact of the postwar Black freedom struggle
on Chicago's Black press—on the coverage they provided and their relationship to the built environment. By the mid-1950s, pivotal events such
as the *Brown* decision and the Montgomery bus boycotts had begun to
draw increased attention from broadcast media and the American popular
press. Although this shift helped to convey the urgency of the struggle to
a wider audience, it undercut coverage provided by Black periodicals—almost exclusively working on a weekly or monthly schedule—which risked
being left behind.[4] This point was reiterated by the brutal 1955 murder of
Black Chicagoan teenager Emmett Till in Money, Mississippi. While the
Defender and *Jet* played a critical role in making Till's slaying a national
scandal, subsequent media coverage demonstrated how the immediacy
of network television and the white dailies allowed them to scoop Black
periodicals on civil rights stories. Ethan Michaeli argues that the need to
provide readers with more immediate coverage of movement flashpoints
was a critical factor in Sengstacke's decision to make the *Defender* a daily
publication.[5]

As his speech at 2400 Michigan Avenue in 1959 demonstrates, Sengstacke
was keenly aware of how the *Defender's* prospects as a daily publication and
its ability to cover the Black freedom struggle were indelibly linked to its
new plant. From a practical perspective, the relocation addressed lingering
production woes and ensured that the newspaper would become "a more
efficient operation" better equipped to respond to developing civil rights
stories on a local and national scale. Just as important, Sengstacke hoped
that the building would help "to rekindle public interest" and reassert the
Defender's value as an organ for Black protest.[6] The relationship between
moving buildings and building the movement would manifest itself in
a more direct way than Sengstacke likely anticipated, as 2400 Michigan

Avenue became a house for the struggle in a literal sense. The Chicago Urban League was a tenant at the *Defender's* offices during the late 1950s and early 1960s, and the plant played host to a range of other civil rights organizations and events. However, these arrangements could not distract from ongoing labor and editorial conflicts as the newspaper's coverage and the relationship between its leadership and rank and file came under increased scrutiny.

Similar tensions could be found half a mile north, where Johnson Publishing was also attempting to reconcile the contents of its magazines with the demands and expectations of its staff and readers. Despite Johnson's assertion that his most prominent publications were "out front, beating the drums and pointing the way," their perceived go-slow approach to civil rights drew widespread disapproval.[7] Even when Johnson attempted to reassure readers that the movement's energy had penetrated the company's offices, such efforts often backfired. In the case of *Ebony's* coverage of the *Brown* decision, readers noted that the magazine's "Backstage" section had managed to print the incorrect date of the Supreme Court's ruling. Imploring the company to take the issue of civil rights more seriously, South Carolinian reader G. L. Ivey declared, "The day of the U.S. Supreme Court's decision should be imbedded so vividly in the minds of all Negroes that it would be an impossibility to forget."[8] In response to these and other criticisms, Johnson expanded civil rights coverage in *Ebony* and *Jet*, revived *Negro Digest*, and moved to open new bureaus in Atlanta and Washington, D.C., key locations in the developing struggle for Black rights.

As the movement spread beyond the South, a group of more politically engaged contributors attempted to expand discussions of civil rights and Black Power within Johnson Publishing's Chicago headquarters. However, the publisher was not always willing to cede control, leading to fraught struggles over editorial philosophy and political representation and contributing to the marginalization of Black radical editors such as Hoyt Fuller and John Woodford both on site and in print. Growing frustrations with Johnson's reticence to support Black militant activists, along with more general critiques of his magazines' gender politics and emphasis on "the happier side of Negro life" saw the company's offices disrupted by a series of protests during the 1960s. For Black activists operating on both the inside and outside of Johnson Publishing, targeting the company's physical locations emerged as a high-profile way to express dissatisfaction and raise

awareness for their cause. At the same time, Black radical periodicals—
most notably *Muhammad Speaks* and the *Black Panther* newspaper—rapidly
gained popularity in Black urban centers across the country. In Chicago
their visibility on the streets of the South and West Sides offered a direct
challenge to the content of the *Defender* and Johnson's magazines, one
that threatened to once again reshape the literal and literary geographies
of Black Chicago.

First Prize for Inadequacy

From its genesis the *Chicago Defender* had consistently presented itself to
readers as a staunch defender of Black rights, with its content organized
around the central principle that "American race prejudice must be destroyed."[9] In keeping with this mission, the newspaper developed close
connections to many of Chicago's most prominent civil rights and social
welfare organizations. During its early years the *Defender* provided enthusiastic support for the Chicago branch of the NAACP, which maintained an
office at 3125 State Street, just a stone's throw away from the newspaper's
first headquarters.[10] Another of Abbott's early passion projects was the
Chicago Urban League (CUL), which was formed during World War I as
one of the first regional affiliates of the National Urban League movement.
Historian Arvarh Strickland notes that Abbott not only used the *Defender*'s
pages to publicize Urban League activity but also pushed for the creation of
a Chicago branch. This ambition was realized in December 1916 when the
first official meeting of the CUL took place at the Wabash Avenue YMCA.
By the 1920s, Abbott had become a fixture on the CUL's executive board
next to other influential Black newspapermen like Claude Barnett of the
Associated Negro Press.[11]

   Shortly after its founding at the Wabash YMCA, the CUL moved its headquarters one mile north to a rented office at 3303 State Street, a few hundred
meters from the *Defender*'s offices. In 1918 the league relocated again, this
time to the first floor of the Frederick Douglass Center at 3032 Wabash
Avenue, an interracial settlement house founded in the early 1900s by Black
activist Ida B. Wells and white unitarian minister Celia Parker Woolley.[12] The
league remained at this address for close to thirty years, gradually expanding
throughout the center in a manner not dissimilar to Abbott's annexation of
Henrietta Lee's home at 3159 State Street. However, whereas the *Defender*
was able to escape the restrictive confines of its first headquarters through

a move to Indiana Avenue, the CUL remained cooped within the Douglass Center. By the 1940s, the league's continued development had created a serious housing problem. Internal memorandums condemned the Douglass Center as a "notorious nuisance which would probably win first prize in any contest for inadequacy and inefficiency."[13] Persistent maintenance issues and the struggle for space were exacerbated by a serious fire in 1949 that caused further damage to an already deteriorated structure.

The CUL's woes were indicative of the systemic housing problems that continued to plague Chicago's Black communities during the postwar era, with restrictive covenants and entrenched redlining practices trapping many Black residents within substandard accommodations.[14] Official league documents described 3032 Wabash Avenue as "depressing and inadequate," pointing to its negative impact on both clients and employees. From a practical perspective, the site inhibited the league's effectiveness as a civil rights and social welfare organization, with staffers unable to provide adequate services to Black patrons.[15] Of even greater concern was the potential damage its Wabash Avenue headquarters was doing to the league's reputation. As internal memos and reports from the CUL's archives at the University of Illinois–Chicago demonstrate, by the early 1950s the building was a public relations disaster. The CUL bemoaned that "the very essence of the League's program is its struggle to win a place in the sun for the shabbily treated minority we represent. Yet the League's present quarters constitute a monument to the whole outmoded idea of maintaining second-class conditions for this minority." Dismissing 3032 Wabash Avenue as a "tragically shabby building," the league declared that it was not a home befitting "an organization which needs to stand proudly before the community as a living example of the principles it represents."[16]

The CUL's leadership appeared split on what to do about its housing situation; some favored a renovation of its existing building, and others suggested that a relocation was the best way to boost its organizational reputation.[17] In 1952 a building committee was formed "to try and do something about the League's own housing problem."[18] Sizable donations were curried from Black press "heavies" such as John Sengstacke and John H. Johnson to help kick-start a funding campaign, and letters detailing the "scandalous" state of its current home were distributed to the league's followers in an effort to generate more widespread support.[19] The building committee quickly identified a number of potential sites, including a three-story office at 1331 Michigan Avenue, half a mile north of the Johnson Publishing offices. However, progress was slow and was complicated by a series of conflicts, with disagreements over how to address the CUL's "housing problem" indicative of broader ideological fractures within the organization.[20] By the early 1950s, CUL affiliates had separated into two camps: a cohort of traditionalists, who favored preserving its largely administrative and politically moderate function, and a more activist-oriented faction, who believed that "there were few, if any, problems confronting the Negro which were outside the purview of the Urban League." These tensions would come to a head in 1955, leading to a six-month shutdown and a reorganization of the league's organizational structure.[21]

At the height of its internal turmoil, the CUL was rocked by news that 3032 Wabash Avenue was in an area designated for redevelopment. The site was quickly purchased by the Chicago Land Clearance Commission, although the league was allowed to continue using the building until it found a suitable replacement.[22] Land clearance and the purchase of private property underpinned the city's aggressive expansion of postwar urban renewal programs. Ironically, this twist provided further evidence of the league's own findings: that a disproportionate number of Black residents had been impacted by the city's efforts to address its "modern problems in transportation, housing, and public welfare."[23] In 1950 Chicago's Black population constituted around 14 percent of its total population. However, the league found that Black residents accounted for nearly 70 percent of persons impacted by urban renewal projects between 1948 and 1956.[24] These patterns of inequality were replicated in urban centers across the country, leading Black writer James Baldwin to famously assert that "urban renewal means Negro removal."[25] In 1956 it appeared that the CUL had stumbled upon an ideal solution when the Illinois Automobile Club placed 2400 Michigan Avenue on the market, and the league agreed to temporarily rent space in the building as it searched for financial backing to buy the site outright. However, before such arrangements could be made, the building was sold, leaving the league's fate in the hands of its new owner, the *Chicago Defender*.

A Clean Break with the Past

Following his appointment as the *Defender*'s publisher, Sengstacke maintained his predecessor's close ties to the Urban League, regularly participating in annual meetings and serving alongside Lester Granger, the league's national secretary, on a committee organized by President Harry Truman to oversee integration in the armed forces.[26] Given this familiarity—not to mention the potential backlash if word got out that he had left one of Chicago's most important Black organizations homeless—Sengstacke was never likely to force the league out of 2400 Michigan Avenue. He did initially push to increase the league's rent, although he backtracked after a hastily arranged conference with members of the organization's executive board. The league's offices were concentrated in the southwest corner of the building, including the entire west section of the third floor running behind the Grand Boulevard Room. The arrangement even included a separate entrance and street address at 2410 Michigan Avenue, providing a level of residential independence that helped the league avoid suggestions of corporate entanglement.[27]

While Sengstacke initially anticipated that the league would be ready to relocate by the completion of the *Defender*'s protracted move into 3435 Indiana Avenue, this target proved unrealistic. The power struggle of the previous decade had left the league's finances "as small and rickety as the building" it previously occupied, and funds raised by the sale of 3032 Wabash Avenue represented at best a down payment on a new site.[28] Convinced that it would be advantageous to stay put until the league was more financially secure, Edwin Berry, the CUL's new executive director, negotiated an extended lease with Sengstacke, one that included the previously threatened rent hike but that was offset by medium-term stability and updated furnishings.[29] Just as Sengstacke's purchase of the former Illinois Automobile Club headquarters was the centerpiece of his expansion plans for the *Defender*, so too did the CUL's occupation of 2400 Michigan Avenue coincide with and help to stimulate a period of tremendous organizational growth.[30] Accordingly, while the league's reformation and the accompanying move from 3032 Wabash Avenue was part of an attempt to engineer "a clean break with the past," it also provided the impetus for the CUL to emerge as "the most powerful organization for interracial goodwill in the city."[31]

The building at 2400 Michigan Avenue quickly became the focal point for the league's ambitious array of social welfare programs, with a steady stream of campaign volunteers, welfare recipients, and jobseekers flowing through its doors. In addition to one-off events and annual funding drives, 2400 Michigan Avenue also served as the home for ongoing projects such as a "Stay in School" campaign.[32] The league's various initiatives—ranging from voter registration to youth unemployment—influenced and came to overlap the *Defender*'s own community engagement projects, with the newspaper's offices becoming the temporary home of an "Opportunity Center" designed to help place young Black college graduates in major industries.[33] During the 1964 presidential election, 2400 Michigan Avenue even hosted a babysitting service for professional Black mothers wanting to vote, with the Boulevard Room serving as a crèche and a fleet of cars waiting to whisk busy parents to and from the voting booth.[34]

As the *Defender*'s audience drew connections between the fight against Jim Crow segregation in the South and their own experiences of racial discrimination in the North, their concerns were noted by new CUL executive secretary Edwin Berry, who appeared altogether less reticent than Earl Calloway or members of the league's traditionalist faction to speak out against the city's entrenched racial problems. Almost immediately after his appointment in 1956, Berry made headlines—and enemies—by publicly denouncing Chicago's status as the most segregated major city in the country, a shameful title exacerbated by the complicity of the city's political and business elite and what Berry described as a "conspiracy of silence among Chicago's mass media."[35] The *Chicago Tribune* warned that Berry was pushing the league to move away from "its traditional role as a social work agency" and to instead embrace "the characteristics of a protest organization."[36] Black publications were more enthusiastic, with *Ebony* highlighting Berry's place "in the vanguard of a massive effort to end segregation and discrimination in the nation's second largest city."[37]

The league's proximity to the *Defender*'s staff helped to cultivate closer relationships between the newspaper's employees and the work of the civil rights organization. Lee Blackwell, the managing editor of the *Defender*'s daily edition, was heavily involved in the league's Youth Guidance Project and served as the chair of its reviewing committee.[38] Louis Martin, who served several stints as the *Defender*'s editor in chief, was a member of the CUL board and a regular at league events held both inside and outside the walls of 2400 Michigan Avenue.[39] Another *Defender* staffer heavily involved in the CUL's activities was Lillian Calhoun, who cut her teeth as the paper's New York correspondent before being hired to help run the organization's public relations team. After rejoining the *Defender* as a features editor, Calhoun continued to help organize CUL events and regularly mined the league's reports and staff expertise to inform her copy.[40] Such connections overlapped with and likely influenced the *Defender*'s increasingly strident coverage of the civil rights struggle. The newspaper eagerly followed the activities of Freedom Riders and other activists across the South, detailing the continued "all-out assault" on Jim Crow segregation. Closer to home, the *Defender* emerged as an outspoken critic of school segregation and the failure of school superintendent Benjamin Willis to address the problem.[41]

Concurrently, the league's occupancy of 2400 Michigan Avenue helped to center the *Defender*'s plant within the city's developing Black activist networks, not just as a media site from which to disseminate news of the movement outward but as an important organizing hub that drew activists' inward. During the late 1950s and early 1960s, the building played host to an array of CUL projects that were more explicitly activist in orientation, including a campaign for integrated housing.[42] Other civil rights groups, many of whom counted *Defender* staffers among their ranks, also made use of the building. Chuck Stone, who joined the *Defender* as its editor in chief in 1963, used the space to host public meetings about the ongoing fight for school desegregation in collaboration with the Chicago branch of the NAACP.[43] Another organization that staged meetings at the *Defender*'s plant was ACT, a grassroots civil rights organization created in 1964 by a cohort of "super-militant" local activists.[44] ACT used the Boulevard Room to coordinate civil rights rallies on the South and West Sides, and, like other Chicago-based activist groups, relied on the *Defender* for favorable coverage and logistical support.[45]

Discord and Disputes

Compared to its underwhelming headquarters at 3032 Wabash Avenue, the CUL's offices in the *Defender* plant represented a considerable upgrade. Several years after the move to 2400 Michigan Avenue, CUL board president Joseph Evans declared that the league's dramatic revival had allowed it to assume a position of "unprecedented prestige in the community"—a prestige that was rooted in the stature of its offices.[46] This point would be made even more explicit in a February 1961 *Defender* article titled "Chicago Urban League Rebuilds from Ashes," which reflected on the league's dramatic upturn in fortunes since its relocation. The *Defender* noted that "housed unglamorously in the very slums against which it labored, the local branch of the Urban League was nothing more than a ghost of its potential self." Conversely, after the league's move to Michigan Avenue, the newspaper asserted that the "modern and polished offices from which the League operates [are] the outward index of a remarkable rebirth."[47] For the *Defender* the benefits of the relationship were self-evident, with the spatial convergence between newspaper and organization complementing the *Defender*'s editorial efforts to document the struggle for Black rights and extending the long-standing role of Black media buildings as symbols of protest. The *Defender* building's reputation as a house for the struggle was further accentuated by a series of bomb threats made against the league (and, by association, the *Defender*) following its relocation.[48]

However, it is important to note that the league's relationship with the newspaper was not without tension. At times the CUL struggled to maintain its identity as a separate institution, despite attempts to paint its relationship with the *Defender* as one akin to that of "a good neighbor" rather than as a lodger. This problem was exacerbated after the decision to close the league's separate entrance in 1959, meaning that although the organization maintained its distinct mailing address of 2410 Michigan Avenue, visitors were required to access its offices by way of the *Defender*'s main foyer. Organizational autonomy was further eroded by the requirement that all visitors had to sign in before being "directed by the *Defender* receptionist to our receptionist on the second floor."[49] Sengstacke's reputation as a stickler also rankled some league associates, with the organization having to abide by a fastidious rental system that included variable rates for office equipment such as chairs and tables as well as the building's various conference rooms and recreational spaces.[50]

The *Defender*'s own demands for space, coupled with the rapid expansion of the CUL's workforce, meant that cohabitation became increasingly difficult. By the early 1960s, the league found itself occupying three "distinct and distant areas of the building"; Berry complained that the organization's living arrangements left it in the effective position of "operating three branch offices under the same roof."[51] These issues were flagged by visitors like National Urban League staffer Nelson Jackson, who was sent to conduct a review of the Chicago branch in 1962.[52] In his report, Jackson declared that the league's headquarters at 2410 Michigan Avenue left "much to be desired. . . . The executive indicates that he could lose a staff member for a week and wouldn't know where he was."[53] As the league's arrangement with the *Defender* soured, Berry sought to restart the building fund, arguing that a league-owned building would "improve the agency's prestige and image in the community."[54] In the summer of 1964, the league finally acquired its own building, ending close to a decade of occupancy at 2400 Michigan Avenue.[55]

We should also not let the role of the *Defender*'s headquarters as a nexus of Black activism in Chicago distract from other battles being fought within and outside of the newspaper's plant, battles that complicate the site's performative function and the publication's role as a "defender" of Black rights. One ongoing struggle that rumbled on throughout the early 1960s pitted Sengstacke against a familiar and formidable adversary: the newspaper's own typographical and editorial staff. For all of its claims to being a staunch supporter of Black economic advancement, the *Defender*'s attitude toward labor rights had proved to be ambivalent since its founding in 1905. Historian Albert Kreiling argues that this was in keeping with the newspaper's broader outlook and that Abbott proved to be "rather conservative on matters other than race," a position shared by former colleagues like Metz Lochard.[56] The *Defender* routinely encouraged Black workers to place their faith in the benevolence of their employers rather than in collective organizing. At the same time, Abbott stubbornly refused to pay competitive wages and consistently battled in-house efforts to unionize.[57]

When the *Defender* relocated to 3435 Indiana Avenue, a scarcity of well-trained Black technicians meant that Abbott was initially forced to hire an all-white mechanical staff affiliated with the Chicago Typographical Union. However, as the Depression cut profits, office manager Sengstacke staged a symbolic lockout of the *Defender*'s white typesetters and compositors. Although Sengstacke would later frame this decision as a response to criticisms from rival newspapers such as the *Pittsburgh Courier*, which attacked the *Defender* "for keeping whites on their payroll while a disproportionate number of blacks in Chicago were unemployed," the move allowed for the employment of nonunion Black workers at significantly lower rates. Over subsequent decades a regular pattern was established: workers would attempt to create independent unions or join stronger bodies like the Chicago Newspaper Guild or the Chicago Typographical Union, while Abbott, and subsequently Sengstacke, would resist unionization efforts and take punitive measures against staff who pushed for better pay and worker rights.[58] Press operators were routinely fired and reinstated after union arbitration, while sporadic strikes and walkouts persisted, most notably a lengthy standoff during the winter of 1947.[59]

After the purchase of 2400 Michigan Avenue, the *Defender* once again ran into labor trouble. The plant's modernization concerned some production staff, who worried that the "trend toward automation" might put their jobs at risk. Concurrently, the introduction of the *Defender's* daily issue demanded an influx of new editorial and production staff, disrupting the fragile truce that had been established after the 1947–48 walkouts.[60] In 1961 a pay dispute prompted workers to dissolve the company's union and instead seek representation through the Chicago Newspaper Guild. Consequently, the *Defender* declined to enter negotiations and also refused to open its books to justify Sengstacke's claims that the paper "could not afford pay raises."[61] In response, around sixty production and editorial staff chose to go on strike in April. Unwilling to concede, Sengstacke fired union-affiliated staff, leading a National Labor Relations Board (NLRB) examiner to rule that the newspaper's management had "failed to bargain in good faith" and demanding the reinstatement of guild members.[62] The following year, the NLRB launched a legal petition to secure back pay for fired staffers and issued an order for Sengstacke to "cease and desist from discouraging membership in the guild."[63]

After the initial pay dispute, groups of picketers had paraded outside the *Defender's* headquarters. We can picture the glowering Sengstacke, ensconced in his private offices, watching the picketers troop back and forth along Michigan Avenue. With hats pulled low and coats buttoned tight to ward off a "furious spring blizzard," they cast an image that, at first glance, would not seem out of place within the movement's now iconic visual canon—the familiar lines of marchers "armed only with protest placards or articles detailing the economic and social inequalities facing blacks."[64] It is only upon closer inspection that we realize the signs they hold do not read "I am a man" or "Jim Crow Must Go" but instead "On Strike: Chicago Newspaper Guild." While the Seventh Circuit Court of Appeals would ultimately rule in the *Defender's* favor, the visual damage done by this spectacle may have outweighed any financial savings.[65] Such incidents were not simply a direct challenge to Sengstacke's organizational leadership; they were an effort to disrupt or reframe his building's performative function as a house for the struggle. Their effectiveness in doing so provides an important reminder of the spaces that often existed between the public role of Black periodicals as "defenders of the race" and the more complex and often invisible negotiations over labor rights and Black socioeconomic opportunities that occurred at many Black publishing enterprises.

Picket at the offices of the *Chicago Defender*. (Kirn Vintage Stock / Alamy Stock Photo)

Black Progress on All Fronts

Half a mile north at the headquarters of Chicago's other leading Black press enterprise, Johnson Publishing was facing its own challenges. The building's purchase had been financed by Johnson's efforts to "mirror the happier side of negro life," and just as the publisher took enormous satisfaction from his company's "showpiece" home, he reveled in the ability of his magazines to let Black readers "get away from 'the problem' for a few moments."[66] As literary scholar Gayle Wald notes, while Johnson's magazines did not completely ignore the issue of civil rights during the 1940s and early 1950s, they regularly "eschew[ed] reporting on discrimination and segregation in favor of contents that emphasized racial self-affirmation."[67]

Historian Jonathan Scott Holloway is struck by the consistency of *Ebony*'s early content: share Black success stories, celebrate entrepreneurship and conspicuous consumption, and "above all, make sure everyone is smiling and has beautiful skin, hair and teeth."[68]

However, as "the problem" became increasingly difficult to ignore, the dominant editorial philosophy of Johnson's magazines came under renewed attack. The "apparent incongruity between the magazine's fare and the suddenly serious tenor of the news affecting Negro lives," coupled with the impact of an economic recession, prompted *Ebony*'s newsstand sales to drop in 1954.[69] In response, Johnson moved to deemphasize (although by no means completely disregard) the sensational, confessional-type content that had populated much of the magazine's early content in favor of a more serious editorial tone. This shift occurred across the company's canon, perhaps most notably in the newsmagazine *Jet*, with reporter Simon Booker contending that the pocket-size weekly was transformed from "society tidbits and gossip [into] a hard-hitting source of news about black progress on all fronts."[70] The brutal murder of Emmett Till in 1955 was a watershed moment for the magazine; writer Timothy Tyson submits that "no photograph in history can lay claim to a comparable impact in black America" than a close-up image of Till's mutilated face taken by photographer David Jackson and published in *Jet*'s September 15 issue.[71]

Jackson was among the many field operatives sent south following the *Brown* decision in order to help expand the company's movement coverage. It was hard and dangerous work, with the photographer learning to traverse back roads and drive "without lights to get away from suspicious sheriffs."[72] In his autobiography, *Shocking the Conscience*, Booker writes that nothing in his upbringing or journalistic training prepared him for his first trip to Mississippi, where he witnessed "not only raw hatred, but state-condoned terror."[73] Other southern sojourners included *Ebony* associate editor Lerone Bennett Jr. and white freelance photographer Mike Shea. Working together was a persistent problem south of the Mason-Dixon Line; the duo often discussed business on street corners and in the backseats of rented cars rather than risk a segregated café or dining establishment.[74] During an interview with one Southern mayor, Bennett was warned, "If you boys got any of them NAACP fellers up there, you'd best kill them before they get down here."[75] Despite such threats, Johnson Publishing staffers became a regular fixture on the "race beat." *Jet* provided more regular updates on local civil rights struggles, while *Ebony*'s monthly format precluded up-to-date reporting but encouraged in-depth features that explored the emergence of "a new militant Negro" in the South. Returning to Chicago with tales of white violence and Black resistance witnessed on "safari into Dixie," Bennett, Booker, and other Johnson staffers injected a movement sensibility into the newsroom that quickly found its way onto the pages of the company's magazines.[76]

Johnson also sought to establish stronger connections with prominent Black rights activists, including Roy Wilkins, the executive director of the NAACP and the subject of an in-depth *Ebony* profile in 1955, and organizer Daisy Bates, who was lauded for her role in the 1957 Little Rock Crisis, which saw Arkansas governor Orval Faubus mobilize the National Guard to prevent a group of Black students from enrolling at Little Rock Central High School.[77] Undoubtedly the figure courted most aggressively by Johnson was Dr. Martin Luther King Jr., the Atlanta-based Baptist minister whose role in the 1955–56 Montgomery bus boycotts helped to position him as the movement's most visible figurehead. Bennett, who had been a classmate of King's at Morehouse College during the 1940s, collaborated with the minister to produce a series of major *Ebony* profiles exploring his nonviolence philosophy and international travel.[78] With the help of *Jet* editor Robert Johnson—another Morehouse classmate—Bennett also convinced King to pen a regular column titled "Advice for Living," which appeared in *Ebony* during the late 1950s.[79] When speaking or campaigning in Chicago, King was prone to drop by the Johnson plant, even using it to stage press conferences, where he urged Black Chicagoans "to use all their resources to get the federal government to take a more active role in the segregation battle."[80]

An expansion of the company's civil rights coverage on the page was aided by parallel moves off it. In 1956 Johnson opened a branch office in Atlanta, Georgia, a major center for the developing Southern movement. Johnson convinced William Fowlkes, a Black press stalwart and longtime contributor to the *Atlanta World*, to become the chief of his Atlanta bureau. Fowlkes established an office at 208 Auburn Avenue that was intended to function as the "headquarters for advertising and circulation men in the area."[81] The building was sandwiched between the *World*'s offices at 145 Auburn Avenue, which housed its business staff, and 210 Auburn Avenue, which hosted its editorial operations. The location suitably embodied the bureau's operational capacity, with Fowlkes relying heavily on the journalistic infrastructure of the Scott Newspaper Syndicate, described by historian Thomas Aiello as the "grapevine of the Black South," to produce content for Johnson's magazines.[82] Although the bureau did not last, the address remained an important local hub, as the Southern Christian Leadership Conference and later the Student Nonviolent Coordinating Committee (SNCC) established offices in the premises.[83]

Johnson also turned his attentions to the nation's capital. Booker notes that "much of the news germane to the civil rights movement" originated in Washington, D.C., and by the end of 1955 it was clear that a Washington bureau would help to significantly improve the company's coverage.[84] Booker, a Maryland native who had integrated the *Washington Post*'s reporting staff before joining Johnson Publishing, was the obvious choice to become the D.C. bureau chief. However, while the debonair Booker easily slipped back into the cosmopolitan pool of capital journalism, Johnson's efforts to find a suitable home for the bureau were more labored. The publisher was informed that "Washington is a southern town. . . . Nobody is going to rent you any space."[85] After launching the bureau from the U Street offices of Black attorney J. Leon Williams, Johnson finally managed to secure a lease on a two-room suite at 266 Constitution Avenue NW in a building owned by the Standard Oil Company.[86] Quickly outgrowing these offices, the bureau then moved to the Riggs Building at Fifteenth and G Street NW. In 1964 Johnson applied for a lease at his dream "front street" address at 1750 Pennsylvania Avenue, just a few hundred yards from the White House. After the publisher's application was denied, Walter Trohan, the Washington bureau chief of the *Chicago Tribune* and a close personal friend of Booker, threatened to go public with the story. Thanks to Trohan's intervention, Johnson Publishing was able to secure a large suite overlooking Pennsylvania Avenue. Several months later, a crowd of "nearly 1,000 federal officials, business people, and civil rights leaders" crammed into the suite for one of the best views of Lyndon Johnson's inaugural parade available anywhere in the capital.[87]

Editorial changes and the opening of regional bureaus were seen as evidence of Johnson's movement sensibilities by organizations such as the NAACP, who recognized the publisher at its 1958 Freedom Fund dinner for his "steadfast support of the continuing struggle for [the] full employment of civil rights."[88] Johnson also deepened his relationship with organizations such as the Urban League, becoming a vice president and helping to promote funding drives and other activities.[89] However, such accolades and personal connections did little to quiet criticism from other quarters, not least his colleagues within the Black press. *New York Age* editor Chuck Stone described *Ebony* as "an apostle of *ex posto facto* militancy" whose participation in the movement was limited to that of a "frightened passenger."[90] *Los Angeles Tribune* publisher Almena Lomax was similarly nonplussed, launching an extraordinary attack after Johnson's citation at the NAACP's Freedom Fund dinner. Lomax contended that Johnson's magazines were "in no way identified with the Negro struggle" and that civil rights activists would be hard-pressed "to find an influence in Negro life which has been as detrimental to stability, militancy, and racial solidarity than the Johnson publications."[91]

A Little World of Our Own

In response to continued criticisms, Johnson decided to revive *Negro Digest*, which had been shelved in 1951.[92] The man entrusted with overseeing its return editing was Hoyt Fuller, who had worked as an associate editor at *Ebony* during the 1950s before growing disenchanted with the magazine's philosophy.[93] Given his previous experience, Fuller was unsure whether to accept Johnson's offer, privately confiding to friends that "I KNOW it is a mistake and that I will regret it."[94] Ultimately, Fuller accepted and the second run of the *Digest* began in May 1961.[95] However, as historian Jonathan Fenderson notes, Fuller's vision for the magazine was at odds with Johnson from the outset. Although the publisher's decision to reboot was clearly based on an effort to capitalize on growing demands for racial equality, he had little desire to see the *Digest* become a militant outlet.[96] Fuller's plans were altogether more ambitious and significantly more radical. He saw an opportunity to provide militant young Black writers "with a platform and a forum" to articulate their ideas, something that contributed to the *Digest*'s emergence as a leading space for critical commentary on the Black experience. During the years immediately following its reintroduction, the magazine published work by a wealth of young Black artists and intellectuals, including sociologist and Black Studies pioneer Nathan Hare, author Frank London Brown, and anti-apartheid campaigner Richard Rive.[97] Under Fuller's leadership the *Digest* grew into a leading voice for the Black Arts movement and a vital outlet for Pan-African thought, something that contributed to its eventual renaming as *Black World*.[98]

These philosophical tensions defined Fuller and Johnson's relationship throughout the *Digest*'s second run and contributed to the magazine's ambiguous and often marginal position within the company's roster. Fuller quickly surmised that Johnson was "not particularly disposed toward me" or the publication.[99] In fairness it should be noted that Johnson continued to publish the *Digest* at a loss into the 1970s, a decision that appeared to run counter to his usual preoccupation with the bottom line, albeit one likely influenced by the *Digest*'s reputation as a serious Black literary journal, which helped to offset criticisms of the company's more consumer-oriented periodicals.[100] However, the publisher provided little support for the *Digest*'s development and in some ways appeared to actively undermine the magazine. Perhaps the most notable example of this was his reluctance to allow corporate advertising in the *Digest*, removing a potentially significant revenue stream and contributing to its position as "last and least" among Johnson Publishing's roster of magazines.[101] The company's marketing arm was also instructed not to promote the publication, while art director Herbert Temple was frequently asked to prioritize typesetting and graphic design for *Ebony* and *Jet* over that of the *Digest*.[102]

Tellingly, Johnson's neglect of the *Digest* manifested itself through the magazine's visibility at the company's headquarters. As Johnson's first magazine, the *Digest* had been synonymous with his publishing company during its early years, something most clearly shown through its original nomenclature as the Negro Digest Publishing Company. This prominence extended to its physical location, as Johnson declared that the publication's name emblazoned across the door of Earl Dickerson's law library at 3501 South Parkway offered "music to [his] soul."[103] Signage for the *Digest* was prominent at 5619 State Street and 5125 Calumet Avenue, Johnson's first independent offices. However, by the late 1940s *Ebony* had usurped the *Digest* as the company's most popular periodical, and when Johnson unveiled his new offices at 1820 Michigan Avenue, the *Digest*'s name was notably absent from its exterior. Instead, the company's employees and readers could get "a good feeling out of seeing the neon-lighted *Ebony* sign more than a mile away from our office on Chicago's famed Michigan Avenue."[104] Even after the *Digest* was reintroduced in 1961, the building's entrance plaque was not updated, effectively rendering the magazine invisible on the exterior of its own offices.[105]

Internally, this marginality extended to the daily activities of the *Digest*'s staff, with Fuller's archival papers at Atlanta University Center documenting his "exhausting" and often lonely negotiation of the company's offices.[106] Johnson later declared that he had a "secret office in the heart of my company" where he kept a list of essential employees, and, given Fuller's treatment, it seems unlikely that the *Digest*'s editor was included.[107] The magazine was perennially understaffed, meaning that Fuller produced the *Digest* almost single-handedly for long periods. Furthermore, whereas *Ebony* and *Jet* had a dedicated editorial team with their own distinct spaces, the *Digest*'s contributors were scattered throughout the company's headquarters, making even simple editorial or production queries an arduous affair. To document his frustrations at such treatment, Fuller began to produce a satirical newsletter titled "JPC-iana," which appears to have been circulated among sympathetic colleagues. Early editions detail the regular slights directed toward Fuller, as well as Johnson's broader misuse of company employees. On one occasion Fuller details how, with the *Digest* behind schedule, two artists were commandeered from their work and taken to Johnson's home "to draw up place-cards for some 50 guests expected at a sit-down dinner party that night."[108]

Given Johnson's enthusiasm for policing his staff, something that saw him characterized as an "overseer" and the company's offices labeled as a "plantation" by disgruntled employees, such dissent could have been potentially dangerous.[109] As Adam Green notes, the publisher's "legendary tendency to micromanage" spread to almost all areas of the company's operation and had a significant impact on the day-to-day politics of its Chicago offices.[110] Johnson took pride in being "all over the building all the time"; one of his favorite hobbies was to stake out the lobby with the goal of catching employees who arrived late.[111] Well into the twilight of his career, Johnson continued to regularly patrol the corridors of his company's offices in order to police editorial activities and to "check in" on his workforce. In a 1997 profile by *N'Digo*, published when Johnson was almost eighty, Charles Whitaker, a former *Ebony* senior editor turned journalism professor, made a point of stressing that "no detail is too small to escape his notice."[112]

However, when it came to Fuller and the *Digest*, Johnson seemed unusually distant. Fuller often found it impossible to schedule face-to-face meetings with Johnson and was regularly forced to communicate with him through written letters or via intermediary employees such as Johnson's personnel director, LaDoris Foster.[113] This neglect levied a significant personal cost; less than eighteen months after his return to Chicago, Fuller was confiding to friends that he had "almost reached the point where I have to force myself to come to work," describing his situation as "depressing, and a little frightening."[114] The editor's correspondence with Johnson became increasingly fractious as time progressed, with Fuller complaining, "I have asked you for practically nothing, and I have not been on the receiving end of much consideration in return."[115] The editor's professional isolation led to him threatening his resignation on multiple occasions.[116] It was a situation that would only worsen following the company's move to a new headquarters during the early 1970s, when Johnson repeatedly stonewalled Fuller and shut him out of company events such as film screenings and corporate lunches.[117]

Yet this neglect also created the space necessary for Fuller to mold the magazine in his image. Carole Parks, who later joined the publication as an associate editor, recalled, "We had a little world of our own. . . . We could do whatever we wanted." Particularly after the magazine's renaming as *Black World*, Fenderson argues, both editors "used Johnson's neglect as an opportunity to further depart from JPC's metanarrative and publish writing that reflected their own politics."[118] Largely freed from the shackles of Johnson's oversight, the *Digest* emerged as arguably the most influential in a new wave of "little Black magazines" that included the *Liberator*, a New York–based Black monthly founded in 1960, and *Freedomways*, a quarterly Pan-African publication started the following year.[119] Critically, the *Digest*'s influence as a voice for Black arts and radical politics contrasted with—and was facilitated by—its liminality within the walls of the Johnson Publishing headquarters. Operating on both the physical and ideological margins of the company's canon, the *Digest* worked to critique, complicate, and even undermine aspects of Johnson's core editorial philosophy from the inside.

To Fight for Total Equality

While *Negro Digest* remained something of a Black sheep within the Johnson Publishing family after its relaunch, its content reflects a broader effort to shift discussions of Black activism and racial politics in both the company's magazines and its headquarters. During the years following the *Brown* decision, a small but influential left-wing bloc emerged within the company. Along with Fuller, other members of this cohort included Era Bell Thompson, *Ebony*'s international editor, who risked imprisonment to help publicize atrocities in colonial Africa; photographer Francis Mitchell, whose later work for the SNCC has been highlighted by visual scholar Leigh Raiford as playing a key role in legitimating its "program of radical democracy"; *Jet* editor Robert Johnson, a trusted confidante of Dr. King; and Allan Morrison, the long-serving *Ebony* editor who was labeled in private as a "fierce Marxist."[120] Perhaps the most visible member of this group was Lerone Bennett Jr., described by Pan-African theorist John Henrik Clarke as part of a "generation of new black thinkers who . . . matured within the eye of the civil rights storm."[121] By the early 1960s, Bennett's growing reputation as a popular historian and public intellectual had made him something of a celebrity.[122] Following the 1962 release of his first book *Before the Mayflower*, "Backstage" reported that dozens of company employees "stood in line before Bennett's office, books in hand, to get his autograph."[123]

This group was soon joined by new contributors; according to historian Korey Bowers Brown, shifts in the movement's trajectory and geography, as well as the expectations of his readers, forced Johnson to "recruit young writers with militant sensibilities."[124] Among them was David Llorens, a SNCC operative who joined the *Digest* as an assistant editor.[125] Other additions included Alex Poinsett, who was entrusted with penning much of *Ebony*'s coverage of the local fight against school segregation.[126] Not all members of the company's audience welcomed these additions; indeed, Poinsett's later reporting on Black Power activists such as Eldridge Cleaver led some readers to describe him as a "racist revolutionary."[127] Nevertheless, they had a considerable impact on the contents of Johnson's magazines, perhaps most clearly traceable through special issues such as "The WHITE Problem in America," published in August 1965, which took aim at "all those whites who have 'stood in the doorways' to keep the Negro back." These sentiments, alongside the magazine's growing coverage of Black radical activism, were highlighted by the *Philadelphia Tribune* as evidence of *Ebony*'s transition "from materialism to militancy."[128]

Similar changes were afoot at the *Defender*, where the need to engineer a more substantive response to the coalescing freedom struggle saw the newspaper cycle through a series of new editors in chief, beginning with Alex Wilson in 1959. Two years earlier Wilson had been brutally beaten by a white mob while attempting to report on the ongoing crisis at Little Rock High School in Arkansas, where state governor Orval Faubus had deployed the Arkansas National Guard to block Black students from integrating the school.[129] Footage of Wilson's assault had circulated across the country, helping to cement his reputation as a fearless reporter committed to documenting the civil rights story. His promotion was heavily publicized by the *Defender*, who linked it to his refusal "to run from a jeering, howling mob" in Little Rock.[130] However, Wilson was increasingly absent from the newspaper's plant—the result of a neurological condition that emerged shortly after the beating and that contributed to his premature death in 1960.[131]

Upon Wilson's passing, Metz Lochard and Louis Martin helped to guide the publication before Sengstacke made the ill-fated decision to rehire white editor Ben Burns.[132] The appointment was met with anger in some quarters, with staffers such as cartoonist Chester Commodore going so far as to boycott the newspaper's plant.[133] Just weeks after his return, Burns confided to Enoch Waters, who had left the *Defender* to join the Associated Negro Press several years earlier, that he was struggling "to get my head above water."[134] Burns would soon be gone, claiming, "In the inflamed racial climate of the 1960s, for a white to edit a black newspaper had become impossible."[135] Interracial relationships were also strained at Johnson Publishing, where some Black contributors bristled at the possibility of "reverse integration" drawing a wave of white employees into the company's plant.[136] After word broke of plans for a white editorial hire, a petition was passed around 1820 Michigan Avenue to catalog concerns ranging from fears that the "white minority might want to date Negro girls" to the question of exactly where white employees should be placed. Johnson later recalled, "They wanted to know where his desk would be. They didn't want it at the front of the room. I didn't want it at the back. We compromised and put it in the middle."[137]

Simmering racial and ideological conflicts spilled into open rebellion in the *Defender*'s newsroom following the appointment of Chuck Stone as editor in 1963. A Black press stalwart who had previously worked at publications such as the *New York Age* and the *Afro-American*, Stone believed in "picketing, boycotting, buying black, [and] employing every democratic measure to fight for total equality."[138] In keeping with this tradition, he attempted to push the *Defender* toward a more militant position, declaring, "We are the only newspaper in Chicago which is enthusiastically—and kind of noisily too—committed to an immediate, swift, uncompromising and total dissolution of all racial barriers." Stone's strident and, at times, slanderous rhetoric saw him labeled by supporters and detractors alike as "the angry man of the Negro press," an editor who was unafraid to focus his acerbic commentary on any target, regardless of race, class, or political affiliation.[139] This included many of Chicago's civil rights groups, even those with whom he shared a roof. Through his aptly named weekly column, "A Stone's Throw," the editor launched repeated attacks against the Chicago Urban League for its perceived conservatism, contending that the organization was "more concerned with sociological orchestration than in concrete civil rights achievements."[140]

While Stone's movement sensibilities played a role in his initial hiring, it quickly became apparent that Sengstacke was having second thoughts about the appointment. Their relationship deteriorated as Stone's coverage of the battle to desegregate Chicago's public schools became increasingly defamatory; at one point the editor compared school superintendent Benjamin Willis to Nazi propaganda minister Joseph Goebbels.[141] Matters came to a head after Stone decided to go after city mayor Richard Daley, describing the politician as a "phony" and imploring Black readers to vote him out of office. Editor and publisher became embroiled in a series of explosive conflicts.[142] On one occasion, in front of the entire newsroom Sengstacke furiously tore up a story Stone had written on housing discrimination.[143] Such incidents were a reminder of Sengstacke's willingness to engineer set-piece confrontations at the *Defender*'s plant as a means of exerting his authority, echoing his earlier battles with Abbott's widow, Edna Denison. The publisher also made a point of encouraging Daley's participation in the 1964 Billiken Parade, a decision that drew fire from readers who declared, "Bud Billiken personifies the spirit of goodwill, and Daley has shown no goodwill toward Negroes."[144]

Perhaps the most open display of editorial defiance enacted at Johnson Publishing came from John Woodford, one of the company's youngbloods. The editor remembers his early days at the company fondly, recalling, "We had a sort of clique that would agitate for more coverage" of Black radical and third world politics.[145] However, Woodford quickly grew frustrated with the relatively slow pace of change. These frustrations became more acute after activist James Meredith's "March against Fear" in 1966 and the emergence of Black Power; Woodford met with repeated stonewalling in his efforts to provide positive coverage of Black Power activists and organizations. Johnson's deference to corporate advertisers was another persistent point of contention, and Woodford also locked horns with more moderate *Ebony* contributors such as Carl Rowan, whom Woodford viewed as "a favorite of the liberal White elite because he espoused their imperialistic, antisocialist foreign-policy line."[146]

Two events in 1968 helped to irreparably weaken Woodford's faith in the company's effectiveness as a voice for Black protest. The first was Johnson's reluctance to address the imprisonment of Black radical activists like former SNCC chairman H. Rap Brown and federal attempts to suppress the Black Panther Party and other Black Power organizations, both of which, Woodford said, were "strictly *verboten*."[147] The second was the publication of *Ebony*'s 1968 special issue on "The Black Soldier," which featured advertisements for the U.S. armed forces and uncritically celebrated the role of Black GIs in fighting the "resourceful and lethal Viet Cong" at a time when many progressive Black leaders and publications were denouncing U.S. intervention in Southeast Asia.[148] In response, Woodford dramatically quit by posting a "Martin Luther–like manifesto, defiant and full of self-inflating invective, on several walls in *Ebony*'s offices." In addition to *Ebony*'s contentious special issue, the editor highlighted the company's failure to support incarcerated Black Power activists, its reluctance to speak out against American complicity in South Africa's apartheid regime, and "countless other reasons which I take as insults to the Afro-American community."[149]

Given his editorial censorship, it is striking that Woodford chose to embrace the physical potential of the newsroom as a tool to directly challenge his publisher's ideological and editorial philosophy. The preservation of Woodford's manifesto in the archival papers of editors like Hoyt Fuller and Robert Johnson demonstrates an afterlife for his act of defiance, perhaps as a rallying cry for other staffers frustrated by the company's editorial policies or their own alienation.[150] In this regard, the manifesto can be read as both a continuation and escalation of dissident undercurrents that were swirling within the Johnson Publishing offices, undercurrents that included private memorandums and Fuller's "JPC-iana" and that extended to employee characterizations of the headquarters as a "plantation."[151] More broadly, Woodford's note and Stone's newsroom confrontations with Sengstacke are just two examples of comparative battles being waged in Black newsrooms across the country, as Black press buildings became the staging ground for conflicts between militant editors and more commercially minded Black publishers accused "of abandoning their industry's long tradition of strident racial protest."[152]

TO WHOM IT MAY CONCERN:

BECAUSE THE SPECIAL ISSUE IS ESSENTIALLY (SEE ARMY AD) EVIL

BECAUSE JPC REFUSES TO HELP THE JAILED HUEY P. NEWTON

BECAUSE JPC REFUSES TO ATTACK BY NAME AND IN PRINT THE U.S.
PROPS OF SOUTH AFRICA

BECAUSE JPC REFUSES TO COVER CASTRO'S CUBA

AND FOR COUNTLESS OTHER REASONS WHICH, ALL IN ALL, I TAKE
AS INSULTS TO THE AFRO=AMERICAN COMMUNITY AND TO MYSELF
IN PARTICULAR; ESPECIALLY THE UNCLE TOM DECLARATIONS IN TIME MAGAZINE,
DECLARATIONS OF FLUNKY=ISM AND GUTLESSNESS AND MORAL ACNE AND IGNORANCE

I HEREBY TAKE THE ADVICE OF CHARLES SANDERS, WHO SAID WHEN
YOU FIND YOURSELF UNALTERABLY OPPOSED TO THE MAN WHO PAYS YOU, YOU SHOULD QUIT;=*

AND SO I DO, AS OF NOW.

JOHN WOODFORD

ASS'T EDITOR
MESSAGE TO JPC FROM JNW

"...MOST AMERICAN NEGROES, EVEN THOSE OF INTELLIGENCE AND COURAGE,
DO NOT FULLY REALIZE THAT THEY ARE BEING BRIBED TO TRADE EQUAL
STATUS IN THE UNITED STATES FOR THE SLAVERY OF THE MAJORITY OF
MEN. WHEN THIS IS CLEAR, ESPECIALLY TO THE BLACK YOUTH, THE
RACE MUST BE AROUSED TO THOUGHT AND ACTION AND WILL SEE THAT
THE PRICE ASKED FOR THEIR COOPERATION IS FAR HIGHER THAN NEED
BE PAID..."

W.E.B. DU BOIS

Woodford Manifesto. (Robert and Naomi Johnson Papers, Emory University Special Collections)

Building the Black Radical Press

Woodford wasn't out of work for long. After plastering his manifesto across the walls of 1820 Michigan Avenue, the editor made a beeline for the offices of *Muhammad Speaks* on the corner of Seventy-Ninth Street and Champlain Avenue. The official newspaper of the Nation of Islam, a Black nationalist sect headed by enigmatic leader Elijah Muhammad, *Muhammad Speaks* began publication in 1960 as a "militant monthly dedicated to justice for the Black Man."[153] Founded in the New York home of Malcolm X, an influential Muslim minister and one of the organization's most recognizable public spokespersons, the publication initially functioned as little more than a personal mouthpiece for "The Honorable Elijah Muhammad." However, historian Khuram Hussain suggests that, under Malcolm's direction, the periodical gained plaudits for editorial quality and extensive coverage "of news events pertinent to Black communities."[154] The minister's influence prompted Elijah Muhammad to shift the publication from New York to Chicago, the Nation of Islam's national base of operations, in 1961.[155] A few years later, after Malcolm's highly public split from the sect, the editorial invective directed toward its former protégé by *Muhammad Speaks* likely played a role in his assassination.

While the relocation reiterated the indelible link between the newspaper and the sect, Muhammad appeared happy to cede control of *Muhammad Speaks* to non-Muslim writers, a decision likely predicated on the scarcity of experienced journalists within the organization. This began with Dan Burley, a stalwart of Chicago's Black press who contributed to what seemed like every major Black periodical in the city over the previous three decades, including multiple stints at the *Defender* and as a correspondent for the Associated Negro Press.[156] Burley's *Defender* connections may also have facilitated a short-term relationship between his former and current bosses, as *Muhammad Speaks* was printed out of 2400 Michigan Avenue during its formative years in Chicago.[157] Upon Burley's death in 1962, the reins to *Muhammad Speaks* were taken up by Richard Durham, another experienced Black journalist who had twinned work for the *Defender* and *Ebony* with the development of a successful career in radio broadcasting.[158] Under Durham's leadership the newspaper's circulation continued to rapidly expand, helped in large part by the Nation of Islam's practice of requiring male members to sell a certain number of copies every week. By the time Woodford joined *Muhammad Speaks*, the Nation was claiming a weekly circulation in excess of 350,000, a figure that dwarfed the *Defender*'s readership and, indeed, the readership of every other Black commercial newspaper in the country.[159]

Another Black radical periodical that gained a large following during this period was the Black Panther Party's community newspaper, which began publication in 1967, one year after the party's own founding. Conceived as a four-page newsletter and published from the party's headquarters in Oakland, California, the *Black Panther* offered economic support to rank-and-file members, who were able to keep ten cents from each twenty-five-cent copy sold. Readership figures are notoriously unreliable, but Jessica Lipsky suggests that the newspaper's circulation had reached 250,000 by the end of its first year in print.[160] Like *Muhammad Speaks*, it was a highly effective promotional and recruitment tool, one that enabled party leaders to communicate their message and purpose to a broad audience and lay the groundwork for the creation of new chapters across the country. In 1968 an Illinois chapter of the Black Panther Party was founded in Chicago by former SNCC members Bobby Rush and Bob Brown, who, along with city council member Sammy Rayner, established a party office at 2350 West Madison Street. Located just yards away from the *Defender*'s West Side offices, the Panther's offices became the de facto local distribution center for the *Black Panther* and an important new space for the production and dissemination of Black print culture within Chicago.[161]

Although neither the Panther's West Side offices nor the Seventy-Ninth Street offices of *Muhammad Speaks* were as visually compelling as the Michigan Avenue addresses of the *Defender* and Johnson Publishing, their respective openings provided a reminder of how Black radical publications were challenging the position of Chicago's leading Black periodicals. To be sure, this was hardly a new development. As earlier chapters demonstrate, the *Defender* reputation for "race militancy" had come under fire from publications like the *Chicago Whip*, which took aim at the *Defender*'s more socially conservative content and its reluctance to support initiatives such as the *Whip*'s "Don't Buy Where You Can't Work" campaign.[162] During the late 1940s and early 1950s, anticommunist pressure saw left-wing editors such as Metz Lochard briefly forced out of the *Defender*. Lochard went on to establish the *Chicago Globe*, a short-lived weekly designed to "espouse the progressive views once endorsed" by Sengstacke's publication, which was intentionally located at 2705 Michigan Avenue, just a few hundred yards from its rival's headquarters.[163] As for Johnson, his enthusiastic embrace of the middle ground had drawn consistent criticism since his company's formation, something that only increased following the emergence of publications such as the *Liberator* during the 1960s.

However, the tremendous popularity of *Muhammad Speaks* and the *Black Panther* offered a different kind of challenge. As scholars such as Fred Carroll argue, their rapid growth was indicative of how the rise of Black Power and a groundswell of Black radical activism was both nurtured by and fed into an increased demand for radical Black literary and journalistic perspectives.[164]

Both papers were undoubtedly party organs; *Muhammad Speaks* in particular was consistently peppered with content related to the Nation of Islam's conspiratorial and pseudoscientific religious theories. However, the two papers' incisive coverage of issues such as police brutality, their disdain for the existing political system, and their support for Black diasporic struggles and liberation movements found a wider audience. When contributors to *Muhammad Speaks* and the *Black Panther* criticized the *Defender* or described the content of Johnson's magazines as "pitiful," these sentiments were not only damaging because of the huge numbers of people they reached.[165] They also hurt because they suggested that these publications had lost their way within Black Chicago's shifting literary and ideological terrain.

Nowhere was this clearer than on the streets of the city itself. During the 1950s and 1960s, Johnson's circulation model had moved decisively toward a subscription base, meaning that even as the audience of publications like *Ebony* continued to expand, they became a less visible presence on many local newsstands.[166] While the *Defender*'s newsboys maintained the paper's presence in Black communities on the South and West Sides, during the second half of the 1960s they suddenly found themselves competing with an army of "immaculately dressed Black Muslims" and dashing *Black Panther* salesmen. It was a battle that, in its own way, paralleled the efforts of Black Power activists to "reclaim" the streets of urban America, and, in the case of the Nation of Islam, its self-professed intentions to "take over the South Side."[167] Hussain argues that Black Muslims and Panther members aggressively hawked papers "on the street corners of black commercial centers across the country," with locations such as the Panther's West Side headquarters and the *Muhammad Speaks* Seventy-Ninth Street offices becoming important nodes in a radical geography of Black urban communications. Where pedestrians had previously heard "Buy the *Defender*" or "Get the World's Greatest Weekly," they were now bombarded with cries of "Salaam Alaikam, come back to your own, read *Muhammad Speaks!*" and "We're the Panthers, want to see? Buy the paper!"[168]

Eager to expand his newspaper's influence further, Elijah Muhammad sought to purchase a new home that would better reflect its enormous popularity and would rival the impressive headquarters of Chicago's premier Black print institutions. In November 1969 *Muhammad Speaks* unveiled a "modern miracle" to its readers; a four-story, sixty-thousand-square-foot printing plant located at 2548 Federal Street, which, when accounting for

Muhammad Speaks Building. (Chicago Sun-Times Collection, Chicago History Museum)

its renovation and the installation of new equipment, was reported to have cost $1.5 million.[169] The plant quickly became the nerve center of the Nation of Islam's sprawling South Side business empire, embodying its organizational emphasis on Black self-sufficiency and community solidarity. Not only had it been purchased without the need for white investment, but *Muhammad Speaks* contended that the relocation would help to create "more than one hundred highly skilled jobs for black people."[170] It was a formidable statement of intent, one that, as the crow flies, lay just a third of a mile southwest of the *Defender*'s Michigan Avenue offices. However, while the *Defender*'s plant may have been almost visible from the roof of *Muhammad Speaks*' new headquarters, the latter's editorial politics helped to disrupt the connection between Chicago's "mainstream" Black publications and the Michigan Avenue Corridor.

To Be Truly Representative

For media historian Jane Rhodes, the enormous, albeit relatively fleeting, readerships enjoyed by *Muhammad Speaks* and the *Black Panther* during the

late 1960s and early 1970s reflected widespread desire for "a decidedly radical, audacious brand of African American journalism," one that represented
a clear challenge to the content of more moderate Black publications.[171]
In the case of the *Defender* and Johnson Publishing, such challenges not
only manifested themselves through the pages of locally circulating Black
radical publications, or the purchase of new Black press edifices such as the
Muhammad Speaks plant on Federal Avenue, but are also traceable through
more direct methods. Outside their Chicago headquarters, as well as at
satellite offices across the country, critics staged pickets and public protests
to express support for maligned editors and to demand that the *Defender*
and Johnson Publishing implement editorial policies that were "truly representative of the black community."[172] In doing so, they highlighted how
the symbolic function of Black media buildings as a house for the struggle
could be strategically turned against their inhabitants as a means of en-
gendering change and drawing attention to a variety of ideological and
philosophical concerns.

One such incident occurred at the *Defender*'s plant in October 1964.
During his short stint as the newspaper's editor in chief, Chuck Stone's
militant posture and uncompromising commitment to the "total dissolution
of all racial barriers" had proved controversial but had also garnered strong
support among some sections of the *Defender*'s newsroom and its broader
audience.[173] Even as Stone's efforts to reshape the newspaper's copy fed
the breakdown in his relationship with Sengstacke, other parties warned
that his dismissal would not be well received by local activists. After Stone's
inevitable firing, supporters gathered outside the *Defender*'s plant to protest
Sengstacke's decision.[174] No doubt encouraged by Stone himself, who left
"convinced that Sengstacke intended for the newspaper to be a cog in Mayor
Daley's machine," protesters established a picket line and brandished signs
demanding his reinstatement.[175] Others wrote to Sengstacke personally,
accusing him of hiding in the newspaper's offices instead of addressing the
issue at hand. Even *Defender* contributor Carole Anderson got in on the act:
"I wonder what kind of man you are[,] Mr. Sengstacke, sitting behind the
desk of a newspaper office afraid of truth and controversy."[176] Like earlier
labor pickets, such actions and characterizations flipped the symbolic function of 2400 Michigan Avenue on its head. When Sengstacke had opened
the *Defender*'s new building, he had positioned it as a vital outpost in the
struggle for racial equality. To his critics, it was now a refuge that shielded

him from public scrutiny. Sengstacke, in other words, had pulled up the drawbridge.

At Johnson Publishing *Ebony*'s proclivity for "cheesecake" content and its focus on light-skinned Black celebrities had long been a source of disapproval, and by the 1960s such material seemed increasingly out of touch with growing calls for Black pride and the demands of Black feminist activists. A cursory glance through *Ebony*'s cover images during the first half of the decade reveal what Maxine Craig describes as a "pigmentocracy that reinforced the link between color and class."[177] In 1965 *Liberator* journalist Eddie Ellis offered a searing takedown of the publication in a two-part article titled "Is Ebony a Negro Magazine?" which declared that the magazine "has NO identification with, or loyalties to, the other 30 million BLACK captives in America."[178] The following year, the publication of an *Ebony* cover story that answered the question "Are Negro Girls Getting Prettier?" with images of almost exclusively light-skinned Black models, prompted a furious response from local campaigners. As activist Molly Martindale recalls, a group of Black women "stormed across town to the offices of Johnson Publishing" to demand the issue's immediate retraction.[179]

At practically the same time, a group of protesters were forming a picket line outside the company's New York offices, located on the third floor of Rockefeller Center.[180] Carrying copies of the magazine's most egregious covers, the group marched back and forth along the Avenue of the Americas to broadcast their contempt for *Ebony*'s regressive depiction of Black beauty and gender politics. Evelyn Rodgers, who reported on the demonstration in a *Liberator* article provocatively titled "Is Ebony Killing Black Women?" reiterated the charge that *Ebony* "stands today as a classic illustration of middle-class Negro attempts to assimilate themselves into the mainstream of white American life."[181] When the picketing was over, Rodgers, along with comrades such as Eddie Ellis and Dona Humphrey, orchestrated a meeting with *Ebony* vice president William Grayson to discuss the magazine's "glorification of white aesthetic standards."[182] In response, Johnson assigned editor Phyl Garland to produce an article on the "natural" hairstyle. When it was published in June 1966, the feature was pointedly introduced by a cover image of twenty-year-old Chicagoan activist Diana Smith, one of the very same activists who had confronted Johnson in his offices several months earlier.[183]

Three years later, Johnson's Chicago headquarters found itself at the center of another public backlash. The December 1969 picket was headed by poet

Don Lee (later known as Haki Madhubuti) and actress Val Gray Ward, both influential figures within Chicago's Black arts scene, and included representatives from close to a dozen Chicago-based Black arts and cultural organizations. Once again *Ebony* was the focal point for discontent, with protesters drawing attention to the magazine's upbeat coverage of Richard Nixon's inauguration—something that was only exacerbated by revelations that the company's Washington, D.C., offices had hosted an inaugural event for "the GOP Committee of Concerned Afro-Americans."[184] More broadly the group contended that Johnson's editorial policy had "resulted in an abundance of stories and/or pictures, particularly in *Ebony*, which either ignore an emerging sense of pride among black people, [or] fail to entertain, inform, or otherwise convey any useful information necessary to the intellectual development or functioning of black people in their struggle for black liberation."[185]

After parading up and down Michigan Avenue for several hours, the group issued a statement to onlooking journalists voicing their complaints in greater detail. At the time of their picket Johnson was out of town, but the publisher asked editor Alex Poinsett to invite the group into 1820 Michigan Avenue so that he could address them via conference call.[186] Some journalists were dismissive of the group's intentions, with *Baltimore Sun* columnist Ernest Furgurson describing the protesters as "rotten apples" and sneering at their efforts to get Johnson's magazines "to tell it the way *they* see it."[187] Nevertheless, like earlier protests against "Are Negro Girls Getting Prettier?" the picket does seem to have made an impression. At a follow-up meeting, group members were able to formally present their requests to Johnson, including the establishment of an internship program for Black youth, more support for works published by radical Black writers, and increased engagement with local Black community organizations. The group also demanded greater institutional support for *Negro Digest* and a name change to better reflect the magazine's editorial philosophy.[188]

If the multiple pickets staged at Johnson Publishing buildings during the 1960s complicate their symbolic function as a house for the struggle and underscore the extent to which some African Americans believed that Johnson's magazines were failing in their efforts to be "truly representative of the Black community," they also shed light on the company's often complex relationship with Black activists.[189] Don Lee's role in the 1969 picket offers an illustrative case study, as the poet received favorable coverage in Johnson's publications during the lead-up to and aftermath of the protest.

Indeed, just months earlier, Lee had visited the Johnson plant as a guest, not as a protester, where he had conducted interviews with David Llorens as part of an in-depth profile that was published in the March 1969 issue of *Ebony*.[190] Poet Lita Hooper relates that Llorens's profile of Lee, which hailed the poet as an "acclaimed creator of black art," helped him garner national attention and played a significant role in cementing his local popularity.[191] Lee's combative relationship with Johnson Publishing reflected the willingness of other Black radical activists to take a public stand against the editorial politics of Johnson's magazines while benefiting from the exposure provided by access to and coverage in these same publications.

The protest also underscored the deepening connections between the company's staffers and a rich network of local Black activism and community organizing. Lee had grown close to Hoyt Fuller upon the latter's return to Chicago, and although the editor feigned ignorance of the 1969 picket, he was heavily implicated in its organization. Jonathan Fenderson characterizes the picket as an "inside job," arguing that Fuller "helped organize the protest as a last-ditch effort to change the name of and increase the resources allocated to" the *Digest*.[192] Similarly, Alex Poinsett's description of the protesters' actions as "worthwhile" in the *Defender* appeared to at least tacitly endorse the picket and its potential ramifications.[193] For editors like Fuller and Poinsett, these actions represented an extension of their ongoing efforts to reshape the company's internal politics. It also demonstrated a keen awareness of how best to target Johnson, a man whose professional career had consistently shown him to be preoccupied with optics. Protesters correctly surmised that where more subtle challenges to the publisher's editorial authority had proven ineffective, a perceived attack on his prized possession—the company's showpiece headquarters—could bear greater fruit.

In keeping with his literary emphasis on "the happier side of Negro life," Johnson attempted to turn the pickets into a positive. By stressing his willingness to "run articles by blacks who've picketed us" in subsequent interviews, Johnson sought to emphasize his own commitment to the cause.[194] To his credit the publisher did appear receptive to protesters' demands, perhaps a reflection of his belief that, at least for a limited period, forthright support for the Black freedom struggle was "not only sound editorial policy, but also good business."[195] After meeting with the picket's ringleaders, Johnson agreed to review his editorial policies and tone.[196] Most significantly, he moved to abandon the use of "Negro" within his magazines, beginning with the *Digest*, which was formally retitled *Black World* several months later. Johnson's apparent willingness to resolve the conflict may well have been influenced by its potential threat to an ambitious new project that was already under way one mile north of his company's Michigan Avenue plant: a custom-built corporate headquarters that he envisioned as the ultimate monument to his own business accomplishments, the unparalleled success of his publishing company, and the enduring power of Chicago's Black press.

6

A Poem in Marble and Glass

On a mild spring day in May 1972, hundreds of onlookers converged on the block of Michigan Avenue between Eighth and Ninth Streets. They had gathered to celebrate the opening of Chicago's latest Black press landmark, the new Johnson Publishing offices. A project more than a decade in the making, 820 Michigan Avenue was the culmination of John H. Johnson's long-standing ambition to build his own headquarters from the ground up. Among those present at the building's unveiling was city mayor Richard Daley, who lauded the structure as "an inspiration, not only to other blacks, but to other citizens of all races."[1] Johnson went further, declaring that the "miracle on Michigan Avenue" was a testament to both the unprecedented success of his publishing empire and the broader gains made by African Americans since he had launched *Negro Digest* three decades earlier out of a corner office of the Supreme Life Building at 3501 South Parkway.[2] With little sense of hyperbole, he described the building as "a poem in marble and glass which symbolizes our unshakeable faith that the struggles of our forefathers were not in vain."[3]

As detailed in the previous chapter, Johnson's magazines—most notably his flagship publication, *Ebony*—continued to attract criticism into the 1960s. Whereas Johnson positioned his company on the front lines of the fight for racial equality, detractors believed it "rode in the caboose as a frightened passenger."[4] For its most vocal critics, Johnson Publishing appeared to be "headed distinctly in the wrong direction, straight into the pockets of white businessmen profiting off the delusions of many Afro-Americans."[5] Such concerns—amplified by the growing influence of radical Black periodicals like the *Black Panther* and *Muhammad Speaks*—exacerbated ideological and philosophical tensions within the company's newsroom and sparked a series of building pickets. In response, Johnson ceded greater control to leftist editors and hired new contributors who sought to reshape the company's publications. Along with the renaming of *Negro Digest* as *Black World* in 1970, perhaps the clearest editorial manifestation of this shift can be seen through a series of incisive *Ebony* special issues, including "The Black Revolution" in 1969 and "Which Way Black America" in 1970, that documented how Black activists were continuing to reshape "a society built largely on the assumptions of black inferiority."[6]

The construction of a new headquarters provided Johnson with another opportunity to rewrite popular understandings of his company's relationship to the Black freedom struggle and its representation of Black America. The result was "$8 million worth of Black pride"—an eleven-story edifice lavishly decorated in "Black liberation themes" and boasting amenities like a soul food canteen, lounges where employees could "get their Afros styled," an in-house library "of more than fifteen thousand volumes on Black life and history," and one of the largest corporate collections of African and African American art in the world.[7] When placed against the backdrop of the Black Power movement and a cresting wave of Black cultural nationalism during the late 1960s and early 1970s, 820 Michigan Avenue can be read as an architectural and aesthetic reaction to criticisms of both Johnson as an individual and the editorial politics of his magazines. Later employees would describe the building as "its own loud protest"—an unapologetic celebration of Black pride and "a visual pronouncement that black America had arrived in all its striving, outrageous, hip and fashionable glory."[8]

However, whereas many onlookers shared these sentiments, to others the building appeared to represent little more than a personal vanity project, one that exposed the limitations of Black capitalism as a strategy for community advancement. As a gaudy exhibition of Black consumerist excess, readers and visitors alike expressed concern that 820 Michigan Avenue was less a monument to Black pride than a "lavish monstrosity," one that provided little tangible support for overpoliced and underprotected Black urban communities.[9] Furthermore, while Johnson framed the building's opening as a reclamation of a historically Black space within central Chicago, to others it reinforced his long-standing equation of professional achievement with proximity to Chicago's predominantly white downtown business district. Such issues can be mapped onto growing tensions between middle- and working-class African American communities in Chicago—exacerbated by the impact of urban revolts, the ongoing disruption of urban renewal, and diverging economic opportunities—which positioned 820 Michigan Avenue as a visible flashpoint for competing debates over the promise of Black capitalism, the search for a Black aesthetic, and the relationship of Johnson's publications to the communities they claimed to represent.

New Decade, Old Problems

Although the formal unveiling of 820 Michigan Avenue would not occur until 1972, its genesis can be traced to a much earlier time. Johnson had investigated the possibility of constructing his own offices before purchasing the Hursen Funeral Home at 1820 Michigan Avenue in the late 1940s. Even as he continued to expand the premises during the 1950s through the acquisition of adjoining land and property, the publisher retained his dream of building a headquarters from the ground up.[10] In 1959 the publisher was presented with another opportunity to pursue this ambition when Chicago's city planners informed him of plans to build an expressway through the Eighteenth Street Corridor.[11] Like the Urban League's forced move from Wabash Avenue several years earlier, Johnson Publishing's potential relocation was a direct consequence of the city's wide-ranging postwar redevelopment efforts. These efforts were further expanded after Richard Daley's successful reelection to a second term, with the mayor promising to oversee one of "the most dramatic and ambitious" urban renewal programs in the nation.[12]

Johnson entrusted his wife, Eunice, who had been a valued confidante and contributor since the company's inception, with the task of finding "a place on a front street" that was closer to the city's thriving downtown business district.[13] After an exhaustive search, Eunice identified a vacant lot on Michigan Avenue around one mile north of the company's existing location. Its esteemed neighbors included the Crane Company Building at 836 Michigan Avenue, a twelve-story skyscraper built in the Classical Revival style and completed in 1912, and the imposing Conrad Hilton Hotel, which took up the majority of the block between Eighth Street and Bilbo Drive.

When its construction was completed in the 1920s, the building—then known as the Stevens Hotel—gained notoriety as the largest hotel in the world.[14] A veritable "city within a city," the Stevens housed a bowling alley, movie theater, ice cream shop, miniature golf course, and even a hospital.[15] Falling into receivership during the Great Depression, the hotel was revived by Conrad Hilton and by the early 1960s had reestablished its reputation as one of the city's most glamorous locales.[16]

Just as his efforts to purchase the Hursen Funeral Home had been met with white resistance, Johnson's initial inquiries about the vacant lot at 820 Michigan Avenue were rebuffed once the sellers realized that he was African American. Unperturbed, the publisher hired a white lawyer to purchase the land in trust and was able to secure the lot for $250,000 in cash. However, no sooner had the site been secured than Johnson discovered the city's planners had decided to route the Southwest Expressway through the Twenty-Fourth Street Corridor, close to the *Chicago Defender* plant at 2400 Michigan Avenue. This new development threatened the future of both his existing headquarters at 1820 Michigan Avenue and the proposed new plant one mile north, as the publisher had planned to finance the construction of his new building by selling his old one to the city. Johnson would spend close to a decade searching for alternative financing, moving from bank to bank in an effort to secure seed money or prospective leases.[17]

In the meantime, the publisher set about finding a suitable architect for the project. Johnson's magazines had regularly championed the work of pioneering Black architects like Paul Williams, the first Black member of the American Institute of Architects, and the publisher believed that hiring a Black designer would carry tremendous symbolic potential.[18] While early Black Chicagoan architects such as Walter Bailey had passed away by the end of World War II, a new generation had begun to emerge. This included Georgia Louise Harris Brown, who became one of the first licensed Black female architects in the United States after graduating from the University of Kansas in 1944 and would be involved in the design of prominent Chicago structures such as Promontory Apartments and 860 Lake Shore Drive before relocating to Brazil.[19] Another member of this cohort was Wendell Campbell, who helped to establish the National Organization of Minority Architects in 1971 and whose notable projects include a remodeling and expansion of the DuSable Museum of African American History (formerly the Ebony Museum of Negro History and Art) complex in Washington Park.[20]

Perhaps the most influential African American of this generation was John W. Moutoussamy, an ambitious and talented designer whom architectural historian ElDante Winston describes as "the Godfather of black architects in Chicago."[21] After serving in the U.S. Army during World War II, Moutoussamy enrolled at Illinois Institute of Technology (IIT) to pursue an architectural degree.[22] There he came under the influence of Mies van der Rohe, a leading voice for architectural modernism, who had transformed IIT into one of the nation's foremost architecture programs following his escape from Nazi Germany during the 1930s.[23] After graduating in 1948, Moutoussamy worked for Chicago-based firms Schmidt, Garden, and Erickson, where he developed his craft under the tutelage of modernist Paul McCurry, and PACE Associates, where he contributed to the redevelopment of the Illinois Automobile Club into the new *Chicago Defender* plant.[24] Moutoussamy subsequently joined Dubin, Dubin, and Black, one of the city's leading architectural firms. Initially brought on as an associate, Moutoussamy quickly made partner, the first Black architect to achieve this standing at a major Chicago architectural firm.[25]

One of Moutoussamy's first major projects for his new firm was a Federal Housing Administration housing project stretching southwest from the corner of Thirty-Fifth Street and Rhodes Avenue, just a few streets behind the Supreme Life Building at 3501 South Parkway. Over the previous ten years much of the area had been cleared by Chicago's Department of Urban Renewal, and plans for a new public housing complex were approved in 1965. The thirteen-acre site, upon which a series of high-rise apartment buildings and two-story townhouses were built, was named Lawless Gardens in honor of Theodore Lawless, a prominent Black philanthropist who headed a consortium of African American investors who had been working on the project since the early 1960s. This group included John Johnson, who threw his weight behind the venture along with other local businessmen and civic leaders. At the project's ground-breaking ceremonies in 1967, a hard-hatted Johnson posed for local media and announced that the complex was "a great thing for this community." Johnson's enthusiasm was shared by Mayor Richard Daley, who declared, "This splendid new housing complex . . . will exemplify the spirit of Chicago."[26]

It is unclear whether Johnson and Moutoussamy were acquainted before their involvement in the Lawless Gardens project, although it is certainly possible that their paths had crossed through their connections to organizations such as the Chicago Urban League or by means of their overlapping social circles as well-respected members of Chicago's Black elite. Regardless of the specific context of their first meeting, Johnson quickly warmed to Moutoussamy, approving of his contributions to the Lawless Gardens complex and other urban renewal projects in predominantly Black neighborhoods on the South and West Sides.[27] For his part, the architect admired Johnson's tenacity and business acumen, describing him in later interviews as a "straightforward, smart, tough man."[28] Convinced that Moutoussamy was the right man for the job, Johnson secured the services of Dubin, Dubin, Black, and Moutoussamy, and stepped up his efforts to advance the project. The publisher's plans initially stretched to a thirty-story multiuse skyscraper that would be financed by the sale of prospective leases. However, a lack of willing investors and the intransigence of white lenders thwarted such grand ambitions.[29] Frustrated by repeated setbacks, Johnson decided to go it alone.

Climbing Jacob's Ladder

The publisher was aided in this effort by the continued development of his publishing enterprise, with increasing revenues providing the necessary capital to help get his building project off the ground. *Ebony*'s success underpinned much of the company's growth, with the magazine's circulation guarantee raised to $1 million a month in 1967 and yearly advertising revenues spiraling beyond $5 million.[30] Cost-cutting measures, including the closure of several satellite offices, freed additional funds, and by the summer of 1969 subsurface inspections and other preliminary work were in full swing.[31] After approving Moutoussamy's architectural plans, Johnson hired the Corbetta Construction Company to break ground on the project in early 1970, with the condition that at least 40 percent of the construction workers employed on the project would be Black.[32] Aside from some minor hiccups, including a strike by heavy equipment operators, work progressed smoothly. However, Johnson was yet to secure additional funding, and by the autumn of 1970 his need for interim financing had become acute. At the last minute, the publisher secured backing from the Metropolitan Life Insurance Company and construction was able to continue uninterrupted.[33]

Like many architects of the period, Moutoussamy's work can be situated within the emergence of the "Second Chicago School" during the decades following World War II. As part of the massive infrastructure and development projects that enveloped the city during this period, a new generation of Chicago architects began to reshape the South Loop and central business district through the construction of steel-and-glass high-rise office and commercial structures.[34] Heavily influenced by the work of Mies van der Rohe, and rooted in Modernist design and the International style, these buildings were distinctive in their revealed skeletal frames, absence of ornamentation, and privileging of line and light. Among the new buildings helping to "usher in the age of Modern and International style architecture" along Michigan Avenue was the Essex Inn at 800 Michigan Avenue. Completed in 1961, shortly after Johnson's purchase of the adjacent lot, the Essex provided a classic articulation of the "glass-box modern style" that became vogue among the city's architects during the 1950s and 1960s.[35]

However, Johnson had informed Moutoussamy that he did not want his company's new headquarters to be a generic variation of the many glass-and-steel Modernist buildings that proliferated across the Loop during the 1950s and 1960s. The architect recalled that "one of the very first things we decided . . . was that the building had to reflect the kind of company it would house."[36] In a city where "new office structures sprout like beanstalks," Johnson envisioned his new corporate headquarters as a lasting monument to Black entrepreneurial achievement, a "unique modern building that would convey Johnson Publishing's business success and architectural taste."[37] The publisher wanted a building that would be both striking and classy, an elegant symbol of Black cultural sophistication and economic power. In short, 820 Michigan Avenue needed to be more than just a suitably impressive home for the nation's most popular Black publishing company. It had to provide a physical testament to, vision for, and celebration of Black pride and racial progress in postwar America.

Faced with this task, Moutoussamy created an immediately recognizable eleven-story, 110,000-square-foot structure. Its façade was dominated by two columns stretching up from the ground level. The use of inward-facing columns and cantilevered floor slabs, which Moutoussamy used to avoid placing load-bearing walls directly next to neighboring structures, had the benefit of allowing the building's façade to project farther onto Michigan Avenue, creating an illusion of size and grandeur.[38] While its design remained rooted in the International style, with a lack of ornamentation and an emphasis on form and structure, the building's sculptural quality

Johnson Publishing Company Building. (John H. White /
Environmental Protection Agency, National Archives)

was somewhat unusual. ElDante Winston suggests that the architect was
inspired by an earlier office building concept by Mies van der Rohe titled
"Office Building of Reinforced Concrete," which featured deeply recessed
windows and striking horizontal spans on each floor.[39] Moutoussamy may
also have taken cues from Brutalism, a form of architectural modernism
that became a popular style for large-scale civic and educational projects
during the postwar period. Characterized by their imposing, almost fortress-like appearance, as well as a heavy use of concrete, Brutalist buildings projected an air of solidity that would have resonated with Johnson's

ambitions for his new headquarters. Moutoussamy's design echoed the appearance of structures such as 55 West Wacker Avenue, a Brutalist office building completed shortly before work began on the new Johnson Publishing headquarters.[40]

However, while the heavy use of concrete was certainly in keeping with the material mores of Brutalism, Johnson was keen to imbue 820 Michigan Avenue with a sense of longevity and good taste. Early on in the design process, the publisher declared that he wanted an abundance of marble "so that the building would express permanence and would have character without flamboyance." Johnson and Moutoussamy finally agreed on the "robust, dimensional beauty of walnut Travertine," which was used to encase the building's concrete exterior.[41] As for the liberal use of window space, Johnson rationalized this design choice as a reflection of his company's "openness to truth, openness to light, openness to all the currents swirling in all the black communities of this land."[42] As Aurora Wallace notes, an emphasis on transparency would become a trend in media architecture during the late twentieth and early twenty-first century, something that invited public scrutiny and stressed corporate and civic responsibility.[43] For 820 Michigan Avenue, an architectural blending of ominousness and openness embodied the dual mission of the company's magazines and their new headquarters as both safe and free spaces from which to defend Black people and "work toward a heightened sense of communal and civic identity."[44]

Other aspects of the building's exterior design could be interpreted as both a nod to Black history and a celebration of African American upward mobility. When viewed from the front, the combination of its columns and the equally spaced horizontal spans created the illusion of a ladder, a powerful and recurrent symbol in African American folklore.[45] Through spirituals like "We Are Climbing Jacob's Ladder," enslaved people used ladder imagery as a metaphor for the ascent from slavery to freedom. In the twentieth century, this sentiment was expanded to address the ongoing struggle for racial equality, with activists such as Paul Robeson helping to revive its popularity during the 1940s and 1950s. In a landmark 1969 essay for *Freedomways*, Black activist Jack O'Dell used the image of Jacob's ladder as part of a wide-ranging assessment of the Black freedom movement in the aftermath of Dr. Martin Luther King Jr.'s assassination.[46] In the case of 820 Michigan Avenue, the building's "rungs" led up to an enormous *Ebony/Jet* sign on its roof, providing what architectural critic Lee Bey describes as "a perfect metaphor for John Johnson's achievement and the achievements of those his publications wrote about."[47]

However, this design also highlighted the differences between the imagery of Jacob's ladder as employed by activists such as Robeson and O'Dell and the Johnson Publishing building on Michigan Avenue. Robeson, whose connections to left-wing and anticolonial organizations such as the Council on African Affairs prompted the U.S. State Department to revoke his passport, understood the song's power to be rooted in a rich Black oral and activist tradition. SNCC stalwart Bob Moses and other grassroots activists drew courage from its lyrics during voter registration drives in Mississippi.[48] O'Dell, a former Communist Party member and influential labor organizer, invoked the image of Jacob's ladder as an avenue upward to social transformation.[49] For these figures the symbolism of Jacob's ladder was rooted in a class-conscious reading of Black struggle and the centrality of collective action and grassroots community activism to the pursuit of racial justice. By contrast, the culmination of the "ladder" displayed on the exterior of the Johnson Publishing building—the names of his most popular magazines—appeared to consolidate Johnson's belief that true Black freedom would be born out through an embrace of American consumer capitalism and a conciliatory politics of racial uplift and bootstraps entrepreneurialism.

Similarly, despite its undoubtedly striking exterior design, Moutoussamy's plans for the building were in many ways deeply conservative. The architect was heavily invested in the Miesian school of architectural modernism and its pragmatic real-world applications. His loyalty to the form contrasted with the ambitions of budding Black architects such as Melvin Mitchell, whose work during the 1960s was energized by an effort to develop a distinctly Black architectural aesthetic that possessed "significant visual and functional differences from the cold sterile aesthetic of International Style modern architecture."[50] Moutoussamy saw little radicalism in his design; indeed, while Johnson's bombastic rhetoric stressed the structure's architectural innovation and significance, for Moutoussamy it appeared that 820 Michigan Avenue was just another building. In later interviews he describes the structure in profoundly ambivalent terms, expressing his dissatisfaction with various features and downplaying its cultural significance. More revealingly, the architect provides a dismissive and characteristically blunt portrayal of the building's true function: "It's like a big advertisement. That's what [Johnson's] in—advertising."[51]

A Castle Fit for a King

As the exterior of 820 Michigan Avenue neared completion, Johnson turned to its interiors. To achieve his goal of creating "one of the city's most spectacular showplaces" he enlisted the help of Arthur Elrod, a white interior designer based in the desert resort town of Palm Springs, California.[52] A Southerner by birth, Elrod was raised in rural South Carolina and studied design at Clemson University before attending the Chouinard Art Institute, a renowned West Coast design school. After establishing a firm with business associate and long-term romantic partner Hal Broderick in the mid-1950s, Elrod quickly became a go-to interior designer of vacation homes for A-list clients in Palm Springs, where he was arguably as well known for his flamboyant parties as his lavish interiors. Writer Adele Cygelman describes Elrod as "one of the most influential designers of the twentieth century," and his name is most readily connected to the Elrod House, an extraordinary Palm Springs residence he contracted architect John Lautner to design in 1968, which would later receive international attention through its starring role in the 1971 James Bond film, *Diamonds Are Forever*. By 1974, when Elrod's career was tragically cut short in an automobile accident that also claimed the life of his associate William Raiser, he had cemented a reputation as one of the country's most daring and sought-after interior designers.[53]

On the recommendation of his wife Eunice, Johnson had initially hired Elrod to oversee the design of an apartment in the Carlyle Building, a condominium complex located in the exclusive Gold Coast neighborhood on Chicago's Near North Side, which the couple and their children John and Linda moved into during the late 1960s.[54] Their previous home was in the upmarket South Side community of Drexel Square, located on the northwest corner of Washington Park, which had been a bright spot of the Black metropolis during the 1930s and 1940s.[55] However, the area was in decline by the 1960s, and Johnson was eager to move on. In his autobiography Johnson explains that he had originally planned to purchase a single unit at the Carlyle, but after a white woman living in the adjacent condominium had complained about the prospect of Black neighbors, the publisher bought her out and created one huge living space.[56] Author Stephen Birmingham refutes this characterization, suggesting that the acquisition was amicable and untainted by racial prejudice. Whatever the politics behind the creation of Johnson's mega-apartment, he wasted little time in setting Elrod and Raiser loose on the space, creating what *Architectural Digest* described as the "ultimate residence" in a detailed photo essay published in its November 1972 issue.[57]

Johnson's satisfaction with the outcome of his Carlyle condominium, coupled with Elrod's interest in the challenge of designing an office space, led to the designer being entrusted with the interiors of 820 Michigan Avenue. The result was extraordinary. Aided by an open checkbook from their client, Elrod and his design team created one of the most spectacular and unusual office spaces in corporate America. Each floor was individually themed and boasted bespoke color palettes and patterns designed to reflect the specific tasks and responsibilities of its workers to ensure that "employees would feel it is their own."[58] On the ground floor, visitors entered the building via an expansive two-story lobby crafted from the same walnut travertine used on its exterior and featuring sixty feet of red sofas and walls lined with Bronze and Mozambique wood. Carpet runners led to a bank of elevators whose interiors were routinely changed to match the season. The second floor was an open-plan space reserved for large company meetings, public events, and parties, with a series of paneled lighting and color-blocked diagonal carpeting. The floors directly above were reserved primarily for storage and file collection, creating a separating layer between events and working space and future-proofing in anticipation of the company's continued expansion.[59]

On the fifth level, dark blue carpeting and bold geometric patterns complemented the company's computer operations and customer service departments. Nestled alongside these departments were the offices of the Johnson Publishing Book Division. Since its formation in the early 1960s, the book division had emerged as one of the largest Black-owned book publishers in the country. A little over a decade after its formation, the division had published more than forty titles on a variety of different subjects, including *The Ebony Cookbook*, a hugely popular collection of "American Negro recipes" curated by food editor Freda DeKnight, and Lerone Bennett Jr's best-selling Black history text, *Before the Mayflower*.[60] The sixth floor, featuring a green, olive, and charcoal color scheme that extended from flooring to cabinetry and even desk telephones, hosted the mailing, circulation, community relations, and public affairs departments. It also included a private office for Gertrude Johnson, Johnson's mother, which the publisher had installed as a symbol of her material investment in the company during its early years. Renewed with fresh flowers every day, the space was a constant source of delight for Gertrude, who never tired of calling up old friends to boast about her son's accomplishments: "I just drove down here in a chauffeur-driven Cadillac that he gave me, and I'm sitting in my office in his building."[61]

The seventh floor, which included the editorial offices of *Jet*, *Black Stars* (a monthly entertainment magazine introduced in 1971), and the recently renamed *Black World*, was covered in a distinctive animal-skin-design carpet and rich brown leather wall coverings. This color scheme extended into the company's library, which included thousands of volumes "written by, or about black people."[62] By contrast, Eunice Johnson's office was entirely beige and white, with a mirrored desk, textured walls and ceilings, molded furniture, and a sofa suspended from the wall. The eighth floor was largely reserved for *Ebony* staffers, with open-plan work spaces decorated with geometric carpets and rich orange and brown hues backing onto private offices inhabited by senior and managing editors. "Seemingly floating in the center of the floor" was a boat-shaped conference room encased in sheer glass walls and featuring luxuries such as an automated movie screen that descended from a ceiling trap—a world away from the cramped and gloomy confines of early buildings inhabited by Black Chicago publications as they attempted to navigate the "perilous sea of journalism" seven decades earlier.[63] The eighth floor also housed the company's photo archives, an "irreplaceable record of 20th-century African American life and culture" containing tens of thousands of color transparencies, black-and-white photographs, and drawings.[64]

Another glass-walled conference room graced the building's gold-and-gray-themed ninth floor, which housed Johnson's working office as well as those of the company's senior administrative and advertising staff. This floor also featured what would quickly become one of the building's most popular visitor attractions: a dedicated awards room displaying mementos and prizes from the company's storied history. These included the 1966 Spingarn Award, presented to Johnson by the NAACP for his "contributions to the enhancement of the Negro's self-image"; a 1968 Pulitzer Prize received by staff photographer Moneta Sleet for his work covering Martin Luther King Jr.'s funeral; photographs and letters from American presidents and international heads of state; and other notable artifacts.[65] The tenth floor

Johnson Publishing Building canteen. (Alexandre Georges / Palm Springs Art Museum. Courtesy of Georges Estate.)

was dominated by the company's mauve, tangerine, and yellow canteen, where employees and visitors enjoyed all-you-can-eat soul food lunches for a dollar a day. As an added perk, the cafeteria included an open-air balcony "for summertime relaxing with luncheon guests." Next door, eyes were drawn to the psychedelic orange and brown swirls that decorated the walls of one of the building's most memorable spaces: its test kitchen. Organized around a central island, the effervescent space popped with color and featured a range of built-in modern appliances. Although Freda DeKnight had succumbed to cancer in 1963, the company's legendary food editor would have no doubt approved of "arguably the most distinctive test kitchen ever created."[66]

A second balcony on the building's eleventh and most exclusive floor extended outward from Johnson's lavish executive suite, which encompassed the entire level. The company elevators opened into a large reception area, usually manned by one of the publisher's personal secretaries and decorated with eye-catching zebrawood and red alligator furniture. Moving deeper into Johnson's "inner sanctum," visitors encountered another conference room, a dining room, and the publisher's main office, all furnished in rich shades of red, brown, and gold, and linked by a remote climate and audio system as well as electronic doors and drapes controlled from a concealed panel in Johnson's oversized desk.[67] In addition to state-of-the-art office equipment and furnishings, the floor boasted a range of features designed to ease the mind of the high-flying Black corporate executive, including a gymnasium, a massage table, and a barber's chair. There was even a private apartment containing a bedroom and a bathroom with sauna. It was an ostentatious setting befitting Johnson's status as the world's most powerful Black publisher and a proud continuation of his predecessors' building prowess. Four decades earlier Anthony Overton's view from the top of the Overton Hygienic Building at 3619 State Street had positioned him as "the proverbial master of all he surveyed." Now Johnson was the city's undisputed Black print icon, sitting atop an "11-story castle" fit for a king.[68]

Its Own Loud Protest

If the exterior of 820 Michigan Avenue helped to convey a sense of stability and utilitarian beauty, the building's interiors provided an unashamedly joyful manifestation of Black cultural mores. The riotous mixture of colors, textures, and patterns complemented the eclectic and distinctly modern editorial content of Johnson's periodicals, with the company's roster of magazines and the décor of its new headquarters conspiring to create a cohesive whole out of their differing and at times dissonant parts. For future Johnson Publishing staffer Eric Easter, the building was "its own loud protest—a visual pronouncement that black America had arrived in all its striving, outrageous, hip and fashionable glory." For architectural critic Lee Bey, the interiors of 820 Michigan Avenue provided an effusive vision of African American mod décor.[69] Cultural historian Maurice Berger describes the space as "a daring social statement" and "an important showcase for black cultural expression." Echoing these sentiments, visual artist David Hartt characterizes the building's decor as a "clear and exuberant expression of black taste, resolutely modern, colorful, and complex."[70]

Completed around the same time as the publication of literary critic Addison Gayle's 1971 anthology, *The Black Aesthetic*, 820 Michigan Avenue can be understood as Johnson's own contribution to this provocatively ambiguous concept.[71] While never developing into a fully formed theory of Black cultural production, the notion of a Black aesthetic was central to the Black Arts Movement, which emerged in tandem with the Black Power movement during the latter half of the 1960s. As the "spiritual sister of the Black Power concept," the Black Arts movement stressed the need for new literary and artistic forms that spoke to the political demands and material desires of Black people.[72] In an influential 1968 essay published in *Drama Review*, theater critic Larry Neal declared, "The Western aesthetic has run its course: it is impossible to construct anything meaningful within its decaying structure." Black Chicagoan poet Don Lee articulated this feeling in an altogether more combative way: "We must destroy Faulkner, dick [and] jane, and other perpetrators of evil. It's time for DuBois, Nat Turner, and Kwame Nkrumah."[73]

Within Johnson Publishing itself, the search for a Black aesthetic was spearheaded by Hoyt Fuller, who used *Negro Digest* to promote the work of Black writers and artists who were grappling with their role in the Black Revolution.[74] *Ebony* also made space for discussions of Black cultural nationalism and radical art. David Llorens's March 1969 profile of Don Lee and Larry Neal's article "Any Day Now: Black Art and Black Liberation," published in August of the same year, provided two instructive examples of the magazine's efforts to grapple with the search for a Black aesthetic.[75] Such content was complemented by the work of art director Herbert Temple, whose cover illustrations offered their own interpretation of how the Black freedom struggle was "redefining deeply rooted values in a society built on the assumption of black inferiority."[76] After the move to 820 Michigan Avenue, senior editors were invited to help design their own offices, providing a fascinating insight into the overlap between taste, literary production, and personal politics. In a nod to his transnational heritage, *Ebony* editor Hans Massaquoi made his office into a treasure trove "of both German literature and African art," while Lerone Bennett Jr's decision to decorate his office with "contemporary black liberation themes" reflected his reputation as a writer who was "far more militant than the magazine he edited."[77] Fuller's archival papers suggest annoyance at the move to 820 Michigan Avenue, which Johnson used as an excuse to freeze wages and also disrupted progress on initiatives championed by Fuller, including a book series with the Atlanta-based Institute of the Black World and a proposed African bureau.[78]

Nevertheless, the building's aesthetic flourishes, not least the design of his own office, appeared to complement Fuller's ongoing efforts to champion Pan-African and Black nationalist artists and intellectuals such as Amiri Baraka and David Graham Du Bois.[79]

For cultural nationalists such as Ron Karenga, the iconoclastic leader of the West Coast–based U.S. Organization, a Black nationalist group, the search for a Black aesthetic demanded that Black people embrace African artistic and cultural traditions to help unlock the power of a shared racial heritage. At the same time, Karenga argued that Black art must resolutely face forward, becoming "part of the revolutionary machinery that moves us to change."[80] This merging of Black past and future became a key feature of Johnson's new building, with the publisher boasting of its success in blending the key elements of postwar Modernist architecture—concrete, steel, and glass—with traditional African materials such as bronze and wood. Similarly, reception areas and conference rooms melded patterned Hermes leather—a signifier of postwar American consumer excess—with "African sculpture(s) and masks." Perhaps the clearest example of such design choices could be found in Johnson's executive suite, which blended "ancient African art and futuristic furniture design."[81] This overarching aesthetic was united through installations by some of the nation's leading Black artists, including collagist Romare Bearden and painter Jacob Lawrence, that graced the publisher's private quarters.

The individual pieces housed on the building's eleventh floor formed part of a larger collection of African and African American artwork on permanent display throughout 820 Michigan Avenue. Johnson had long endeavored for his offices to be used for "exhibitions of outstanding photography and art," and the construction of 820 Michigan Avenue allowed this function to be dramatically expanded.[82] As the company's new headquarters took shape, an art selection committee headed by Herbert Temple solicited prominent artists to submit their work for consideration.[83] Upon its completion the building housed nearly two hundred individual art pieces, a collection that Johnson championed as "the world's largest and most representative corporate collection of black artists' work."[84] Unsurprisingly, signature pieces by figures such as Bearden and sculptor Richard Hunt, whose enormous bronze installation *Expansive Construction* took pride of place in the building's lobby, drew widespread attention. However, artwork could be found in all areas of the building, including the sixth-floor reception area, which

Johnson Publishing Building, sixth-floor reception area.
(Alexandre Georges / Palm Springs Art Museum. Courtesy
of Georges Estate.)

featured a painting by Eldzier Cortor and a Dogon mask from Mali.[85] Collectively, the range of artists and artworks represented "aimed to promote an Afrocentric point of view that was accessible to wider audiences and part of the larger national Black Arts Movement."[86]

Its Own Loud Protest?

For Johnson the relationship between Moutoussamy's architectural design, Elrod's interiors, and the building's myriad attractions and amenities combined to produce "a really bold, positive statement about the company's commitment to the black people it serves."[87] This sentiment was at the forefront of a sprawling visual tour published in the September 1972 issue of *Ebony* that introduced the magazine's audience to the company's new headquarters for the first time. Spread across forty pages, the feature promised to guide readers through the whole building "from lobby to Executive Suite, from shipping room to the editorial offices." The length of the photo essay was a major reason behind the September issue being the largest, color-wise, in the magazine's history.[88] Just as earlier *Ebony* photo essays had used the company's offices as an extension of its editorial efforts to normalize and celebrate Black achievement, so too did the magazine's 1972 tour present 820 Michigan Avenue as a model of "iconic blackness articulated to equally naturalized and sanctioned symbols of class respectability [and] achievement."[89] It was a suitably indulgent photo spread for an unabashedly performative space—not simply an impressive architectural and design endeavor but a site where "black creativity could blossom and the production of black magazines would be a joy."[90]

While the building's amenities and colorful interiors were the main attraction of *Ebony*'s photo tour, the presence of company employees played an important part of making 820 Michigan Avenue legible to a broader audience. The magazine expressed hope that readers would enjoy not only the building's dynamic interiors but also meeting "some of the men and women who have helped make EBONY a success." Tellingly, the magazine's September 1972 "Backstage" section asserted that the company was "more than an edifice—no matter how impressive" and took the opportunity to remind readers of "the talent, the hard work and the dedication" of the people who worked within it.[91] By so publicly acknowledging the debt the company owed to its employees, Johnson effectively positioned 820 Michigan Avenue as a tribute to the company's staff. Similarly, through emphasizing his employees' enjoyment of the new headquarters and the incorporation of their ideas into Elrod's design process, the publisher promoted 820 Michigan Avenue as a collaborative and profoundly democratic endeavor. From this perspective, the building's eclectic furnishings and interwoven design ideas complemented the broader impact of the company's magazines as "the shared accomplishment of an eclectically diverse and talented staff: one whose varied experiences and social orientation equipped it to represent postwar black life in uniquely ambitious ways."[92]

Yet at the same time, it is undeniable that the completion of 820 Michigan Avenue helped to reinforce Johnson's role as the company's patriarch and undisputed leader. The publisher often took advantage of the building's amenities to assert his professional dominance, with its soul food canteen a regular site for such displays. In extracts from his satirical newsletter "JPC-iana," Fuller recalled that Johnson's propensity to jump the lunch queue, and even stand behind the serving counter picking out choice cuts with his bare fingers, "turned the stomach" of rank-and-file employees.[93] A strict disciplinarian, Johnson's penthouse offices reportedly contained "a 'give 'em hell' room" where employees were brought to face his "legendary wrath."[94] Johnson's tendency to wait in the lobby to catch out tardy employees, a tactic he had regularly employed at the company's previous offices, also provided ample opportunities to assert his authority. Indeed, the building's glass-fronted, two-story lobby ensured that such encounters became far more of a public performance following the company's relocation, with onlookers provided a prime window seat to Johnson's dressing downs. Walking the floors and riding the elevators of his new headquarters were part of Johnson's daily routine and underpinned his efforts to be "all over the building all of the time."[95]

For Johnson, this ubiquity was an important part of embellishing his self-anointed role as an everyman: "I know my people, I socialize with them, and we're friends."[96] However, for many employees, the publisher's public displays of spatial dominance directly undermined the building's potential as a site where "black creativity could blossom and the production of black magazines would be a joy."[97] This was certainly the case for editor Monroe Anderson, who joined *Ebony* shortly after the building's completion. Although Anderson initially delighted in the building's "incredible" interiors, he soon tired of Johnson's "militaristic" leadership style, something that ensured employees' movement through the company's new headquarters remained highly regulated. For Fuller, Anderson, and other staffers, the building's stylish interiors could not offset Johnson's overbearing management style. After all, what difference did good design make when the publisher was constantly "scream[ing] at people" or "dress[ing] down his editors out in the hallway"? From a similar perspective, features such as ladies' lounges where staff could "keep their Afros styled" were seen as a case of style over substance, one that, alongside continued descriptions of the company's offices as a "plantation" by disgruntled workers, suggested that its eye-catching amenities and ostentatious interiors obscured a conservative and highly toxic workplace culture.[98]

This institutional conservatism also continued to shape the role of women within Johnson Publishing and their positionality with the company's new headquarters. The relative absence of Black women in the building's construction and design process was indicative of the company's often-fraught gender politics both on and off the page. Similarly, the detailed photo essay published in the September 1972 issue of *Ebony* reified the enduring gender disparities between the company's secretarial and administrative staff and more senior editorial and advertising roles. While Johnson used the building's opening as an opportunity to announce the appointment of three female vice presidents, Black women continued to be underrepresented in executive positions.[99] The company's deeply hierarchical organization and its deference to societal gender norms was best encapsulated by its top floor executive offices, a space almost completely dedicated to consolidating Johnson's status as a "race man." Rumors about the publisher's use of his private apartment and his alleged proclivity for "pretty women" further enforced the role of 820 Michigan Avenue as a symbol for Black male heterosexual power.[100]

Perhaps most intriguingly, given Johnson's emphasis on 820 Michigan Avenue's symbolic value to Black America, the demand for Black-authored critical perspectives emanating from the Black Power and Black Arts movements, and the unabashedly heterosexist politics of cultural nationalists like Ron Karenga, the publisher appeared to harbor few reservations over ceding artistic control of the building's interiors to Elrod, a white Southerner and an openly gay man.[101] Undoubtedly, Elrod's distinctive style and dynamic use of color, texture, and pattern produced a striking vision of "afrocentric modernism that was well-turned, avant garde and quite hip."[102] At the same time, the designer's role in bringing 820 Michigan Avenue to life complicates its presentation as an "authentically" Black space. Elrod's influence over the building's interior design provides us with another example of Johnson's desire to elevate his company as a voice for, and symbol of, Black identity and achievement, and his concurrent use of white contributors to help advance this project. In this regard, Elrod's influence can be connected to the earlier impact of figures such as Ben Burns and Stephen Deutch, as well as that of white architectural photographer Alexandre Georges, who was entrusted with depicting 820 Michigan Avenue in *Ebony*'s photo-editorial tour.[103]

A Poem in Marble and Glass

Although *Ebony* initially informed readers that it would be moving into its new South Loop location sometime in the spring of 1971, the building's completion dragged on toward the end of the year.[104] After further delays Johnson decided to push ahead with the relocation in early December, moving his staff into the floors that had been fully furnished and holding an impromptu assembly to document the occasion.[105] The new address appeared on the masthead of *Jet* for the first time on December 16, and exactly five months later a grand opening ceremony and open house event marked the building's official "coming out" party.[106] A section of Michigan Avenue was closed off for the ceremony, which was conducted on the street outside the building. A diverse mix of celebrities, politicians, and businessmen was in attendance, including Mayor Richard Daley and *Chicago Tribune* publisher H. F. Grumhaus. Also present was Supreme Life chairman Earl B. Dickerson, who, close to three decades after Johnson had started *Negro Digest* out of the lawyer's offices at 3501 South Parkway, had a front-row seat to the next and most dramatic phase in the company's building history.

The ceremony was directed by *Ebony* senior editor Lerone Bennett Jr., who, irrespective of his ideological differences with Johnson, remained one of the publisher's most strident public defenders.[107] After an opening invocation by Kenneth Smith, a prominent local minister and community leader, Bennett offered a characteristically forceful address to the gathered audience. Apropos of his position as the company's in-house historian, the editor connected the unveiling of 820 Michigan Avenue to the longer history of Black Chicago, declaring, "It is a matter of great importance that this occasion is unfolding here near the shores of Lake Michigan where Chicago's Black father, Jean Baptiste DuSable, started it all nearly 190 years ago." Drawing a direct line between the city's spatial past and present, the editor contended that DuSable's cabin "and this gleaming building are linked in time and spirit." Furthermore, beyond representing a reclamation of downtown Chicago as a Black space, Bennett emphasized the building's broader function as both "a major economic milestone in the history of Black people" and a reflection of "the collective movement of Black America." Echoing Bennett's words, Johnson declared the building to be "a poem in marble and glass which symbolizes our unshakeable faith that the struggles of our forefathers were not in vain and that we shall indeed overcome in this land in our times."[108]

Black business and civic leaders responded in kind. George Johnson, the president of Black cosmetics firm Johnson Products, contended that 820 Michigan Avenue was "the most magnificent structure that we have in the downtown section of Chicago" and could barely contain his glee that "a Black man has put it here." Jesse Jackson, the head of the influential Chicago-based civil rights organization PUSH, offered a more prophetic reading of the relocation, suggesting that "the ramifications of the success of Johnson Publishing Co. are certainly greater than the building. . . . To thousands in the valley, one signal on the mountain means hope."[109] Prominent Black publications such as the *Chicago Defender*, *Pittsburgh Courier*, and *Los Angeles Sentinel* championed the structure as "a 'living monument' to the creative, productive, and administrative/managerial abilities of Afro-Americans" and emphasized its significance as the first Black-designed and -owned building on the Chicago Loop.[110] The building's opening ceremonies also formed the basis for a special edition of Black public affairs television program *Black Journal*, which aired on PBS the following year.[111]

Perhaps the most pleasing response to the opening of 820 Michigan Avenue, at least from Johnson's perspective, came from white onlookers and media outlets. The opening of earlier Black media buildings in Chicago had gone largely unnoticed by white publications, which provided little space to explore Black life outside of geographically coded narratives of racial pathology. *Ebony* contributor Jack Slater articulated this myopia in a more visceral way, asserting, "All the white press is interested in . . . is piss in the hallways and blood on the stairways."[112] However, the pomp and circumstance surrounding the construction and public unveiling of 820 Michigan Avenue piqued interest. *Jet* reported that "more than 1,000 luminaries from throughout the country" attended the building's opening ceremony, with the presence of Daley and other influential members of Chicago's business and political elite helping to draw a swarm of journalists and photographers to the event.[113] Johnson was keen to maximize press coverage, enlisting female staff members as tour guides and holding two evening receptions to ensure comprehensive access.[114] In response, many local journalists picked up the narrative threads put out by the publisher and other company representatives to stress the building's physical and symbolic importance.

Writing for the *Chicago Sun-Times*, Rob Cuscaden contended, "If ever a building was the symbolic image of its occupants, that structure is surely the new Johnson Publishing Co. Building at 820 S. Michigan."[115] Leaning heavily on the company's building history as a metaphor for Johnson's professional trajectory and the rising fortunes of African Americans writ large, Cuscaden contrasted the "cramped" confines of *Ebony*'s birthplace at 5619 State Street with Moutoussamy's imposing design for Johnson's new corporate home, which "from its broad, forceful horizontals of sleek Travertine marble to its wide expanses of glass . . . says—quietly, simply but unequivocally [*sic*]—success."[116] *Chicago Daily News* fashion editor Peg Zwecker was another figure to champion the new building as an elegant example of Black sophistication and cultural mores, describing the structure as "a dream come true."[117] Zwecker's colleague Patricia Moore was equally forthcoming, penning an article on the new Johnson Publishing "super-pad" that focused on the otherworldly design of Johnson's executive suite. Moore declared, "The lavishly appointed top floor . . . is literally the crowning testimony to Johnson's considerable financial success."[118] The building's unique style also drew the attention of lifestyle magazines such as *Interior Design*, which published a detailed photo essay in the autumn of 1972.[119]

Many among *Ebony*'s audience were also quick to express their delight at the building's opening and to link its completion to the success of Johnson's enterprise and the broader gains made by African Americans during the decades following World War II. North Carolinian reader Marianna Raynor declared that Johnson Publishing was "letting the world know where the black business stands, and it happens to stand eleven stories tall in the lives of many black readers." For Brooklynite Blanche McLeod, the building was a powerful demonstration of "what our race can do when we really set our minds to it."[120] Writing from Pittsburgh, Phyllis Smith attested that 820 Michigan Avenue was "enough to make every black person 'burst at the seams' with pride." Echoing Johnson's emphasis on the building's potential as a unifying racial symbol, Californian reader Dean Wakefield posited that the structure was "an inspiration to all black people no matter how militant or conservative we profess to be."[121]

Extravagance and Empty Fanfare

For Johnson the public response to 820 Michigan Avenue offered a moment of triumphant vindication. At the building's opening, the publisher declared that it "would have taken a building twice the size of this new structure to house all of the creditors and cynics" during his company's early years as he scrambled to secure readers and advertisers out of its "back street" offices on the South Side.[122] Just a few decades later Johnson had become one of the most influential publishers in the history of African American journalism and held total control over one of the largest Black-owned businesses in the country.[123] A few months after the building's opening, he was named American Publisher of the Year by the Magazine Publishers Association.[124] Shortly thereafter he purchased popular AM broadcast outlet WGRT, making it Chicago's only Black-owned radio station.[125] Soon, Johnson was a regular feature on the boards of major companies such as Twentieth Century Fox, Chrysler, and the Greyhound Corporation.[126] Yet more than any other professional accolade, he believed that 820 Michigan Avenue was the ultimate testament to both his own ability to "succeed against the odds" and the remarkable rise of his media empire. It is no surprise that Johnson would later describe the building's opening as the proudest moment of his life.[127]

It is easy to see how the building provided a compelling symbol for Black economic and cultural advancement, one that, within the context of the early 1970s, became intimately connected to the broader appeal of Richard Nixon's "Black capitalism" initiatives. During his successful 1968 presidential campaign, Nixon had used appeals to Black economic development as a way of complementing his widely criticized "Southern Strategy," which sought to increase political support for the Republican Party across the South through direct appeals to white racism. As business historian Robert Weems notes, because economic development and racial integration were not necessarily intertwined, Nixon could promote the notion of "Black capitalism" without alienating Southern whites. Conversely, these appeals helped the Republican forerunner to avoid being labeled a conservative reactionary like third-party candidate George Wallace, despite his similarly enthusiastic use of the "race card." With the promise of federal projects and private-sector funding to help promote Black business development, Nixon shrewdly offered Black militants "a monetary incentive to repudiate notions of 'Burn, Baby, Burn.'"[128]

The effectiveness of this strategy highlighted the multivalency of Black Power as a political and rhetorical concept. While the white press was quick to label any self-identifying Black Power activist as "radical" or "subversive," it is important to observe that beyond widespread demands for Black pride and self-empowerment, the philosophical and ideological beliefs of Black Power advocates varied significantly.[129] For revolutionary Black Power activists whose thinking was rooted in the rich and overlapping traditions of popular front politics, labor organizing, and anticolonialism, the pursuit of Black Power was predicated on dismantling the inherent racism of the American political and economic system. For others, Black Power meant the development of Black economic power within the doctrine of free enterprise capitalism. Expressed in a different way by Nixon in the immediate aftermath of Martin Luther King Jr.'s assassination in April 1968, these militants were interested not in separation but in "a piece of the action." By co-opting the conservative economic underpinnings of Black nationalist thought, Nixon was able to secure the support of prominent Black celebrities and entrepreneurs along with that of notable Black Power advocates such as Floyd McKissick, whose belief in the merits of Black capitalism saw him "openly switch from being a black militant to being a black Republican."[130]

Given Johnson's enthusiastic and oft-repeated belief that the best route to racial advancement was by embracing conspicuous consumption and the full integration of African Americans into capitalist society, it is unsurprising that the publisher emerged as a prominent supporter of both Nixon and the premise of Black capitalism. Just a few days before the president's inauguration in January 1969, Johnson was among a select group of Black leaders who met with Nixon and his urban affairs adviser, Daniel Patrick Moynihan, to discuss his plans for Black economic development.[131] Two months later Johnson was in Washington, D.C., to watch Nixon sign an executive order establishing an Office of Minority Business Enterprise (OMBE) and a National Advisory Council for Minority Enterprise. Within months of his company's relocation, the OMBE was using 820 Michigan Avenue to stage press conferences and announce the introduction of new minority enterprise projects.[132] Such initiatives were celebrated by figures like soul singer James Brown, another prominent Nixon supporter, who declared that 820 Michigan Avenue was "the baddest [building] I have ever seen."[133] For Brown and other self-styled community spokespeople, Johnson's new corporate edifice offered a compelling example of how an adherence to capitalist principles could help propel Black America toward the promised land.

However, not all observers shared this view. Several months after the building's official opening, the *San Francisco Sun Reporter* published a highly critical review of the relocation. As the newspaper noted, the tremendous success of Johnson Publishing Company depended on the financial support of Black patrons, who continued to pour time and money into the enterprise. As one of Chicago's "most spectacular showplaces," 820 Michigan Avenue was certainly a striking visual addition to the city's skyline. However, for the *Sun Reporter* it was hardly a conscientious use of its readers' hard-earned dollars. Indeed, the paper argued that "for all intents and purposes, Johnson Publishing seems bent upon squandering its money on extravagance and empty fanfare." Rejecting Johnson's claims that the building was a bold statement about his company's "commitment to the Black people it serves," the *Sun Reporter*'s columnist suggested instead that the ostentatious structure provided compelling evidence that the publisher and his magazines were "less committed to the welfare of the Black community than to a yearning for wasteful, Cadillac-type flair."[134] Similar criticisms were scattered throughout reader responses to the building's public unveiling. Whereas the majority appeared to believe that 820 Michigan Avenue was "enough to make every black person 'burst at the seams with pride,'" some expressed despair that so many within the Black community appeared "to prize emulating something that may stand for nothing."[135]

Such rumblings of discontent extended beyond editorial commentary and personal correspondence to include firsthand reactions to the building. If the company's previous headquarters had become an important tourist destination during the 1950s and 1960s, then the lavish interiors and symbolic resonance of 820 Michigan Avenue ensured that this role was dramatically expanded. Even before the building's formal unveiling, *Ebony* reported that daily busloads of local schoolchildren were arriving for guided tours.[136] Within months of its opening, the magazine was begging readers to call ahead if they intended to visit in order to reduce waiting times and "make the task easier for our tour guides."[137] Less than two years after Mayor Daley had helped Johnson; his wife, Eunice; and his mother, Gertrude, cut the ribbon across its doors, the magazine estimated that a scarcely believable two hundred thousand visitors had passed through the building's impressive two-story lobby.[138] This included Charles Whitaker, a tenth-grade student and future *Ebony* editor, who recalls being "awed" by the structure. For some editors the building's relentless floor traffic was a practical concern: it was often difficult to concentrate on the task at hand with "the distraction of 20 youngsters peering through their office doors."[139]

While most visitors declared the building to be "breathtakingly beautiful" and "a most spectacular showplace," some found its interiors a gaudy display of consumerist excess. This was exacerbated by tour guides, who

Johnson Publishing Building, executive suite bathroom and sauna. (Alexandre Georges / Palm Springs Art Museum. Courtesy of Georges Estate.)

were instructed to brag about lavish touches such as leather-covered typewriters and "tropical flowers . . . flown in every day."[140] The chief offender was Johnson's penthouse office, described by the *Chicago Daily News* as "like part of an extravagant movie set," which raised hackles as well as eyebrows. The suede-covered walls, electronic drapes, and marble-clad sauna evoked "wisecracks about diamond-studded floors" from students on guided tours, and Johnson's explanation that he "wanted to make the place a showcase of what successful blacks can do in business" fell on deaf ears.[141] Other visitors were more direct. After touring Johnson's private suite, one local minister reportedly informed the publisher that he now knew "what God would have done if he hadn't run out of money."[142] Johnson's desire to show off his new headquarters exacerbated such concerns. In self-aggrandizing interviews, he boasted that he didn't have time for the luxuries of his private suite, meaning that the "lovely stacks of Yves Saint Laurent towels" in his sauna remained practically untouched. Conversely, staged images of Johnson "working out" in his exercise room while still wearing a suit and tie seemed little more than a portrait of brazen egotism.[143]

Accountable to the Black Community

Such criticisms were damaging not merely because they positioned John-son as an out-of-touch member of the Black bourgeoisie but also because they undermined the key foundations upon which the building's symbolic function rested, beginning with the promise of Black capitalism as a model for Black advancement. In large part due to his appeals to Black economic development, Johnson had stuck by Nixon into the early 1970s, voting for him in 1972 as he had done in 1968.[144] However, by Nixon's second term it had become clear that initiatives such as the OMBE provided little sub-stantive support for Black businesses and that federally sanctioned "Black capitalism" projects were hindered by underfunding, political intransigence, and financial mismanagement. The unfulfilled promise of such initiatives was arguably best embodied by the debacle of Floyd McKissick's Soul City, a planned community in North Carolina that received support from the OMBE and the Department of Housing and Urban Development but was unable to survive "the uneasy marriage between black capitalism and . . . federal bureaucracy."[145]

At the same time, the amorphous appeal of Black capitalism helped Nixon to redirect Black demands for economic justice, contain domestic Black radicalism, and begin the rollback of Great Society–era social welfare programs—outcomes that were in all likelihood the true rationale for Nixon's support of Black capitalism in the first place. By co-opting Black Power's rhetoric of pride and economic self-determination, Nixon was able to marry Black radical politics to ideas of free-market capitalism. By celebrating "minority" enterprise as a model of racial progress, he was able to undermine more radical demands for reparations and economic redress.[146] Indeed, if 820 Michigan Avenue was "its own loud protest," then this was a protest that was dramatically different from the kind that had ripped through many of the nation's cities during the long, hot summers of the previous decade. As a literally constructive rather than destructive form of Black Power protest, the Johnson Publishing headquarters was an inherently conservative and ultimately inadequate symbol of both Black demands for self-determination and the ongoing struggle for racial justice.

These tensions manifested themselves on both a local and national level. During the second half of the 1960s, continuing civil rights activism and racial unrest had shed new light on the city's deeply segregated and fundamentally unequal political and economic foundations. The Chicago Freedom Movement, which rocked the city throughout 1965 and 1966, represented the most ambitious civil rights campaign outside of the American South. Two years later King's assassination sparked an explosion of deadly rioting in Black communities on the South and West Sides that left hundreds injured and saw entire blocks razed to the ground. Against the backdrop of persistent racial tension, the framing of 820 Michigan Avenue as a unifying and feel-good story of Black success carried clear political implications, with the eagerness of the city's white daily papers to reiterate Johnson's claims that the building represented "a good, symbolic thing for black people" reflecting a widespread desire to shift attention away from lingering racial inequalities.[147] Similarly, for politicians such as Mayor Daley, the public unveiling of the building provided a valuable opportunity to reclaim Chicago's status as a "promised land" for Black residents. In his remarks at its opening ceremony, Daley described the structure as "an inspiration, not only to other blacks, but to other citizens of all races," and ended by reminding onlookers that "there are other great opportunities for black citizens in the city."[148]

Daley's presence at the unveiling of 820 Michigan Avenue can be understood as part of a concerted public campaign to win back African American support, with a series of flashpoints during the late 1960s and early 1970s placing the relationship between Chicago's mayor and its Black residents under increasing strain. The most contentious issue remained the murder of Black Panther leader Fred Hampton, who was killed by a team of FBI agents and Chicago police officers during an early morning raid on Hampton's West Side apartment in December 1969. Activist Don Rose would later recall that the mayor's defense of the officers involved in the raid, paired with his condemnation of the Panthers and other local Black Power organizations, "turned the black community . . . against the [Democratic] machine and against Daley in particular."[149] As support for Daley soured, his connections to Johnson came under increased scrutiny. The pair had a cozy relationship; Johnson was even able to extract planning permission for a basement parking lot at 820 Michigan Avenue that exited directly onto Michigan Avenue, something that hadn't been approved since a regulatory change to the city's building codes during the nineteenth century.[150] In return, Johnson publicly backed Daley's 1971 reelection campaign, a position that put him at odds with many sections of Chicago's Black community.[151]

Criticisms of the building's extravagant design, of its relevance as a protest symbol, and of the role of figures like Daley in its unveiling all fed into the most significant question that accompanied its completion—namely, the ability of Johnson's publications to speak to an increasingly divergent Black community. Taking advantage of the legislative gains made during the movement years, a new generation of white-collar Black workers had prospered in Chicago during the late 1960s and early 1970s. Black professional workers complemented the strength of the city's African American business elite, helping to solidify its reputation as "the black business capital of America."[152] At the same time, deindustrialization, economic downturn, and the continued disruption of urban renewal had devastated many of Chicago's poor and working class African American communities. Research by civil rights organizations such as the Chicago Urban League found that by the mid-1970s approximately one-third of the city's Black population was unemployed and that more than half of Chicago's Black residents were trapped in hyper-segregated neighborhoods and "experiencing extreme and worsening poverty."[153]

While Johnson insisted that he was aware of such poverty, seeing the sumptuous views over Lake Michigan "from his opulent penthouse office" provided visitors and readers with a striking reminder that the publisher was both spatially and socioeconomically aligned with the top third of the African American population—the people largely represented in *Ebony* and his other publications—and distanced from where he started, "down there somewhere with the other two-thirds."[154] Professionally, this dislocation was exacerbated by the South Loop location of 820 Michigan Avenue, which placed further distance between Johnson Publishing and its South Side roots. On a personal level it was reinforced by Johnson's relocation from Drexel Square to the overwhelmingly white confines of the Gold Coast. Indeed, by the early 1970s Johnson's relationship with the South Side appeared to be largely confined to his role as an absentee landlord. Shortly before the opening of 820 Michigan Avenue, a handyman named Ira Talmer had died after the third-floor porch of a building owned by Johnson at 5142 Greenwood Avenue collapsed during remedial work. While tenants placed blame for the accident on the building manager rather that Johnson himself, their descriptions of the building's poor condition were hardly a glowing endorsement of Johnson's sympathy for the common man.[155]

In a curious twist, by the early 1970s the space left by Johnson's personal and professional retreat from the South Side had begun to be filled by Black-owned small business projects that took their names from the publisher's own magazines. This included Ebony Real Estate, which opened in June 1970 at 7903 Ashland Avenue; the Ebony Reduction Salon, a "weight reducing emporium," which opened in March 1969 at 757 West Seventy-Ninth Street; and the Ebony Oil Company located at 620 West Fifty-Ninth Street, whose president, John Dickey, was described by the *Chicago Defender* as "a rare breed of business man in the black community."[156] On the Near North Side these endeavors were joined by the Jet Community Market at 1022 North Larrabee Street, which was formally opened in March 1970. Formerly known as the Cabrini-Green Community Market, the building had been burned out during the riots that occurred after King's assassination. Its unveiling was celebrated by company president Henry Watson as the realization of a long-standing ambition to see "a community supermarket owned by black people living and working in and around a CHA [Chicago Housing Authority] housing project."[157]

In many ways the Jet Community Supermarket offered a more compelling vision of the dream supposedly embodied through 820 Michigan Avenue and imprinted within Johnson's magazines: the dream of how Black businesses could unite and uplift African American communities. The market, maintained under the watchful eye of manager Ernest McGee, may not have boasted the funky interior stylings of Johnson's showpiece headquarters, but it had "many colorful displays and well-stocked shelves." There was no soul food canteen, but consumers wanting African American culinary staples such as "catfish, buffalo, silver bass or red snapper" could find them in the fish department, or they could head over to the produce section to pick up family favorites such as "fresh collard, turnip or mustard greens." The market was not eleven stories tall and certainly didn't house a major collection of Black art. However, Watson hoped it would still have "a significant and beneficial impact" on the lives of local residents. Although the market was just a mile west of Johnson's luxury complex at the Carlyle, one doubts the publisher ever set foot inside. If he had done so, he might have seen something truly remarkable—a corporation truly owned by and accountable to the Black community.[158]

Conclusion

A little over three years after the formal opening of the Johnson Publishing headquarters at 820 Michigan Avenue, *Ebony* marked its thirtieth anniversary. The occasion provided John H. Johnson and the magazine's staff with an opportunity to reflect on the publication's dramatic rise over the previous three decades. From an initial circulation of twenty-five thousand, *Ebony*'s total audience, when accounting for pass-on readership, had breached 7 million per issue by the mid-1970s.[1] The magazine's enormous popularity underpinned the continued rise of Johnson Publishing as a whole, with *Black Enterprise* placing Johnson Publishing behind only Motown Industries in its 1975 rankings of the nation's top Black businesses.[2] For Johnson, this success vindicated his editorial prerogative to "mirror the happier side of Negro life" and his belief that "image power is a prerequisite of economic and political power"—both ideas that were embodied not only through his magazines' pages but also through the spaces and places within which they were produced. The centrality of the company's building history to this narrative of racial progress was acknowledged in *Ebony*'s anniversary issue, which connected the opening of its Washington, D.C., bureau with the political and legislative gains of the civil rights era and mapped Black progress during the postwar era onto its own ascent from "a one-room office in the Supreme Life Insurance Co. building" at 3501 South Parkway to its imposing Michigan Avenue headquarters.[3]

Several months earlier the *Chicago Defender* had celebrated a notable landmark of its own: the publication's seventieth anniversary. To mark the occasion, the *Defender* released a special commemorative issue in May 1975 that celebrated its continued efforts to give voice to Black America and to "the lingering struggle for justice and equality." An accompanying photo essay traced its improbable rise from a kitchen table at 3159 State Street to an imposing publishing plant at 2400 Michigan Avenue, a transition that spoke to how "an impossible dream 70 years ago has taken on the flesh and blood of living reality today."[4] Just as the newspaper's founder, Robert Abbott, had dramatized this transformation by exhibiting "the complete office equipment of the first *Defender*" at earlier sites such as 3435 Indiana Avenue, so too did John Sengstacke preserve the famous folding table and a kitchen chair as "a little memento" of the publication's humble origins in his present offices.[5] Recognizing the indelible connection between the *Defender*'s impact and its building history, the Society of Professional Journalists took the newspaper's anniversary as an opportunity to announce that its Michigan Avenue plant had been selected as a "Historic Site in Journalism," an honor that acknowledged both the *Defender*'s reputation as a "strong journalistic voice for the black community" and the role of its offices in furthering this mission.[6]

Through such accolades and retrospective accounts, the *Defender* and Johnson Publishing added further strands to the dense and overlapping spatial histories that had been constructed by Chicago's Black press over preceding generations—histories that had indelibly linked their physical locations with their role as a "voice for the race" and their editorial content to the visibility and functionality of their buildings. During the late nineteenth and early twentieth centuries, the humble offices inhabited by many of Chicago's Black media concerns reflected their precarious economic and social status. For Robert Abbott and others who eschewed traditional links to Black religious and fraternal organizations in an attempt to build a modern, commercially oriented Black press, it seemed as though "the wolf [was] at each door."[7] However, as the onset of the Great Migration swelled Chicago's African American population, the city's Black press and its buildings grew in tandem. For Southern sojourners heeding the clarion call of publications like the *Chicago Defender*, the Black press was a vital tool in helping them adjust to life in the urban North. In turn, many migrants saw Black publishing offices as symbols of economic and social opportunity and as prominent landmarks in the landscape of the Chicago's emerging Black metropolis. These sentiments were welcomed by Abbott, who understood the critical role that the built environment could play in the relentless quest for greater advertising and circulation. Not without reason did the publisher contend that "every additional reader to the *Chicago Defender* is another brick in our wall of protection, another beacon light in our tower of success."[8]

Buoyed by its emergence as the "dean" of Chicago's Black newspaper group, the *Defender*'s move to Indiana Avenue during the early 1920s helped to bolster its self-appointed role as the "world's greatest weekly."[9] The *Defender*'s offices were just one part of a vibrant Black newspaper row that flourished during this period as Chicago's Black press thrived as part of a golden age of Black business development on the South Side. Just as Black media concerns battled to map and remap the contours of the African American city, so too did they seek to embellish (or diminish) the centrality of their own and other Black press buildings within Black Chicago's literal and literary landscapes. For the upstart *Chicago Whip*, critiques of the *Defender*'s content and relationship with Black Chicago were manifested through attacks on the newspaper's offices and its proximity to "vice spots . . . beneath its very nose."[10] For publications like the upmarket and aspirational *Chicago Bee*, architecture became a way of conflating the character of its content with the character of its building. Thus the *Bee*'s elegant Art Deco headquarters on State Street became a physical extension of "what the *Bee* stands for."[11] More broadly, Chicago's Black periodicals created new conceptual and rhetorical frameworks to advance the South Side as a "spatial articulation of . . . the Black metropolis vision." In different ways and with varying degrees of success, these ideas were encapsulated through the notion of "Defenderland," Abbott's name for "a South Side bound together in its identity by the newspaper," and the promise of "Bronzeville," a racialized literary and cultural geography characterized and popularized by the periodicals that inhabited it.[12]

As the form and function of Chicago's Black press began to change during and after World War II, Black periodicals used their buildings to represent and respond to these changes in different ways. For the *Defender* the built environment became a means of rebutting popular narratives of Black press decline. Rejecting coverage that linked the shrinking circulation and influence of Black newspapers with their failure to "modernize plants and beef up skimpy staffs," Abbott's successor, John Sengstacke, pushed for the development of "a substantial *Chicago Defender* Office and Community Building" to counteract economic and legal pressures.[13] While Sengstacke's ambitions to construct a new corporate headquarters from the ground up would be unfulfilled, the newspaper's acquisition of 2400 Michigan Avenue provided a powerful message to readers and detractors alike: that the *Defender* remained "an important national institution with a rich tradition and considerable influence."[14]

Concomitantly, the increasingly capacious offices inhabited by Johnson Publishing Company during the 1940s and early 1950s, culminating in publisher John H. Johnson's widely celebrated renovation of the Hursen Funeral Home at 1820 Michigan Avenue, served as notable landmarks in its rapid emergence as the nation's leading Black press institution. As cataloged through documentary series such as *One Tenth of a Nation*, the company's "luxurious editorial offices [were] eloquent testimony" to both its own success and the broader ascendancy of Black newsmagazines in postwar America.[15]

Yet even as the move to larger and more impressive buildings solidified the enduring or emerging power of the *Defender* and Johnson Publishing, their relocation to Michigan Avenue placed increased distance between Chicago's leading Black press enterprises and the heart of the South Side community that had nurtured their development. For Johnson this was further complicated by his apparent conflation of first-class accommodations with the city's predominantly white downtown business district. In response, the publisher chose to emphasize the structural barriers impeding his acquisition of 1820 Michigan Avenue, an argument that positioned its eventual purchase not as a retreat from but a victory for "the race."[16] In the case of the *Defender*, the newspaper's relocation was rationalized as part of an expansion program that would allow the publication to better navigate its dual responsibilities to Chicago's Black communities and the national African American populace. For both enterprises, their new offices were a vital weapon in "the battle for civic authority and public relations under the guise of public interest."[17] As exhibition spaces, historical galleries, civic hubs, and popular tourist attractions, these sites became a veritable "crossroads of the world," helping to realize the earlier desire of Robert Abbott for Black media buildings to become "the meeting place for all the people."[18]

At the same time, the continued visibility of Chicago's Black media buildings positioned them as important symbols for—and, at times, prominent battlegrounds in—the ongoing struggle for civil rights and racial justice. The *Defender*'s cohabitation with the Chicago Urban League during the late 1950s and early 1960s provides us with perhaps the most explicit example of how the civil rights movement "came home" for Chicago's Black press during the decades following World War II. As publications like the *Defender* and companies like Johnson Publishing grappled with their relationship to and depiction of the Black freedom struggle, their offices became highly politicized and deeply contested sites, ones that could provide "evidence" of their commitment to the cause or serve as canvases upon which to project criticisms of the publications they housed. Such contestations reflect the multivalent functionality and performativity of Black media buildings, something that would become even more pronounced when Johnson Publishing's new corporate headquarters was unveiled during the early 1970s. Celebrated in some quarters as a riotous monument to Black cultural and economic power, the building was derided by others as a self-serving shrine to the political impotency and failed promises of Black capitalism.

The mixed response to the unveiling of 820 Michigan Avenue can be linked to broader debates about the role and responsibility of the Black press in a "post–civil rights" America. Historically, Black publications had been defined by their role as a "fighting press," something perhaps more clearly demonstrated through the Double V campaign during World War II, which was seen as an act of sedition by the federal government but also pushed the readership of Black publications to unprecedented heights. During this period the *Defender* was one of a dozen Black-owned and -operated newspapers with a weekly circulation of more than one hundred thousand. However, by the early 1970s the only Black newspaper that could lay claim to such numbers was *Muhammad Speaks*. Writing in 1973, *Los Angeles Times* correspondent Francis Ward warned that the Black press was "fighting for its institutional life—caught between a highly vocal segment of blacks who criticize it as outdated . . . and the rising costs of production and news gathering which have forced it to depend more and more on white advertisers."[19]

At a ceremony marking the unveiling of 2400 Michigan Avenue as a "Historic Site in Journalism," Sengstacke did little to hide his annoyance at "the state of the black press and the economic progress of black America in general."[20] Given the broader pressures facing Black publications, the plant's designation as a historic site seemed less an appreciation of the *Defender*'s continuing role as "an outstanding representative of modern black journalism" and more a reminder that the newspaper's most significant contributions were confined to the past.[21] While the format of Johnson's magazines helped to offset circulation and advertising declines for longer than outlets such as the *Defender*, by the late 1990s the cracks that had begun to appear on the travertine marble façade of 820 Michigan Avenue reflected the company's increasingly shaky economic foundations.[22] When Johnson died in 2005 the company was forced to take out a lien on its offices after failing to pay a contractor for maintenance work.[23] By the time the building was sold to Columbia College Chicago, in 2010, it was operating at little more than 50 percent capacity.[24] Less than a decade later its conversion into condominiums provided the backdrop to the company's bankruptcy filings as the house that Johnson built threatened to crumble away altogether.[25]

There is another story here—a story about where Chicago's Black media buildings fit into narratives of Black press decline and how they map onto the "decades of economic disaster, social change and the ravages of urban renewal" that have continued to impact many of the city's working-class Black communities since the triumphant opening of 820 Michigan Avenue.[26] By the 1980s, the Chicago Bee Building was a derelict monument to the faded glory of Chicago's Black newspaper row. When journalist Ethan Michaeli joined the *Defender* several years later, the state of the newspaper's plant reflected its own fall from grace. Sequestered amid rows of derelict apartment buildings, warehouses, and factories, the broken-down building "looked as if it was part of a bygone era."[27] Similarly, by the time 820 Michigan Avenue was sold, it was seen as a "decaying relic" ready to be picked clean by "the buzzards of urban progress"—no longer its "own loud protest" but a symbol for the failed promises of Black economic development and a reminder of the racial fault lines that continue to divide Chicago.[28] For some activists the city's failure to protect its Black media landmarks formed part of a larger conspiracy "to let our community deteriorate to the point where it will have to be all torn down so that it can be gentrified."[29]

It is also a story about community resistance and the continuing role of Chicago's Black press as a voice for the city's African American residents. During the 1980s and 1990s, the rehabilitation of the Chicago Bee Building as a community branch of the Chicago Public Library became central to ongoing debates over neighborhood renewal, urban inequality, and African American history. From a similar perspective, Black media buildings emerged as linchpins in the struggle to establish the Black Metropolis–Bronzeville District and to secure protected status for iconic South Side locations such as the former *Defender* plant at 3435 Indiana Avenue, the Overton Hygienic Building at 3619 State Street, and the Supreme Life Building at Thirty-Fifth Street and Martin Luther King Jr. Drive (renamed in 1968 in tribute to the fallen civil rights icon).[30] Efforts to restore Bronzeville to its former glory have been aided by the *Defender*'s return, with a relocation to 4445 Martin Luther King Jr. Drive in 2009 applauded as "a move back to its African American roots in location and mission."[31] More recent attempts by Black activists to save the Johnson Publishing Building on Michigan Avenue—which led to a landmark designation but were unable to rescue its iconic interiors from being gutted—also suggest that for many community members, Black publications and their buildings remain something worth fighting for.

This is a story that is beyond the boundaries of this book, but it is one that reinforces, rather than diminishes, the historic significance of Chicago's Black press and its relationship with the built environment. Through their lives and afterlives, in guises old and new, Chicago's Black media buildings continue to shape the city's Black public sphere and the relationship between its Black media outlets and the communities they serve. From kitchen tables, rented storefronts, and backstreet offices to multimillion-dollar plants and publishing houses, the buildings owned or inhabited by the *Chicago Defender*, Johnson Publishing, and a host of other Black media concerns offer a powerful insight into the history of Chicago's Black press and its role in shaping the real and imagined geographies of Chicago's Black metropolis. As potent symbols of Black progress and as powerful reminders of a dream deferred, they provide us with a new language to explore the relationship between media production, racial protest, and spatial politics in the making and remaking of the modern American city.

Notes

Introduction

1. "Tribune Opens Great Contest on Birthday," *Chicago Tribune*, June 10, 1922.

2. Solomonson, *Chicago Tribune Tower*; Keegan, *Chicago Architecture*, 56.

3. "Notables Join in Dedication of News Building," *Chicago Tribune*, July 9, 1929; Leslie, *Chicago Skyscrapers*, 168.

4. "A Monument to Service," *Pittsburgh Press*, June 25, 1929.

5. Solomonson, *Chicago Tribune Tower*; Leslie, *Chicago Skyscrapers*.

6. Junger, *Becoming the Second City*, x.

7. Wallace, *Media Capital*, 5.

8. "A Monument to Service."

9. Stamper, *Chicago's North Michigan Avenue*, 61; Guarneri, *Newsprint Metropolis*, 4.

10. In keeping with my efforts to center the South Side within broader discussions of Chicago's physical and mediated landscape, readers should assume north-south addresses are on the South Side unless explicitly stated. For example, South Indiana Avenue will be referenced as Indiana Avenue. "5,000 Inspect Defender's New Plant," *Chicago Defender*, May 14, 1921.

11. Sandburg, *Chicago Race Riots*, 51; Drake and Cayton, *Black Metropolis*.

12. For more on historical definitions and constructions of the Black press, see Wolseley, *Black Press, U.S.A*; J. Rhodes, "The Black Press"; Gallon, *Pleasure in the News*.

13. "In Memoriam," *The Root*, November 21, 2010.

14. *The Black Press*, PBS, 1999.

15. "The Negro Newspaper," *Chicago Defender*, June 4, 1921.

16. "Salutatory," *Broad Ax*, July 15, 1899.

17. "Chicago," *Ebony*, February 1978; "Today Show Interview, June 1970," box 25, folder 17, ASFP.

18. Pasley, *Tyranny of Printers*; Adelman, *Revolutionary Networks*.

19. Valle, *Massachusetts Troublemakers*, 56–58.

20. *American Newspaper Directory*, 121.

21. Gray, "Type and Building Type," 87.

22. Wallace, *Media Capital*, 4; Guarneri, *Newsprint Metropolis*; Ericson, Riegert, and Åker, Introduction to *Media Houses*.

23. Wallace, *Media Capital*, 5.

24. *Centennial Newspaper Exhibition*, 191.

25. L. Rhodes, *Ethnic Press*, 3–4.

26. *Centennial Newspaper Exhibition*, 205; *Chicago and Its Resources*, 30.

27. *Centennial Newspaper Exhibition*, 244.

28. "To Our Patrons," *Freedom's Journal*, March 16, 1827.

29. For an introduction to Black press scholarship, see Gallon, *Pleasure in the News*; J. Rhodes, "The Black Press"; Vogel, Introduction to *The Black Press*; Wolseley, *Black Press, U.S.A*.

30. *The Black Press*, PBS, 1999.

31. Vogel, Introduction to *The Black Press*, 1.

32. Fagan, *Black Newspaper*, 26.

33. Gooden, *Dark Space*, 23.

34. Sernett, *North Star Country*, 184.

35. Gardner, *Black Print Unbound*, 62.

36. Alexander, *Race Man*, 34.

37. Zucchino, *Wilmington's Lie*.

38. Wallace, *Media Capital*, 5.

39. "After 38 Years, Defender Moves," *Chicago Defender*, April 11, 1959.

40. Walker, "The Promised Land," 12.

41. "Failure Is a Word I Don't Accept," box 22, folder 10, HWFP; "Publishing Company Operated by Blacks," box 2, folder 1, BBP.

42. "New JPC Building Dedicated," *Jet*, June 1, 1972.

43. "In Memoriam."

44. Ballantyne, "Reading the Newspaper," 52.

45. Anderson, *Imagined Communities*.

46. "A Hard Zell," *Chicago Tribune*, October 19, 2000.

47. Ballantyne, "Reading the Newspaper," 52.

48. Wallace, *Media Capital*, 7.

49. Rodgers, "Journalism," 68.

50. Stamper, *Chicago's North Michigan Avenue*, 62–63.

51. "Lifting a River Out of Its Bed," *Popular Mechanics*, May 1929.

52. "The Chicago Daily News," *Indiana Times*, June 18, 1929.

53. Reed, "Third Chicago School?" 163.

54. Hirsch, *Making the Second Ghetto*, 17.

55. Drake and Cayton, *Black Metropolis*; Bone and Courage, *Muse in Bronzeville*, 1.

56. Clarence Page, "The Other Chicago," *Chicago Tribune*, June 8, 1997.

57. "Working Out a Fine," *Chicago Tribune*, December 1, 1894.

58. "Policy Patrons Robbed by Trick," *Chicago Tribune*, May 2, 1903.

59. "Brundage and Hoyne Join to Punish Rioters," *Chicago Tribune*, August 1, 1919; "Riots Spread," *Chicago Tribune*, July 30, 1919.

60. Hirsch, *Making the Second Ghetto*.

61. Spear, *Black Chicago*; Philpott, *Slum and the Ghetto*.

62. Baldwin, *Chicago's New Negroes*; Green, *Selling the Race*, Knupfer, *Chicago Black Renaissance*.

63. Reed, *Chicago's Black Metropolis*; "Publisher's Page," *Black Enterprise*, June 1974.

64. A. Burns, *Storefront to Monument*; Hirsch, *Making the Second Ghetto*; Semmes, *Regal Theater*.

65. "Chicago Defender Plans Guide Service," *Chicago Defender*, May 13, 1933.

66. Sandburg, *Chicago Race Riots*, 51.

67. A. Burns, *Storefront to Monument*, 5.

68. Baldwin, *Chicago's New Negroes*, 22.

69. Bone and Courage, *Muse in Bronzeville*, 1.

70. Schlabach, *Along the Streets*; Knupfer, *Chicago Black Renaissance*.

71. Green, *Selling the Race*, 2.

72. "Our Office," *Chicago Defender*, January 6, 1912.

73. Michaeli, *Defender*, 335.

74. "New JPC Building Dedicated."

75. "The Black Press," *Nieman Reports*, Fall 2003.

76. "Chicago Defender Returns to South Side," *WBEZ*, April 30, 2009; Commission on Chicago Landmarks, "The Black Metropolis–Bronzeville District"; "Former Home of *Ebony* and *Jet* Reopens as Modern Apartments," *Chicago Crusader*, June 27, 2019.

77. C. Wilson, *Whither the Black Press?*; Boyd, *Jim Crow Nostalgia*; Hyra, *New Urban Renewal*.

78. Green, *Selling*, 2.

79. Waters, *American Diary*.

80. In this regard I draw inspiration from the work of Stephanie Camp, Saidiya Hartman, and other scholars who have embraced the speculative as part of efforts to retheorize the histories of marginalized people and communities. Camp, *Closer to Freedom*; Hartman, *Wayward Lives*.

81. Guarneri, *Newsprint Metropolis*, 4.

Chapter 1. A Card Table and a Kitchen Chair

1. Pacyga, *Chicago*, 71.

2. Leslie, *Chicago Skyscrapers*.

3. Burg, *Chicago's White City*, xiii.

4. *Picturesque World's Fair*, 11; Junger, *Becoming the Second City*, 126.

5. Reed, *All the World*, 76.

6. Bederman, *Manliness and Civilization*, 40.

7. Paddon and Turner, "African Americans," 21–22.

8. Quoted in Burg, *Chicago's White City*, 218; "Working People Go to the Fair," *Chicago Tribune*, June 5, 1893.

9. "West African Folk," *Chicago Tribune*, May 4, 1893.

10. Reed, *Black Chicago's First Century*, 206.

11. Belles, "Black Press in Illinois"; Walker, "Promised Land."

12. Penn, *Afro-American Press*, 238; Rudwick and Meier, "Black Man in the 'White City,'" 354.

13. Blight, *Frederick Douglass*; Duster, *Crusade for Justice*.

14. "Eight Negroes Lynched," *Free Speech*, May 21, 1892.

15. McMurry, *Keep the Waters Troubled*, 199.

16. Penn, *Afro-American Press*.

17. Wells et al., "Reason Why."

18. "Two Notable People Are Married," *Chicago Tribune*, June 28, 1895.

19. Duster, *Crusade for Justice*, 205.

20. Grossman, *Land of Hope*, 130.

21. Ottley, *Lonely Warrior*, 6.

22. Michaeli, *Defender*, 3.

23. Reed, *Black Chicago's First Century*, 341.

24. Baldwin, *Chicago's New Negroes*, 29.

25. Purnell and Theoharis, Introduction to *Strange Careers*, 1–42.

26. "Miss Ida Wells Here," *Brooklyn Citizen*, December 7, 1894.

27. Walker, "Promised Land"; Dolinar, *Negro in Illinois*, 117.

28. "A Recapitulation of 25 Years Work," *Chicago Defender*, May 3, 1930.

29. "Abbott, Robert S.," box 1, folder 1, ASFP.

30. Ottley, *Lonely Warrior*, 87,

31. *Colored People's Blue Book*, 105.

32. "Mrs. H. P. Lee," *Chicago Defender*, July 31, 1926.

33. "Chips," *Broad Ax*, October 3, 1903; "Henrietta Lee," 1900 U.S. Census, Chicago Ward 3, District 0058.

34. "Mrs. H. P. Lee"; Hendricks, *Gender, Race, and Politics*.

35. Rice, *Chicago Defender*, 7.

36. "People Who Helped Abbott," *Chicago Defender*, August 13, 1955.

37. "Looking Back," *Chicago Defender*, May 4, 1935.

38. "People Who Helped Abbott."

39. Ottley, *Lonely Warrior*, 95.

40. "The City-Hall," *Chicago Tribune*, September 30, 1882.

41. "Entertained in a Most Lavish Manner," *Broad Ax*, June 30, 1906; "Jacob L. Parks," *Broad Ax*, May 12, 1906.

42. "Chips," *Broad Ax*, April 29, 1905.

43. 1910 U.S. Census, Chicago Ward 2, District 0197.

44. D. Haywood, *Let Us Make Men*, 105.

45. "Looking Back."

46. Michaeli, *Defender*, 23.

47. Carby, *Race Men*, 9.

48. "Mrs. H. P. Lee."

49. Ottley, *Lonely Warrior*, 94.

50. "Thirty Years of Service," *Chicago Defender*, May 4, 1935.

51. Michaeli, *Defender*, 23; "Kitchen Table Illustration," box 1, folder 1, ASFP.

52. "The Week," *Chicago Defender*, July 31, 1926; "The Week," *Chicago Defender*, May 3, 1930; "Dustin' off the News," *Chicago Defender*, May 14, 1949.

53. "Mother of Defender," *Chicago Defender*, May 3, 1930.

54. Gallon, *Pleasure in the News*, 20.

55. "Salutatory," *Broad Ax*, July 15, 1899.

56. Belles, "Black Press in Illinois"; Walker, "Promised Land."

57. Dill, "Growth of Newspapers," 24.

58. "Booker T. Washington and the Rise of the NAACP," *The Crisis*, February 1954.

59. "Chicago," *Appeal*, August 11, 1888; "Dustin' Off the News."

60. "Chips," *Broad Ax*, May 14, 1910.

61. "Miscellaneous Musings," *Chicago Defender*, March 26, 1910.

62. Ottley, *Lonely Warrior*, 93.

63. "Thirty Years of Service."

64. Ibid.

65. Henkin, *City Reading*, 104.

66. "Chicago Address," *Western Appeal*, August 11, 1888.

67. Garb, *Freedom's Ballot*, 61; Spear, *Black Chicago*, 6–7.

68. Spear, *Black Chicago*, 12.

69. "Quinn Chapel," National Register of Historic Places, September 4, 1979.

70. Reed, *Rise of Chicago's Black Metropolis*, 64.

71. "Evidences," *Chicago Advocate*, September 16, 1909.

72. *Colored People's Blue Book*, 132.

73. "Edwin H. Faulkner," *Broad Ax*, August 27, 1904.

74. "Negro Democracy in Chicago," *Broad Ax*, August 12, 1899.

75. "Wisdom Comes by Reading," *Broad Ax*, June 24, 1905.

76. Sandburg, *Chicago Race Riots*, 52.

77. Reed, *Black Chicago's First Century*, 338.

78. Baldwin, *Chicago's New Negroes*, 23–25.

79. Schlabach, *Along the Streets*, 6.

80. Kenney, *Chicago Jazz*, 15.

81. "Rambling about Chicago," *Chicago Defender*, March 4, 1910.

82. Baldwin, *Chicago's New Negroes*, 22.

83. Ibid., 38.

84. Blair, *I've Got to Make My Livin'*, 173.

85. Gasher, "Geographies of the News," 127.

86. Gallon, *Pleasure in the News*, 33.

87. Mackintosh, *Newspaper City*, 61–62.

88. Detweiler, *Negro Press*, 115.

89. Guarneri, *Newsprint Metropolis*, 22.

90. Kenney, *Chicago Jazz*, 18.

91. Blair, *I've Got to Make My Livin'*, 278.

92. Ottley, *Lonely Warrior*, 119.

93. "Looking Back."

94. Digirolamo, *Crying the News*, 374.

95. Michaeli, *Defender*, 27.

96. "Schoolboy Earns Big Money," *Chicago Defender*, October 24, 1914.

97. "One of the Defender's Delivery Wagons," *Chicago Defender*, March 29, 1913.

98. "The Chicago Defender's Auto Delivery Service," *Chicago Defender*, May 16, 1914.

99. Quoted in Stewart, *Migrating to the Movies*, 132.

100. "31st and State a Festive Center," *Chicago Defender*, June 15, 1912.

101. Teresa, *Looking at the Stars*, x.

102. "Our Office," *Chicago Defender*, January 6, 1912.

103. Michaeli, *Defender*, 28.

104. "Jack Johnson," *Chicago Defender*, February 19, 1910.

105. "Booker T. Washington," *Chicago Defender*, March 7, 1914.

106. "May Keiser Stowers Wins Tribune Prize," *Chicago Defender*, April 29, 1911.

107. Michaeli, *Defender*, 31; Rice, *Chicago Defender*.

108. Rice, "Robert Sengstacke Abbott," 51.

109. Thompson, *Black Life in Mississippi*, 20.

110. Jordan, *Black Newspapers*, 140.

111. Simmons, *African American Press*, 36.

112. Michaeli, *Defender*, 40.

113. "Southern White Gentleman Rapes Colored Lady," *Chicago Defender*, November 4, 1911.

114. Michaeli, *Defender*, 41; Bone and Courage, *Muse in Bronzeville*, 42.

115. Reed, *Knock at the Door*, 136.

116. "Editor Abbott Calls Roll of Those Who Aided *Defender*," *Chicago Defender*, May 31, 1930.

117. Waters, *American Diary*, 289.

118. Ibid., 290.

119. Jordan, *Black Newspapers*, 32.

120. Michaeli, *Defender*, 59–60; Spear, *Black Chicago*, 115.

121. "The Empty Chair," *Chicago Defender*, October 16, 1915.

122. Jordan, *Black Newspapers*, 32.

123. Schlabach, *Along the Streets*, 7.

124. Grossman, *Land of Hope*, 68.

125. Sernett, *Bound for the Promised Land*, 3.

126. Henri, *Black Migration*, 63.

127. "Abbott, Robert S.," box 1, folder 1, ASFP.

128. "Northern Invasion," *Chicago Defender*, January 20, 1917.

129. Jordan, *Black Newspapers*, 111.

130. Kornweibel, *Investigate Everything*, 118–20.

131. Michaeli, *Defender*, 72.

132. Washburn, *African American Newspaper*, 105.

133. Kornweibel, *Investigate Everything*, 124–25.

134. "A Book Which Will Live," *Dallas Express*, July 26, 1919.

135. "Chicago Defender Opens New Department," *Chicago Defender*, February 19, 1916.

136. Michaeli, *Defender*, 70; "Dustin' Off the News."

137. "People Who Helped Abbott."

138. "Biography," box 1, folder 1, ASFP.

139. "New Buildings," *Chicago Inter-Ocean*, December 12, 1885.

140. "Abbott Publishing Co.," box 11, folder 5, ASFP.

141. "People Who Helped Abbott"; Rice, *Chicago Defender*, 32.

142. "Chicago Defender Opens New Department."

143. "'Black Belt' the Blackest Belt of Chicago Vice," *Chicago Tribune*, December 17, 1921.

144. "The Other Chicago," *Chicago Tribune*, June 8, 1997.

145. McCammack, *Landscapes of Hope*.

146. Chicago Commission on Race Relations, *Negro in Chicago*, 123.

147. "Flats Blown Up," *Chicago Tribune*, February 28, 1919.

148. "The Homes of Two Colored Families Bombed," *Broad Ax*, November 23, 1918; "Whites Place Bomb on Housetop," *Chicago Defender*, May 31, 1919; Tuttle, *Race Riot*, 158.

149. Lumpkins, *American Pogrom*.

150. Krugler, *1919*, 1.

151. Tuttle, *Race Riot*; Sandburg, *Chicago Race Riots*.

152. Chicago Commission on Race Relations, *Negro in Chicago*, 26–27.

153. "The Riot Area Extending over the Black Belt," *Chicago Tribune*, July 29, 1919.

154. Chicago Commission on Race Relations, *Negro in Chicago*, 26.

155. "Race Riots in Chicago," *Broad Ax*, August 2, 1919; "Showered by Bullets," *Chicago Defender*, August 2, 1919.

156. "Chicagoans Pay Tribute to Mrs. Ridley," *Chicago Defender*, June 27, 1942.

157. H. Haywood, *Black Communist*, 72.

158. "Allen and Harsh Risk Lives to Get *Whip* Copy to Press," *Chicago Whip*, August 9, 1919.

159. "Public Places in Riot Zone to Remain Closed," *Chicago Whip*, August 9, 1919.

160. Chicago Commission on Race Relations, *Negro in Chicago*, xvi.

161. "Tim Samuelson," box 8, folder 4, BEAP.

162. Ottley, *Lonely Warrior*, 191.

163. "Attention Agents and Subscribers," *Chicago Defender*, August 9, 1919.

164. Gardner, *Black Print*, 62.

165. Michaeli, *Defender*, 119; Dolinar, *Negro in Illinois*, 186.

Chapter 2. A Monument to Negro Enterprise

1. "Before Chicago Erupted into Race Riots in 1919, Carl Sandburg Reported on the Fissures," *Chicago Tribune*, July 18, 2019.

2. McWhirter, *Red Summer*, 125–26.

3. Sandburg, *Chicago Race Riots*, 6.

4. *Black's Blue Book*, 43.

5. "Tribune Tower Opens Its Doors," *Chicago Tribune*, July 6, 1925.

6. Sandburg, *Chicago Race Riots*, 52; "Newspapers of the Race," *Kansas City Sun*, May 3, 1919.

7. In 1920 Chicago's African American population was 109,458; by 1930 it had grown to 233,903. Hirsch, *Making the Second Ghetto*, 17; Hayner, *Binga*; Baldwin, *Chicago's New Negroes*; "The Quest for Economic Security," *Ebony*, February 1974.

8. Reed, *Rise of Chicago's Black Metropolis*, 5.

9. Baldwin, *Chicago's New Negroes*.

10. Wallace, *Media Capital*, 5.

11. Ottley, *Lonely Warrior*, 193.

12. "Contract," box 2, folder 3, ASFP.

13. Commission on Chicago Landmarks, "The Black Metropolis–Bronzeville District," 17.

14. "Howard Theater," *The Rotarian*, April 1921; "Among Architects and Builders," *Chicago Tribune*, July 29, 1900.

15. S. Davis, *Chicago's Historic Hyde Park*, 395.

16. *The Jews of Illinois*, 352.

17. "Jews Dedicate a Synagogue," *Chicago Tribune*, October 7, 1901; "To Present Oriental Scene," *Chicago Tribune*, November 2, 1902.

18. Commission on Chicago Landmarks, "Melissia Ann Elam Home."

19. Baldwin, *Chicago's New Negroes*, 50.

20. Best, *Passionately Human, No Less Devine*, 106.

21. "Lease," box 11, folder 1, ASFP.

22. Commission on Chicago Landmarks, "Black Metropolis–Bronzeville District"; "5,000 Inspect *Defender*'s New Plant," *Chicago Defender*, May 14, 1921; Waters, *American Diary*, 125.

23. Michaeli, *Defender*, 134–35.

24. "Biography," box 1, folder 1, ASFP.

25. "3435 Indiana," *Chicago Defender*, April 9, 1921.

26. "Announcement," box 18, folder 27, ASFP.

27. "5,000 Inspect *Defender*'s New Plant."

28. Detweiler, *Negro Press*, 64.

29. Ottley, *Lonely Warrior*, 196–97; Rice, "Robert Sengstacke Abbott," 50.

30. "5,000 Inspect *Defender*'s New Plant."

31. "Mr. George A. Wilson," *Chicago Defender*, June 4, 1910.

32. Renda, *Taking Haiti*, 189.

33. Rolinson, *Grassroots Garveyism*, 25.

34. Grant, *Negro with a Hat*, 260.

35. "Phylon Profile, 1947," box 1, folder 1, ASFP.

36. Michaeli, *Defender*, 125.

37. Kornweibel, *Seeing Red*, 46.

38. "Murals," box 1, folder 7, ASFP.

39. "A Young Artist," *The Crisis*, March 1913, 223; Pinder, *Painting the Gospel*, 36.

40. "Cover," *The Crisis*, December 1918.

41. "5,000 Inspect Defender's New Plant."

42. "Big Business among Blacks in Chicago," *Phoenix Tribune*, November 12, 1921.

43. Ottley, *Lonely Warrior*, 193.

44. Travis, *Autobiography of Black Chicago*.

45. Ingham and Feldman, *African-American Business Leaders*, 75.

46. Howard, "Rise and Fall of Jesse Binga," 61.

47. Hayner, *Binga*.

48. "The Opening of Binga Bank," *Broad Ax*, January 8, 1921.

49. "Congratulations Usher Binga Bank in New Home," *Chicago Defender*, October 25, 1924; "Binga State Bank to Move into New Quarters," *Chicago Defender*, October 18, 1924.

50. Abbott held stock interests in the Binga Bank and was a regular presence at social events held by Binga and his wife, Dora. Cooley, *Moving Up, Moving Out*, 32; Hayner, *Binga*, 63.

51. "Plans, Work, Binga's Secret for Success," *Chicago Tribune*, May 8, 1927.

52. Detweiler, *Negro Press*, 3.

53. "Industry and Business," *Chicago Defender*, August 4, 1928.

54. Gallon, *Pleasure in the News*, 13.

55. Burma, "Analysis of the Present Negro Press," 175.

56. "Black Belt," *Chicago Tribune*, December 17, 1921.

57. "Advertisement," *Editor and Publisher*, April 8, 1916.

58. "The Tribune Tower," *Chicago Tribune*, July 6, 1925.

59. Trodd, "Black Press," 451.

60. Gasher, "Geographies of the News," 127; "The Other Chicago," *Chicago Tribune*, June 8, 1997.

61. "Chicagoland's Shrines," *Chicago Tribune*, July 27, 1926.

62. Guarneri, *Newsprint Metropolis*, 185.

63. Waters, *American Diary*, 70.

64. "Opportunity, March 1929," box 18, folder 23, ASFP.

65. Chicago Commission on Race Relations, *Negro in Chicago*, 559, 564.

66. "We Thank You!," *Chicago Defender*, May 6, 1922.

67. "Interesting Facts," box 11, folder 7, ASFP; "A Bit about Chicago," box 11, folder 1, ASFP; "America's Greatest Institution," box 11, folder 4, ASFP.

68. Ibid.

69. General Manager to Helen Hilts, May 15, 1921, box 1 folder 1, ASFP.

70. "Show Reels of Defender News Plant," *Chicago Defender*, January 21, 1928.

71. "Crowds See Pictures of Chicago Defender Plant," *Chicago Defender*, February 4, 1928.

72. "Chicago Defender Plant in Movies," *Chicago Defender*, June 10, 1933.

73. "Thirty Years of Service," *Chicago Defender*, May 4, 1935.

74. "Chicago, and Race Progress," *Plaindealer*, August 29, 1924.

75. "The Mouthpiece of 14 Million People," *Chicago Defender*, January 14, 1922.

76. "Thirty Years of Service."

77. Michaeli, *Defender*, 136.

78. Rice, "Robert Sengstacke Abbott," 50.

79. "Mouthpiece of 14 Million People."

80. Michaeli, *Defender*, 158.

81. Rice, *Chicago Defender*, 32.

82. "Real Estate Contract," box 2, folder 3, ASFP; "Abbott Purchase," box 2, folder 3, ASFP.

83. Ottley, *Lonely Warrior*, 255; "Robert S. Abbott House," National Register of Historic Places.

84. "A Bit about Chicago," box 11, folder 1, ASFP.

85. "Mouthpiece of 14 Million People."

86. Sandburg, *Chicago Race Riots*, 74.

87. Reed, *Rise of Chicago's Black Metropolis*, 105; *Black's Blue Book*, 43.

88. "Out of Town Notes," *Nashville Globe*, May 31, 1918; *Black's Blue Book*, 50; "The Chicago Negro," *New York Tribune*, July 31, 1919.

89. "First since Reconstruction," *Time*, December 29, 1952.

90. "Allen and Harsh Risk Lives to Get Whip Copy to Press," *Chicago Whip*, August 9, 1919; "Chicago Race Riots Smolder," *San Francisco Chronicle*, August 2, 1919.

91. Spear, *Black Chicago*, 186.

92. "Chicago's Doctors Slandered," *Broad Ax*, April 16, 1921; Chicago Commission on Race Relations, *Negro in Chicago*, 524.

93. "Chicago Whip Chases the Defender," *Chicago Whip*, September 27, 1919.

94. Ibid.

95. "Chicago Office," *Chicago Whip*, December 6, 1919; "Chicago Office," *Chicago Whip*, January 1, 1921.

96. "Society," *Chicago Whip*, August 21, 1919; "Society," *Chicago Whip*, January 17, 1920.

97. "Notice to All Renters!," *Chicago Whip*, March 20, 1920.

98. "Defender Man Joins Whip Staff," *Chicago Whip*, July 31, 1920.

99. McCammack, *Landscapes of Hope*, 45–46.

100. "Living on the Boulevards," *Chicago Whip*, October 4, 1919.

101. "Climbing the Alps," *Chicago Whip*, May 7, 1921.

102. "Vice May Cause More Riots," *Chicago Whip*, December 23, 1922; "Under the Lash of the Whip," *Chicago Whip*, November 18, 1922.

103. "Is Mouth Choked with Dollar Bills," *Chicago Whip*, October 14, 1922.

104. "Dice Rattle Unheeded by Newspaper," *Chicago Whip*, December 9, 1922; "The Press and Its 'Pool of Slime,'" *Chicago Whip*, December 9, 1922.

105. Reed, *Rise of Chicago's Black Metropolis*, 99; "Some Chicagoans of Note," *The Crisis*, September 1915.

106. "Editorial," *Half-Century*, August 1916.

107. Quoted in Reed, *Knock at the Door*, 270.

108. "Let's Chat," *Half-Century*, April 1917.

109. Weems, *Merchant Prince*, 62.

110. Rooks, *Ladies' Pages*; Halliday, "Centering Black Women," 242.

111. Glasrud and Champion, "Anita Scott Coleman," 77–78.

112. "For the Race and America," *Half-Century*, August 1919; Halliday, "Centering Black Women," 243.

113. "The Quest for Economic Security," *Ebony*, February 1974.

114. "Building News," *American Architect* 119, 1921.

115. While Overton biographer Robert Weems contends that Smith was Black, census records categorize him as white. Weems, *Merchant Prince*, 115; "1910 US Census," York, Pennsylvania; Enumeration District: 0131, 15B.

116. "New Hotel to Be Built in Streeterville," *Chicago Tribune*, September 7, 1919.

117. Commission on Chicago Landmarks, "Black Metropolis–Bronzeville District," 10.

118. Ibid., 12.

119. "Back to the 'Good Old Days,'" *Chicago Tribune*, October 21, 1928; "Helping to Beautify City," *Chicago Tribune*, December 19, 1926.

120. Commission on Chicago Landmarks, "Black Metropolis–Bronzeville District," 12.

121. Wilson, *African American Architects*, 24.

122. "Negroes' Bank Shows Big Gains," *Detroit Free Press*, September 27, 1925; "Douglass National Bank," *Chicago Defender*, September 29, 1923.

123. Reed, *Rise of Chicago's Black Metropolis*, 72.

124. "Courier Opens Branch Offices in East and West," *Pittsburgh Courier*, March 1, 1924; "Chicago Office," *Pittsburgh Courier*, March 15, 1924.

125. "Death and Funeral of Doctor Theodore R. Mozee," *Broad Ax*, November 24, 1917.

126. Horne, *Rise and Fall of the Associated Negro Press*, 24–25.

127. "Kashmir Chemical in New Quarters," *Richmond Planet*, May 8, 1920.

128. "Newspaper Men Launch 'Boost Chicago' Campaign," *Chicago Defender*, September 17, 1921.

129. Commission on Chicago Landmarks, "Black Metropolis–Bronzeville District," 10.

130. Rooks, *Ladies' Pages*, 68.

131. Reed, *Rise of Chicago's Black Metropolis*, 104.

132. "When It Comes to Women," *Chicago Bee*, December 9, 1945.

133. Walker, "Promised Land," 33; F. Carroll, *Race News*, 62.

134. F. Davis, *Livin' the Blues*, 108–109.

135. Enoch Waters and Robert Weems contend that Overton's corporate records, as well as an extensive collection of the *Bee*, were discarded following the company's dissolution during the 1980s. Waters, *American Diary*, 121; Weems, *Merchant Prince*, 1–2.

136. "A Modernistic Bit for South State," *Chicago Tribune*, October 27, 1929.

137. "Plans Home for Colored Paper on State Street," *Chicago Tribune*, October 27, 1929.

138. "The 'Skyscraper' of Bronzeville," *Urban Remains*, December 28, 2016.

139. "Northwestern Terra Cotta Company Building," 7.

140. Coburn, "Chicago Bee Building," 197–98.

141. "Modernistic Bit for South State."

142. "The Chicago Bee Has Five Planks," *Pittsburgh Courier*, August 10, 1929.

143. Baldwin, *Chicago's New Negroes*, 36.

144. Randall Burkett, "Hammurabi in the (MARBL) House," *MARBL Scholar Blog*, May 1, 2015, https://scholarblogs.emory.edu/marbl/2015/05/01/hammurabi-in-the-marbl-house

145. Green, "Rising Tide of Youth," 239.

146. *Intercollegian Wonder Book*, 214.

147. Reed, *Rise of Chicago's Black Metropolis*, 7; "South Parkway," *Chicago Tribune*, July 16, 1925.

148. Semmes, *Regal Theater*, 17.

149. Howard, "Rise and Fall of Jesse Binga," 67.

150. Greenberg, *To Ask for an Equal Chance*, 21.

151. Reed, *Depression Comes to the South Side*, 9–11.

152. "Cruising Around," *Indianapolis Recorder*, August 23, 1930.

153. Reed, *Depression Comes to the South Side*, 10–11.

154. "Chicago Negro Bank Fails," *Birmingham Reporter*, August 9, 1930.

155. Howard, "Rise and Fall of Jesse Binga," 74–75; Hayner, *Binga*.

156. Weems, *Merchant Prince*, 124.

157. Commission on Chicago Landmarks, "Black Metropolis–Bronzeville District," 10.

158. Reed, *Rise of Chicago's Black Metropolis*, 82.

159. Michaeli, *Defender*, 189.

160. Weems, *Merchant Prince*, 106.

161. Reed, *Depression Comes to the South Side*, 76.

162. "Chicago Defender Good Fellow Movement," *Billboard*, December 31, 1921.

163. "Thanksgiving Baskets," *Chicago Defender*, May 5, 1975; "Sengstacke Radio Interview, 1939," box 24, folder 6, ASFP.

164. Michaeli, *Defender*, 133.

165. Rutkoff and Scott, "Pinkster in Chicago," 318; "Bud Has Visitors," *Chicago Defender*, August 3, 1929.

166. Bone and Courage, *Muse in Bronzeville*, 63–64.

167. Michaeli, *Defender*, 182.

168. "A Few Sidelights on Bud's Big Jubilee," *Chicago Defender*, August 22, 1931.

169. Bone and Courage, *Muse in Bronzeville*, 64.

170. McCammack, *Landscapes of Hope*, 108.

171. Rutkoff and Scott, "Pinkster in Bronzeville," 317.

172. "Slums and Rebuilding," *Chicago Tribune*, April 16, 1930.

173. Herbst, *Politics at the Margin*, 65.

174. For more on the South Side's politics of naming, see Bone and Courage, *Muse in Bronzeville*; Schlabach, *Along the Streets*.

175. Michaeli, *Defender*, 207.

176. Drake and Cayton, *Black Metropolis*, 383.

177. "Congratulations, Mr. Mayor," *Chicago Defender*, September 14, 1935.

178. "His Civic Duty," *Chicago Defender*, August 3, 1935; "Their Decision Final," *Chicago Defender*, September 7, 1935.

179. "Newspapers of the Race"; Sandburg, *Chicago Race Riots*, 52.

Chapter 3. A Building on a Front Street

1. Schrenk, *Building a Century of Progress*.

2. Ganz, *1933 Chicago World's Fair*.

3. Ibid., 112.

4. Bey, "Century of Progress," 126.

5. Reed, *Depression Comes to the South Side*, 141–42; "Negro Day at Fair Flops," *Chicago Defender*, August 19, 1933.

6. Bey, "Century of Progress," 126.

7. Reed, *Depression Comes to the South Side*, 141.

8. Meier and Rudwick, "Negro Protest," 162.

9. Leslie, "Chicago Bee Building," 198.

10. "Visitors Swarm Offices of Abbott Publications," *Chicago Defender*, July 8, 1933.

11. "Bud Welcomes Fair Visitors," *Chicago Defender*, June 3, 1933.

12. "Fair Visitors See Defender Plant," *Chicago Defender*, July 22, 1933; "Kansans Attend Boule and Visit World's Fair," *Chicago Defender*, August 19, 1933; "Californian Here on Visit Sees Fair," *Chicago Defender*, June 3, 1933.

13. "Chicago to Open Doors to World's Fair Visitors," *Chicago Defender*, April 29, 1933.

14. "Chicago Defender Plans New Guide Service for Fair Visitors," *Chicago Defender*, May 13, 1933.

15. "Are You a Visitor?" *Chicago Defender*, July 15, 1933.

16. Ganz, *1933 Chicago World's Fair*, 115.

17. "Everybody Got Free Ice Cream," *Chicago Defender*, August 26, 1933; "The Billiken Picnic," *Chicago Defender*, August 26, 1933.

18. "John H. Johnson," THM; Johnson and Bennett, *Succeeding against the Odds*, 57.

19. Johnson and Bennett, *Succeeding against the Odds*, 199; "The Press," *Time*, October 23, 1950.

20. Hine, Introduction to *Black Chicago Renaissance*, xv.

21. Reed, *Rise of Chicago's Black Metropolis*, 28; McCammack, *Landscapes of Hope*, 23.

22. Semmes, *Regal Theater*, 24.

23. Drake and Cayton, *Black Metropolis*, 379.

24. *Census Data of the City of Chicago, 1934*, 684.

25. "John H. Johnson," THM; John and Bennett, *Succeeding against the Odds*, 74.

26. Travis, *Autobiography of Black Chicago*.

27. Bone and Courage, *Muse in Bronzeville*, 1.

28. Johnson and Bennett, *Succeeding against the Odds*, 61.

29. Schlabach, *Along the Streets*, ix; "Mapping Chicago's Literary History," *Chicago Review of Books*, December 20, 2017.

30. Hine, Introduction, xv.

31. Wright, *Native Son*.

32. Bone and Courage, *Muse in Bronzeville*, 7.

33. Schlabach, *Along the Streets*, x.

34. Johnson and Bennett, *Succeeding against the Odds*, 60–61.

35. Mullen, *Popular Fronts*, 75.

36. Olson, *Chicago Renaissance*, 247.

37. "Center of Attraction," *Chicago Defender*, January 23, 1932.

38. Burt, "Vivian Harsh," 236.

39. Johnson and Bennett, *Succeeding against the Odds*, 68.

40. "John H. Johnson," THM; Mahoney, *Douglas/Grand Boulevard*, 92.

41. Johnson and Bennett, *Succeeding against the Odds,* 67–68, 82.

42. Drake and Cayton, *Black Metropolis*, 463.

43. Quoted in Reed, *Rise of Chicago's Black Metropolis*, 71.

44. "Chicagoans Launch Mammoth Enterprise," *Chicago Defender*, January 17, 1920.

45. Randall, *History of the Development of Building Construction*, 78.

46. Reed, *Rise of Chicago's Black Metropolis*; "Liberty Life Insurance," *Chicago Defender*, May 5, 1923.

47. "Home of Liberty Life Insurance Company," New York Public Library Digital Collections, 1925, https://digitalcollections.nypl.org/items/510d47de-5178-a3d9-e040-e00a18064a99

48. Commission on Chicago Landmarks, "Black Metropolis–Bronzeville District," 27.

49. Puth, "Supreme Life," 9.

50. Johnson and Bennett, *Succeeding against the Odds*, 85.

51. "Our First Twenty Years," box 267, folder 4, CABP; Blakely and Shepard, *Earl B. Dickerson*, 167.

52. "Linking the Ages in Bronzeville," box 7, folder 15, EBD; Schlabach, *Along the Streets*, x.

53. Johnson and Bennett, *Succeeding against the Odds*, 96–97.

54. "John H. Johnson," THM.

55. B. Burns, *Nitty Gritty*, 31; "Recalling the Glory Days of *Reader's Digest*," *New York Times*, October 1, 2010.

56. "John H. Johnson," THM.

57. Blakely and Shepard, *Earl B. Dickerson*, 45; "Martin L. King Drive," reel 56, BPSI.

58. Johnson and Bennett, *Succeeding against the Odds*, 120.
59. Ibid., 91.
60. Michaeli, *Defender*, 256.
61. B. Burns, *Nitty Gritty*, 4, 9; West, "Ben Burns."
62. "Index," *Chicago Tribune*, September 9, 1945.
63. Johnson and Bennett, *Succeeding against the Odds*, 120; B. Burns, *Nitty Gritty*, 31.
64. Holloway, *Jim Crow Wisdom*, 56.
65. Hall, "Fenton Johnson," 220–21.
66. "Editorial Offices," *Bronzeman*, June 1933.
67. Robert S. Abbott, Successful Publisher, Enters Magazine Field," *Birmingham Reporter*, September 27, 1930.
68. "Introducing," *Negro Digest*, November 1942.
69. Green, *Selling the Race*, 138.
70. "Introducing."
71. Holloway, *Jim Crow Wisdom*, 43.
72. Hirsch, *Making the Second Ghetto*, 17.
73. Hall, "On Sale," 191.
74. Johnson and Bennett, *Succeeding against the Odds*, 125.
75. Green, *Selling the Race*, 138.
76. "Remembering John H. Johnson," *Jet*, August 29, 2005; "Mrs. Roosevelt Says," *Negro Digest*, December 1943.
77. "From the Editor," *Negro Digest*, July 1943.
78. "Negro Digest Publishing Co.," *Negro Digest*, January 1944.
79. Johnson and Bennett, *Succeeding against the Odds*, 134.
80. Ingham and Feldman, *African-American Business*, 373.
81. "Chicago Night Club Era Ends with Closing of Club DeLisa," *Jet*, March 6, 1958.
82. "East-West Star Dust," *Pittsburgh Courier*, August 19, 1944.
83. Johnson and Bennett, *Succeeding against the Odds*, 135.
84. "Introduction," *Life*, November 23, 1936.
85. Holloway, *Jim Crow Wisdom*, 63.
86. "Backstage," *Ebony*, November 1945.
87. "Backstage," *Ebony*, December 1945.
88. "Backstage," *Ebony*, October 1946.
89. Stange, "Photographs," 208.
90. "Backstage," *Ebony*, January 1946.
91. "Backstage," *Ebony*, March 1946.
92. Johnson and Bennett, *Succeeding against the Odds*, 165.
93. Hirsch, *Making the Second Ghetto*, 4.
94. "Backstage," *Ebony*, January 1946; "Backstage," *Ebony*, March 1946.
95. Commission on Chicago Landmarks, "Chicago Orphan Asylum," 6.
96. B. Burns, *Nitty Gritty*, 96.
97. Commission on Chicago Landmarks, "Chicago Orphan Asylum," 8–10.

98. Ibid., 22.

99. Knupfer, *Chicago Black Renaissance*, 34.

100. Jackson, *Indignant Generation*, 96.

101. Hricko, *Genesis of the Chicago Renaissance*, 121.

102. Green, *Selling the Race*, 132.

103. Olson, *Chicago Renaissance*, 247.

104. Knupfer, *Chicago Black Renaissance*, 40–41.

105. Commission on Chicago Landmarks, "Chicago Orphan Asylum," 26.

106. Bone and Courage, *Muse in Bronzeville*, 172.

107. Watson, "John H. Johnson," 235.

108. See box 2, folders 10–12, HRCP.

109. "Parkway House Sets Sights on Expansion," *Chicago Tribune*, March 10, 1963.

110. B. Burns, *Nitty Gritty*, 39.

111. Ibid., 46.

112. Jefferson, *Negroland*.

113. B. Burns, *Nitty Gritty*, 46.

114. Ibid., 6.

115. West, "Ben Burns."

116. Green, *Selling the Race*, 162.

117. "Backstage," *Ebony*, January 1947.

118. "Backstage," *Ebony*, November 1946; "Backstage," *Ebony*, December 1954.

119. B. Burns, *Nitty Gritty*, 90; Miller, *Chicago's South Side*.

120. "Backstage," *Ebony*, March 1946.

121. Johnson and Bennett, *Succeeding against the Odds*, 164; Allan Morrison to John Johnson, January 3, 1947, box 1, folder 1, AMMP.

122. "Biography," box 1, folder 1, AMMP; "Allan Morrison, 51," *New York Times*, May 24, 1968.

123. "Backstage," *Ebony*, August 1946; "Backstage," *Ebony*, November 1950.

124. "Backstage," *Ebony*, October 1946.

125. "Backstage," *Ebony*, November 1947.

126. "Backstage," *Ebony*, February 1948; "Backstage," *Ebony*, June 1948.

127. Chambers, *Madison Avenue*, 47.

128. Johnson and Bennett, *Succeeding against the Odds*, 193.

129. Green, *Selling the Race*, 15, 138.

130. "Armless Wonder," *Ebony*, November 1945.

131. "Backstage," *Ebony*, August 1947.

132. Drake and Cayton, *Black Metropolis*, 113.

133. Johnson and Bennett, *Succeeding against the Odds*, 198; B. Burns, *Nitty Gritty*, 111.

134. Tyre, *Chicago's Historic Prairie Avenue*, 26.

135. "The House," *Glessner House Museum*, https://www.glessnerhouse.org/the-house.

136. "Hursen," *Chicago Tribune*, February 24, 1929.

137. "Hursen," *Chicago Tribune*, February 23, 1913.

138. "Hursen," *Chicago Tribune*, March 31, 1929.

139. B. Burns, *Nitty Gritty*, 111.

140. Johnson and Bennett, *Succeeding against the Odds*, 199.

141. Drake and Cayton, *Black Metropolis*, 175.

142. Bachin, *Building the South Side*, 252.

143. "John H. Johnson," THM.

144. Johnson and Bennett, *Succeeding against the Odds*, 199; B. Burns, *Nitty Gritty*, 111.

145. "John H. Johnson," THM.

146. For more on the trickster archetype, see J. Roberts, *From Trickster to Badman*.

147. "Michigan Hoist Maker," *Ebony*, May 1955; "How Two 'Janitors' Bought White Bank," *Ebony*, June 1965.

148. "John H. Johnson," *Washington Post*, September 14, 1980.

149. "Chicago Success Story," box 2, folder 1, BBP; "Ten Negroes," box 150, folder 1, CABP.

150. "John H. Johnson."

151. "Hursen," *Chicago Tribune*, February 23, 1913.

152. "Backstage," *Ebony*, June 1949.

153. "Ebony Opens Its New Building," *Ebony*, October 1949.

154. "Backstage," *Ebony*, September 1949.

155. "*Ebony* Opens Its New Building."

156. Green, *Selling the Race*, 164; "Ebony," box 18, folder 1, SDPC.

157. "*Ebony* Opens Its New Building."

158. B. Burns, *Nitty Gritty*, 112.

159. "Poster," box 2, folder 3, BBP.

160. B. Burns, *Nitty Gritty*, 148; West, "Johnsonland," box 2, folder 7, BBP.

161. "Backstage," *Ebony*, July 1982.

162. Era Bell Thompson to John Johnson, February 18, 1952, box 1, EBTP; Era Bell Thompson to John Johnson, undated, box 1, EBTP; Era Bell Thompson to John Johnson, June 26, 1959, box 1, EBTP.

163. Cairns, *Front-Page Women Journalists, 1920–1950*, xiv.

164. Rooks, *Ladies' Pages*, 131.

165. "*Ebony* Opens Its New Building."

166. "Test Kitchen," *Ebony*, October 1949.

167. "Ebony," *Business Week*, March 22, 1952.

168. "Failure Is a Word I Don't Accept," box 22, folder 10, HWFP; "Publishing Company Operated by Blacks," box 2, folder 1, BBP.

169. Stange, "Photographs," 208.

170. Johnson and Bennett, *Succeeding against the Odds*, 156.

171. "Backstage," *Ebony*, August 1947.

172. Stange, "Photographs," 208.

173. "Ebony Opens Its New Building."

174. Johnson and Bennett, *Succeeding against the Odds*, 84.

175. "Johnny Johnson Introduces Jet," box 150, folder 1, CABP; "Why *Jet*?" *Jet*, November 1, 1951.

176. "Johnson Magic Casts Spell over Three More Magazines," *Ebony*, November 1955.

177. Johnson and Bennett, *Succeeding against the Odds*, 213; "Jet Society Editor," *Jet*, June 4, 1953; Masthead, *Jet*, April 16, 1953; "Tulsa Editor Joins Ebony," box 150, folder 1, CABP.

178. "Mouthpiece of 14 Million People," *Chicago Defender*, January 14, 1922; "Backstage," *Ebony*, August 1952.

179. "Backstage," *Ebony*, July 1953.

180. "The Story of EBONY," *Ebony*, November 1955.

181. "The Negro Press," *Time*, November 7, 1955.

182. "Backstage," *Ebony*, April 1956.

183. "Backstage," *Ebony*, March 1954.

Chapter 4. A Meeting Place for All the People

1. Robert Abbott to John Sengstacke, March 9, 1932, box 8, folder 32, ASFP; Robert Abbott to John Sengstacke, October 6, 1933, box 8, folder 32, ASFP.

2. "Robert Abbott," *Ebony*, June 1955.

3. "Special Tribune to Robert Abbott," *New York Age*, May 28, 1955.

4. "Ebony Opens Its New Building," *Ebony*, October 1949.

5. John Sengstacke to William Dawson, November 28, 1949, box 149, folder 1, CABP.

6. "Report of the President," box 103, folder 4, ASFP.

7. "Chicago Defender, Negro Weekly, to Become Daily," *Chicago Tribune*, December 3, 1955.

8. Ballantyne, "Reading the Newspaper," 52.

9. "Our Office," *Chicago Defender*, January 6, 1912.

10. "Annual Meeting of the Directors, 1933," box 11, folder 2, ASFP; Robert Abbott to John Sengstacke, April 17, 1934, box 8, folder 32, ASFP.

11. Robert Abbott to John Sengstacke, October 13, 1933, box 8, folder 32, ASFP.

12. Michaeli, *Defender*, 159–60.

13. "Notice to All Departments," box 11, folder 3, ASFP.

14. Michaeli, *Defender*, 206.

15. Inter-office communication, August 23, 1933, box 11, folder 2, ASFP.

16. Walker, "Promised Land," 25.

17. Whitaker, *Smoketown*; "Courier Dedicates New Plant," *Pittsburgh Courier*, December 14, 1929.

18. "Formal Opening of New Courier Staff Office," *Pittsburgh Courier*, April 29, 1939.

19. "Cortez Peters Scores in Chicago Demonstration," *Pittsburgh Courier*, August 12, 1939.

20. Waters, *American Diary*, 127.

21. Cairns, *Front-Page Women Journalists*, xiv.

22. "Stage Star Visits Defender Plant," *Chicago Defender*, August 22, 1939; "A Midget Song and Dance Star Visits Defender Office," *Chicago Defender*, August 12, 1939.

23. Waters, *American Diary*, 261–62.

24. Michaeli, *Defender*, 240–41.

25. "John Sengstacke, Abbott's Nephew, Replaces Widow as Head of Defender," *Chicago Defender*, February 7, 1942; "America's Black Press Lord," box 22, folder 8, ASFP.

26. Washburn, *Question of Sedition*, 90–91.

27. "Printers on Strike at Chicago Defender," *Chicago Tribune*, December 7, 1947.

28. Rice, *Chicago Defender*, 74; Carroll, *Race News*, 133.

29. Aiello, *Grapevine of the Black South*; Farrar, *Baltimore Afro-American*, 17.

30. Michaeli, *Defender*, 216.

31. "Unveil New Defender Family of 7 Papers," *Chicago Defender*, December 13, 1952.

32. Trodd, "Black Press," 451; "Defenderland," *Editor and Publisher*, April 26, 1952.

33. "Chicago Defender Honored on Its Golden Anniversary," *Chicago Defender*, December 3, 1955; "Fiftieth Anniversary Program," box 241, folder 27, ASFP.

34. "Announce Defender Daily," *Chicago Defender*, December 10, 1955.

35. Hirsch, *Making the Second Ghetto*, 17.

36. "Sengstacke Statement on Defender," *Chicago Defender*, December 10, 1955.

37. John Sengstacke to William Dawson, November 28, 1949, box 149, folder 1, CABP.

38. *One Tenth of a Nation.*

39. "Report of the President," box 103, folder 4, ASFP.

40. "Big Business among Blacks," *Phoenix Tribune*, November 12, 1921.

41. Carroll, *Race News*, 76.

42. "Looking Back," box 11, folder 7, ASFP.

43. "Daily Defender Makes Debut," *Chicago Defender*, February 11, 1956.

44. Michaeli, *Defender*, 352.

45. "1958 Corporate Structure," box 46, folder 1, ASFP.

46. Ibid.

47. "New Daily Meets Challenge," *Chicago Defender*, May 11, 1958.

48. "Bare $1,000,000 Expansion Plan," *Chicago Defender*, December 10, 1955.

49. "No Motor Row Like Chicago's," *Chicago Tribune*, February 6, 1910; Commission on Chicago Landmarks, "Motor Row District," 9.

50. Buerglener, "Selling Automobility," 165.

51. "Changes Are Many Along 'Motor Row,'" *Chicago Tribune*, January 29, 1911.

52. "Illinois Auto Club Buys Erie-Michigan Corner," *Chicago Tribune*, December 13, 1931; "Illinois Auto Club to Build on South Side," *Chicago Tribune*, December 9, 1934, 22; "Proposed Home for Illinois Automobile Club," *Chicago Tribune*, December 9, 1934.

53. "New Design for Illinois Automobile Club," *Chicago Tribune*, September 15, 1935.

54. "Auto Club Building Sold to Non-Profit Group," *Chicago Defender*, November 5, 1957.

55. "1958 Corporate Structure," box 46, folder 1, ASFP; "$1 Million Building Stake in Bitter Chicago Battle," *Chicago Defender*, July 19, 1958.

56. Michaeli, *Defender*, 353; "1958 Corporate Structure," box 46, folder 1, ASFP; "Building Plans," box 232, ASFP.

57. PACE Associates invoice, September 14, 1959, box 103, folder 15, ASFP; PACE Associates invoice, October 1, 1959, box 103, folder 15, ASFP.

58. "After 38 Years, Defender Moves," *Chicago Defender*, April 11, 1959.

59. "Defender Editorial Staff in New Building," *Chicago Defender*, February 8, 1960.

60. "Defender 'Moving Day' Started in March '59," *Chicago Defender*, May 7, 1960; "Pictorial Review of the Defender's 'Giant Step,'" *Chicago Defender*, May 7. 1960.

61. "An Old Friend Dresses Up," undated, box 104, folder 1, ASFP.

62. "Modern Equipment, Skill Aid Progress," *Chicago Defender*, May 7, 1960.

63. "The Negro Press," *Time*, November 7, 1955.

64. Washburn, *African American Newspaper*, 5.

65. "The National Scene," *Chicago Defender*, December 31, 1955; "Fading Market for Protest Organs," *The Crusader*, November 11, 1955.

66. "Come Along on a Tour of New Defender Plant," *Chicago Defender*, May 7, 1960.

67. "John H. Johnson," THM.

68. "1958 Corporate Structure," box 46, folder 1, ASFP.

69. "Opportunity, March 1929," box 18, folder 23, ASFP.

70. "Julius F. Taylor," *Chicago Defender*, May 19, 1934; "Dustin' off the News," *Chicago Defender*, April 16, 1938; Belles, "Black Press in Illinois," 348.

71. "Non-White Population Changes, 1950–1960," *Human Relations News of Chicago*, July 1961.

72. Bone and Courage, *Muse in Bronzeville*, 8.

73. Frazier, *Black Bourgeoisie*, 150.

74. "Backstage," *Ebony*, January 1947.

75. "Chicago Defender to Become a Daily Tabloid," *Plaindealer*, December 9, 1955.

76. Hayter, *Binga*; Cooley, *Moving Up, Moving Out*.

77. Weare, "Charles Clinton Spaulding," 167.

78. Johnson and Bennett, *Succeeding against the Odds*, 277.

79. Thomas Hayes to John Sengstacke, May 19, 1967, box 25, folder 6, ASFP.

80. Michaeli, *Defender*, 353; "Projected Operating Plans," box 46, folder 1, ASFP.

81. "Non-White Population Changes."

82. "Defender Expansion Plans for West Side Announced," *Chicago Defender*, April 6, 1963.

83. "Opportunity, March 1929," box 18, folder 23, ASFP.

84. A. Burns, *Storefront to Monument*, 5.

85. Snyder, *Making Black History*, 33.

86. Dagbovie, *Early Black History Movement*; Morris, *Carter G. Woodson*.

87. "What the People Say," *Chicago Defender*, February 24, 1934.

88. "Negro History and Literature," *Chicago Whip*, January 29, 1921.

89. Greene, *Selling Black History*, 171–72.

90. Rocksborough-Smith, *Black Public History*, 2.

91. Mullen, *Popular Fronts*, 80–82.

92. Gellman, *Death Blow to Jim Crow*, 60.

93. Mullen, *Popular Fronts*, 99.

94. Rocksborough-Smith, *Black Public History*, 53.

95. A. Burns, *Storefront to Monument*, 17.

96. "Ebony Opens Its New Building."

97. "Late Dr. Charles Johnson Is Named to 'Hall of Fame,'" *Atlanta World*, January 11, 1957.

98. "Ebony Establishes Hall of Fame," *The Crusader*, November 4, 1955.

99. "Ebony Hall of Fame," *Ebony*, November 1955.

100. "Ebony Hall of Fame," *Ebony*, February 1956.

101. "Ebony Hall of Fame," *Ebony*, February 1957; "Ebony Hall of Fame," *Ebony*, February 1958.

102. "Ebony Hall of Fame," *Ebony*, February 1956.

103. "Named to 'Hall of Fame,'" *Atlanta World*, January 11, 1957.

104. "Back to School Stay in School," box 263, CULR; "Backstage," *Ebony*, June 1969.

105. "Yesterday in Negro History," *Jet*, November 26, 1953; West, *Ebony Magazine*.

106. Rocksborough-Smith, *Black Public History*, 65.

107. "B. L. Leavell," *Chicago Tribune*, October 26, 1968.

108. "Presents Merit Awards at Emancipation Day Program," *Chicago Defender*, September 22, 1958.

109. A. Burns, *Storefront to Monument*, 16.

110. Rocksborough-Smith, *Black Public History*, 52.

111. "Ill. Auto Club Building Sold to Non-Profit Group," *Chicago Defender*, November 5, 1957.

112. "200 Meet with Defender Execs," *Chicago Defender*, March 9, 1959.

113. "Mostly about Women," *Chicago Defender*, December 20, 1958.

114. "Room Easily Available to Community Groups," *Chicago Defender*, May 7, 1960.

115. "Chicago Climaxes Brilliant Musical Year," *Chicago Defender*, August 14, 1959.

116. "Idlewilder's Tri-State Party Whirl Replete with Gala Fetes," *Chicago Defender*, May 21, 1960; "At Real Estate Broker's Wives Coffee Sip," *Chicago Defender*, October 20, 1960; "Hammonettes First Affair Is Success," *Chicago Defender*, April 27, 1960; "Housewives Association Meets in New Quarters," *Chicago Defender*, February 16, 1959; "Women to Fete Merchants at June 21 Dinner," *Chicago Tribune*, June 5, 1960.

117. "Idlewilder's Tri-State Party."

118. "Zetas Outline 3-Point Plan," *Chicago Defender*, September 22, 1962; "Defender's Modern Boulevard Room Popular," *Chicago Defender*, May 7, 1960.

119. "The Lee D. Jenkins Mark 20th Wedding Date," *Chicago Defender*, January 9, 1960; "On Stage," *Chicago Defender*, December 30, 1959.

120. "Defender's Modern Boulevard Room."

121. "An Old Friend Dresses Up," box 104, folder 1, ASFP.

122. Hirsch, *Making the Second Ghetto*, 65.

123. Wolcott, *Race, Riots*, 125; "$1 Million Building Stake."

124. "Defender Plays Host to 300 Ad Agency Representatives," *Chicago Defender*, May 16, 1960.

125. "Defender's Modern Boulevard Room."

126. "An Old Friend Dresses Up," box 104, folder 1, ASFP.

127. "Our Office."

128. "Backstage," *Ebony*, March 1946.

129. "Ebony Opens Its New Building."

130. "Tours Dispel Mystery of Negro Section," *Chicago Tribune*, March 13, 1955.

131. B. Burns, *Nitty Gritty*, 114.

132. "3A Class Visits the Defender," *Chicago Defender*, April 9, 1960; "High School Editors Are Defender Guests," *Chicago Defender*, November 11, 1961.

133. "Welcome to Chicago," *Chicago Defender*, August 22, 1959.

134. "Backstage," *Ebony*, July 1953.

135. Ericson, Reigert, and Åker, Introduction to *Media Houses*, 2.

136. "Backstage," *Ebony*, November 1975.

137. Wallace, *Media Capital*, 7.

138. "Publisher's Statement," *Ebony*, November 1975.

139. "Backstage," *Ebony*, January 1954.

140. "First Ten Years Are the Happiest," *Ebony*, November 1955.

141. "The Negro Press"; Rooks, *Ladies' Pages*; Haidarali, "Polishing Brown Diamonds."

142. "Advertisement," *New Journal and Guide*, November 18. 1950.

143. "Backstage," *Ebony*, January 1954.

144. "Female Impersonators," *Jet*, October 2, 1952; "Female Impersonators," *Ebony*, March 1948.

145. "Backstage," *Ebony*, January 1954.

146. Russell, "Color of Discipline"; Drexel, "Before Paris Burned," 134.

147. "Backstage," *Ebony*, July 1953.

148. "Student Group from Europe Will Tour City," *Chicago Tribune*, July 5, 1951; "Andre Bokwango," *Chicago Defender*, October 26, 1960; "50 Foreign Visitors Tour Defender Plant," *Chicago Defender*, January 3, 1962.

149. "First Ten Years."

150. "Letters," *Ebony*, December 1945.

151. "Backstage," *Ebony*, February 1953.

152. "Backstage," *Ebony*, February 1956.

153. "Backstage," *Ebony*, July 1953.

154. "Backstage," *Ebony*, June 1953.

155. Horne, *Rise and Fall*, 99.

156. Renda, *Taking Haiti*, 10.

157. "Inside Haiti," *Ebony*, January 1946.

158. Photographs 1–32, box 32, BBP; "Backstage," *Ebony*, February 1949.

159. Horne, *Rise and Fall*, 123.

160. "Haitian President Guest of White House," *Chicago Defender*, January 29, 1955.

161. "First Ten Years"; "JPC Guestbook," *Ebony*, November 1992; "Haiti Prexy Says U.S. Bias Will Be 'Bad Dream,'" *Jet*, February 17, 1955.

162. Thompson, "What Africans Think about Us," *Ebony*, February 1954.

163. "Dixie Governors Snub President Tubman," *Jet*, November 4, 1954; "First Ten Years."

164. Signed Portrait of John Johnson addressed to President Tubman, WTPC.

165. "Liberia Independence to be Marked Saturday," *Chicago Defender*, July 25, 1959; "Africans Visit Defender Plant," *Chicago Defender*, May 5, 1962; "800 Attend Brilliant Reception," *Chicago Defender*, August 4, 1962.

166. Johnson and Bennett, *Succeeding against the Odds*, 261; "Newsmen Accompany Nixon to Gold Coast Celebration," *Atlanta World*, March 12, 1957.

167. "Cover," *Jet*, July 31, 1958.

168. Meriwether, *Proudly We Can Be Africans*, 172.

169. "Nkrumah Dinner," box 241, folder 31, ASFP.

170. "Return of Saturday's Child," *Ebony*, October 1958; "Departing Nkrumah Tells U.S.," *Jet*, August 15, 1958.

171. "Toure Luncheon," box 241, folder 36, ASFP.

172. "African President Visits the South," *Ebony*, February 1960; "Guinea Strongman Toure on 1st U.S. Tour," *Jet*, November 5, 1959.

173. Blakely and Shepard, *Earl B. Dickerson*, 185.

174. "Founding Fathers," *Chicago Defender*, August 24, 1961; "Chicago Visit of Julius Momo Udochi," box 14, EBDP.

175. Von Eschen, *Race against Empire*, 8.

176. "Backstage," *Ebony*, February 1956.

177. Campbell, *Middle Passages*, 291.

178. "Backstage," *Ebony*, August 1994.

179. "South Africa," *Ebony*, July 1960.

180. Johnson and Bennett, *Succeeding against the Odds*, 199.

181. B. Burns, *Nitty Gritty*, 114.

182. Johnson and Bennett, *Succeeding against the Odds*, 259.

183. "President of Guinea in City," *Chicago Tribune*, October 31, 1959.

184. "Let My People Go," *Ebony*, April 1960.

Chapter 5. A House for the Struggle

1. "Backstage," *Ebony*, August 1954.

2. Ibid.

3. "After 38 Years, Defender Moves," *Chicago Defender*, April 11, 1959; Michaeli, *Defender*, 353.

4. Roberts and Klibanoff, *Race Beat*.

5. Michaeli, *Defender*, 335.

6. "1958 Corporate Structure," box 46, folder 1, ASFP.

7. Johnson and Bennett, *Succeeding against the Odds*, 287.

8. "Letters," *Ebony*, October 1954.

9. Michaeli, *Defender*, 173.

10. Reed, *Chicago NAACP*, 46.

11. CUL Annual Report, 1923, box 1, folder 5, CULR; CUL Annual Report, 1926, box 1, folder 6, CULR.

12. McMurry, *To Keep the Waters Troubled*, 273.

13. Undated memo, A-XVII-39, box 40, folder 472, CULR.

14. "Urban Renewal," box 2, folder 33, CULR; Hirsch, *Making the Second Ghetto*, 17.

15. "Why Our Proposed $100,000 Building," May 3, 1952, box 40, folder 472, CULR.

16. Undated memo, A-XVII-39, box 40, folder 472, CULR; "CUL Newsletter," box 7, folder 6, LBJP.

17. Alexander Allen to Sidney Williams, September 18, 1952, box 40, folder 472, CULR.

18. Sidney Williams to Mary Young, May 2, 1952, box 40, folder 472, CULR.

19. "Building Fund Chatty Letter #1," box 40, folder 472, CULR; "Building Fund Chatty Letter #2," box 40, folder 472, CULR; "Building Fund Chatty Letter #3," box 40, folder 472, CULR; "Building Fund Chatty Letter #4," box 40, folder 472, CULR.

20. Sidney Williams to Building Committee, undated, box 40, folder 476, CULR.

21. Strickland, *History of the Chicago Urban League*, 178, 185.

22. Ibid., 169–71.

23. "A New Look at Chicago's Boom," *Chicago Tribune*, September 25, 1955.

24. "Urban Renewal and the Negro in Chicago," box 2, folder 33, CULR.

25. Interview on WNDT-TV, New York City, May 28, 1963.

26. "John Sengstacke Greets President," *Chicago Defender*, June 12, 1948; Earl Dickerson to John Sengstacke, September 5, 1941, box 183, folder 2, ASFP.

27. Edwin Berry to John Sengstacke, December 8, 1958, box 128, folder 1526, CULR.

28. "Chicago Urban League Overview, Dec. 1958," box 7, folder 112, CULR; "CUL Newsletter," box 7, folder 6, LBJP.

29. John Sengstacke to Edwin Berry, June 6, 1960, box 128, folder 1526, CULR.

30. Strickland, *History of the Chicago Urban League*, 205.

31. "Urban League Aims," *Chicago Tribune*, October 8, 1955, 12; "Urban League Raises $77,135 in Fund Drive," *Chicago Tribune*, July 23, 1956.

32. "Negro Group's Stay in School Drive Starts," *Chicago Tribune*, August 25, 1957; "Urban League Finds Negro Job Answers," *Chicago Tribune*, May 12, 1960; "Sets Kickoff for League Members," *Chicago Defender*, June 11, 1960.

33. "'Opportunity Center' Seeking Negro College Grads," *Chicago Defender*, October 10, 1964.

34. "Babysitting for LBJ Vote," *Chicago Defender*, November 3, 1964.

35. "Mayor Daley Hits Back in Urban League Attack," *Chicago Tribune*, September 5, 1957.

36. "Roles of 2 Negro Groups Confuse Public," *Chicago Tribune*, January 5, 1958.

37. "North's Hottest Fight for Integration," *Ebony*, March 1962.

38. "Finds Community Aids Youth Guidance Project," *Chicago Defender*, November 25, 1959.

39. "Fight against Bias Gaining, League Told," *Chicago Defender*, April 26, 1960; "Louis Martin Plays Role in Civic Affairs," *Chicago Tribune*, June 1, 1957; CUL Minutes, February 17, 1958, box 4, folder 503, CULR.

40. "Negro Housing Is Topic for Conference," *Chicago Tribune*, November 15, 1964; Michaeli, *Defender*, 383–84.

41. "Willis Defends Jim Crow School Policy," *Chicago Defender*, December 7, 1961; "Mississippi and the Law," *Chicago Defender*, July 19, 1961.

42. "Launch Drive to Integrate City Housing," *Chicago Tribune*, January 3, 1960.

43. "A Stone's Throw," *Chicago Defender*, August 24, 1963; Michaeli, *Defender*, 378.

44. "Announce Formation of New Super-Militant Group," *Jet*, May 7, 1964.

45. "ACT Schedules 2 Chicago Rallies," *Chicago Defender*, June 24, 1964; "Lawrence A. Landry," *Chicago Tribune*, June 8, 1997.

46. "$1200 Gift for League's Drive," *Chicago Defender*, July 9, 1960.

47. "Chicago Urban League Rebuilds from Ashes," *Chicago Defender*, February 11, 1961.

48. "League Gets Bomb Threat," *Chicago Defender*, October 16, 1958.

49. "Inter-Office Memorandum," May 21, 1959, box 128, folder 1526, CULR.

50. "Schedule of Rentals," undated, box 128, folder 1526, CULR.

51. "Building Memorandum," October 4, 1960, box 40, folder 479, CULR.

52. Strickland, *History of the Chicago Urban League*, 256.

53. Nelson Jackson to Program Department, July 19, 1962, box 317, folder 3331, CULR.

54. Edwin Berry to Frank Keller, March 31, 1960, box 40, folder 478, CULR.

55. "League Moves," *Chicago Tribune*, July 19, 1964.

56. Kreiling, "Commercialization of the Black Press," 181; "Phylon Profile, 1947," box 1, folder 1, ASFP.

57. "Opportunities," *Chicago Defender*, April 3, 1915.

58. For a more in-depth discussion of the *Defender*'s labor politics, see Bekken, "Relations of Production."

59. Michaeli, *Defender*, 282–83.

60. "Corporate Structure, 1958," box 46, folder 1, ASFP.

61. Bekken, "Relations of Production."

62. "Reinstate 33 Editorial Aids. Defender Is Told," *Chicago Tribune*, December 14, 1961.

63. "NLRB Orders Defender to Rehire 58 Strikers," box 149, folder 10, CABP.

64. "The Chicago Defender Story," box 149, folder 8, CABP; Berger, *Seeing through Race*, 6.

65. "U.S. Court Upholds Defender," *Chicago Defender*, April 16, 1964.

66. Johnson and Bennett, *Succeeding against the Odds*, 157.

67. Wald, *Crossing the Line*, 126.

68. Holloway, *Jim Crow Wisdom*, 64.

69. Roberts and Klibanoff, *Race Beat*, 79.

70. Booker, *Shocking the Conscience*, 84.

71. Tyson, *Blood of Emmett Till*, 75; "Nation Horrified by Murder of Kidnaped Chicago Youth," *Jet*, September 15, 1955.

72. "Backstage," *Ebony*, June 1966.

73. Booker, *Shocking the Conscience*, 3.

74. "Southern Trip," box 4, folder 4, BBP.

75. "Backstage," *Ebony*, November 1954.

76. "The New Fighting South," *Ebony*, August 1955.

77. "NAACP's New Leader," *Ebony*, July 1955; "First Lady of Little Rock," *Ebony*, September 1958.

78. "The King Plan for Freedom," *Ebony*, July 1956; "My Trip to the Land of Gandhi," *Ebony*, July 1959.

79. "Daring Black Leaders," box 3, RNJP.

80. "'Segregation' in Chicago Hit by Rev. King," *Chicago Tribune*, May 28, 1963.

81. "Backstage," *Ebony*, April 1956.

82. Aiello, *Grapevine of the Black South*.

83. Forman, *Making of Black Revolutionaries*, 219.

84. Booker, *Shocking the Conscience*, 84.

85. Johnson and Bennett, *Succeeding against the Odds*, 221.

86. "Backstage," *Ebony*, April 1956.

87. Booker, *Shocking the Conscience*, 86, 248.

88. "Rudolph Bing, John H. Johnson Get Freedom Awards," *Jet*, December 4, 1958.

89. John Johnson to Claude Barnett, May 14, 1960, box 150, folder 1, CABP.

90. Quoted in Roberts and Klibanoff, *Race Beat*, 79.

91. "NAACP Honors Champagne, Caviar and Chitt'lins," *Los Angeles Tribune*, November 21, 1958.

92. "Negro Digest Fans Are a Persistent Breed," box 15, folder 20, HWFP; Hall, "On Sale," 195.

93. Hoyt Fuller to John Johnson, February 12, 1957, box 15, folder 20, HWFP; "Unpublished Autobiography," box 14, folder 31, HWFP.

94. Hoyt Fuller to Otto, February 14, 1961, box 2, folder 28, HWFP.

95. Hoyt Fuller to John Johnson, undated, box 15, folder 20, HWFP.

96. Fenderson, *Building the Black Arts Movement*.

97. "A Matter of Time," *Negro Digest*, March 1962; "Strike," *Negro Digest*, April 1962; "The Black Anglo-Saxons," *Negro Digest*, May 1962.

98. "Editor's Notes," *Black World*, May 1970.

99. Hoyt Fuller to David Llorens, November 1965, box 16, folder 14, HWFP.

100. Carroll, *Race News*, 177.

101. Hoyt Fuller to John Johnson, December 2, 1974, box 22, folder 10, HWFP.

102. "JPC-iana," box 22, folder 10, HWFP.

103. Johnson and Bennett, *Succeeding against the Odds*, 120.

104. "*Ebony* Opens Its New Building," *Ebony*, October 1949.

105. "20 Years of EBONY," *Ebony*, November 1965.

106. Hoyt Fuller to Otto, October 1, 1962, box 2, folder 28, HWFP; Hoyt Fuller to Cloyte Murdock, March 20, 1962, box 2, folder 1, HWFP.

107. "Failure Is a Word I Don't Accept," box 22, folder 10, HWFP.

108. "JPC-iana," box 22, folder 10, HWFP.

109. "The Toughest Bosses in America," *Fortune*, August 1984.

110. Green, *Selling the Race*, 160.

111. "Failure Is a Word I Don't Accept," box 22, folder 10, HWFP; "Monroe Anderson," THM.

112. "The One and Only," *N'Digo*, November 6, 1997.

113. "Backstage," *Ebony*, March 1972, 28; "JPC Editorial Staff," box 15, folder 21, HWFP; Hoyt Fuller to LaDoris Foster, December 22, 1971, box 22, folder 11, HWFP; Hoyt Fuller to John Johnson, June 18, 1962, box 5, folder 16, HWFP.

114. Hoyt Fuller to Otto, October 1, 1962, box 2, folder 28, HWFP.

115. Hoyt Fuller to John Johnson, May 26, 1965, box 22, folder 23, HWFP.

116. Hoyt Fuller to John Johnson, August 6, 1968, box 15, folder 20, HWFP.

117. "JPC-iana," box 22, folder 10, HWFP; Hoyt Fuller to John Johnson, August 7, 1975, box 22, folder 10, HWFP.

118. Fenderson, *Building the Black Arts Movement*, 86–87.

119. Smethurst, *Black Arts Movement*, 208; Tinson, *Radical Intellect*.

120. Richard Giles to Allan Morrison, August 23, 1946, box 1, folder 2, AMP; Johnson and Bennett, *Succeeding against the Odds*, 240; Raiford, *Imprisoned in a Luminous Glare*, 113.

121. "Lerone Bennett: Social Historian," box 1, LBP.

122. West, *Ebony Magazine*.

123. "Backstage," *Ebony*, March 1963, 23.

124. Brown, "Souled Out," 116.

125. "Two Busy Writers Who Are Also 'Real,'" *Negro Digest*, December 1965.

126. "School Segregation Up North," *Ebony*, June 1962.

127. "Letters," *Ebony*, April 1976.

128. "Publisher's Statement," *Ebony*, August 1965; "From Materialism to Militancy," *Philadelphia Tribune*, December 4, 1965.

129. Bates, *Long Shadow of Little Rock*, 92.

130. "Now I Can Work in Peace," *Chicago Defender*, September 16, 1957; "Alex Wilson New Editor of *Defender*," *Chicago Defender*, February 28, 1959.

131. Michaeli, *Defender*, 355; "Alex Wilson, *Defender* Editor-in-Chief, Dies," *Chicago Defender*, October 12, 1960.

132. "Sengstacke Names White Editor," box 149, folder 9, CABP.

133. B. Burns, *Nitty Gritty*, 211.

134. Ben Burns to Enoch Waters, August 1, 1962, box 149, folder 8, CABP.

135. B. Burns, *Nitty Gritty*, 215.

136. "Negro Firm Faced Integration Difficulty," box 2, folder 1, BBP.

137. Ibid.

138. "Chicago's Other Paper," *Southern Illinoisan*, October 20, 1963.

139. Stone, *Tell It Like It Is*; D. Jackson, "Outspoken Mr. Stone," 38.

140. "A Stone's Throw," *Chicago Defender*, May 4, 1964.

141. "A Stone's Throw," *Chicago Defender*, March 14, 1964.

142. "A Stone's Throw," *Chicago Defender*, April 2, 1964.

143. Michaeli, *Defender*, 392.

144. "Feels Defender Has Biased Political Views," *Chicago Defender*, October 19, 1964.

145. Author interview with John Woodford, June 21, 2016.

146. Woodford, "Messaging the Blackman," 4.

147. Ibid., 1.

148. "Negroes in 'The Nam,'" *Ebony*, August 1968.

149. Woodford, "Messaging the Blackman," 6; "Manifesto," box 15, folder 20, HWFP.

150. "Manifesto," box 3, RNJP.

151. "Toughest Bosses in America."

152. Carroll, *Race News*, 153.

153. The publication's original name was *Mr. Muhammad Speaks*. Masthead, *Mr. Muhammad Speaks*, May 1960.

154. Hussain, "Dreaming Differently," 321.

155. J. Rhodes, "Black Press," 295.

156. Stanley, "Dan Burley," 143–47.

157. "Tom Picou," box 8, folder 1, BEAP.

158. S. Williams, *Word Warrior*, 117.

159. Woodford, "Messaging the Blackman."

160. "The Enduring Influence of the Black Panther Party," *Columbia Journalism Review*, August 14, 2019.

161. Commission on Chicago Landmarks, "West Town State Bank Building," 5; J. Williams, *From the Bullet to the Ballot*, 61.

162. Reed, *Depression Comes to the South Side*, 69.

163. Metz Lochard to W.E.B Du Bois, September 11, 1950, WEBP.

164. Carroll, *Race News*, 127, 154.

165. "On Life in the Sudan," *Muhammad Speaks*, August 29, 1969.

166. "Backstage," *Ebony*, October 1964.

167. Farrar, "Black Press," 239; "Muhammad Exhorts Blacks to Buy Chicago's South Side," *Jet*, March 16, 1972.

168. Hussain, "Radical Black Media," 348.

169. "Muhammad Speaks Building," *Muhammad Speaks*, November 7, 1969.

170. "Progress," *Muhammad Speaks*, November 7, 1969.

171. J. Rhodes, "Black Press," 287.

172. "Black Artists Picket Ebony," *Chicago Defender*, December 31, 1969.

173. "Chicago's Other Paper," *Southern Illinoisan*, October 20, 1963

174. "Sengstacke Expands Chi Daily Defender," *Pittsburgh Courier*, October 31, 1964.

175. Michaeli, *Defender*, 392.

176. "The People Speak," *Chicago Defender*, October 15, 1964.

177. Craig, *Ain't I a Beauty Queen?* 137.

178. "Is *Ebony* a Negro Magazine?" *Liberator*, October-November 1965.

179. Martindale, "Women in the Movement," 358.

180. "20 Years of *Ebony*," *Ebony*, November 1965.

181. "Is Ebony Killing Black Women?" *Liberator*, March 1966.

182. Tinson, *Radical Intellect*, 96.

183. "The Natural Look," *Ebony*, June 1966.

184. "National Hotline," *Pittsburgh Courier*, March 29, 1969; "Changing of the Guard," *Ebony*, March 1969.

185. "Blacks Object to Editorial Line of Ebony," *Los Angeles Times*, December 31, 1969; "Black Artists Picket."

186. "Ebony, Jet Hit," *Chicago Daily News*, December 30, 1969.

187. "The Year in Perspective," *Baltimore Sun*, January 1, 1970.

188. "Ebony Chief to Review Policies," *Chicago Daily News,* January 2, 1970.

189. "Black Artists Picket."

190. "Black Don Lee," *Ebony*, March 1969.

191. Hooper, *Art of Work*, 10.

192. Fenderson, *Building the Black Arts Movement*, 17.

193. "Black Artists Picket."

194. "The Long Journey to Wealth," *Chicago Daily News*, August 9, 1973.

195. "Felicitations to 'Ebony,'" *The Crisis*, December 1965.

196. "*Ebony* Chief to Review Policies."

Chapter 6. A Poem in Marble and Glass

1. "Daley Lauds Publisher at Ribbon-Cutting Fete," *Chicago Defender*, May 17, 1972.

2. Johnson and Bennett, *Succeeding against the Odds*, 313.

3. "New JPC Building Dedicated," *Jet*, June 1, 1972.

4. Johnson and Bennett, *Succeeding against the Odds*, 287; Roberts and Klibanoff, *Race Beat*, 79.

5. "Is Ebony a Negro Magazine?" *Liberator*, October-November 1965.

6. "The Black Revolution," *Ebony*, August 1969; "Which Way Black America?" *Ebony*, August 1970.

7. Johnson and Bennett, *Succeeding against the Odds*, 314; "*Ebony* Magazine's New Home," *Ebony*, September 1972.

8. "In Memoriam," *The Root*, November 21, 2010.

9. "Ebony Lavishes $8 Million on New Building," *San Francisco Sun Reporter*, October 14, 1972.

10. "Ebony Opens Its New Building," *Ebony*, October 1949; "Backstage," *Ebony*, March 1954.

11. Johnson and Bennett, *Succeeding against the Odds*, 306.

12. "Daley, Victor, Maps Chicago's Renewal," *New York Times*, April 9, 1959.

13. Johnson and Bennett, *Succeeding against the Odds*, 306.

14. "Corner Stone of Largest Hotel in World Laid," *Chicago Tribune*, March 17, 1926.

15. "Heartbreak Hotel," *Chicago*, August 2006.

16. "Stevens Hotel Gets New Name," *New York Times*, November 1, 1951.

17. Johnson and Bennett, *Succeeding against the Odds*, 306–307.

18. "How to Build a Home," *Ebony*, March 1949; "Negro Architect Builds Sinatra Home," *Ebony*, January 1957.

19. "Georgia Louise Harris Brown," *Washington Post*, September 30, 1999.

20. "Black Architects," *Ebony*, July 1983; "Wendell Campbell," THM.

21. "At Home in Chatham," *New City Design*, November 19, 2015.

22. "Ill. Tech Honors Several S.W. Side Students," *Chicago Tribune*, June 13, 1948; "John W. Moutoussamy," December 28, 1983, Art Institute of Chicago.

23. "Architect John Moutoussamy," *Chicago Tribune*, May 9, 1995.

24. PACE Associates invoice, September 14, 1959, box 103, folder 15, ASFP.

25. Commission on Chicago Landmarks, "Johnson Publishing Company Building," October 5, 2017.

26. "T. K Lawless Housing Complex Is Dedicated," *Chicago Defender*, June 22, 1967; "Begin $10 Million T. K Lawless Housing Complex in Chicago," *Jet*, July 6, 1967.

27. "Groundbreaking Set Today for Englewood Project," *Chicago Defender*, November 14, 1967.

28. Art Institute of Chicago, "John W. Moutoussamy."

29. Johnson and Bennett, *Succeeding against the Odds*, 307.

30. "Ebony Ad Lineage Climbs 10.9%," box 19, folder 7, BBP; "Ebony Magazine," box 2, folder 2, BBP.

31. "Soil Testing Services," August 1, 1969, JWMP.

32. Johnson and Bennett, *Succeeding against the Odds*, 308; "Corbetta Construction Company," February 2, 1970, JWMP.

33. "Strike Halts Big Builders," *Chicago Tribune*, March 10, 1970; "Corbetta Construction Company," February 20, 1970, JWMP.

34. "A New Look at Chicago's Boom," *Chicago Tribune*, September 25, 1955.

35. "Downtown Invasion Continues," *Chicago Tribune*, September 18, 1960; Commission on Chicago Landmarks, "Essex Inn," December 1, 2016.

36. "*Ebony* Magazine's New Home."

37. Commission on Chicago Landmarks, "Johnson Publishing Company Building."

38. Art Institute of Chicago, "John W. Moutoussamy."

39. Commission on Chicago Landmarks, "Johnson Publishing Company Building."

40. For a primer on Chicago Brutalism, see http://chicagobrutalism.com.

41. Commission on Chicago Landmarks, "Johnson Publishing Company Building."

42. "*Ebony* Magazine's New Home."

43. Wallace, *Media Capital*, 143–44.

44. Gardner, *Black Print Unbound*, 62; A. Burns, *Storefront to Monument*, 5.

45. The concept of Jacob's ladder has been incorporated into more recent Black architectural designs, such as the Harvey B. Gantt Center for African-American Arts and Culture in Charlotte, North Carolina. "Harvey B. Gantt Center," *Architect*, November 30, 2012.

46. "Climbin' Jacob's Ladder," *Freedomways*, Winter 1969.

47. "Chicago's Historic JPC Building Goes Up for Sale," *Chicago Crusader*, November 22, 2010.

48. Hale, "Black as Folk," 127.

49. Singh, Introduction to *Climbin' Jacob's Ladder*, 7.

50. Mitchell, *Crisis of the African-American Architect*, 110.

51. Art Institute of Chicago, "John W. Moutoussamy."

52. *"Ebony* Magazine's New Home."

53. Cygelman, *Arthur Elrod*; "The Life and Happy Times of Arthur Elrod," *Los Angeles Times*, April 21, 1974.

54. Johnson and Bennett, *Succeeding Against the Odds*, 254–55.

55. Pruter, *Doowop*, 12.

56. Johnson and Bennett, *Succeeding against the Odds*, 309.

57. Birmingham, *Certain People*; "Architectural Digest," series 1, box C, HCB-AEA.

58. "New Office Building," box 2, folder 1, BBP.

59. *"Ebony* Magazine's New Home."

60. "Backstage," *Ebony*, January 1973.

61. "John H. Johnson," THM.

62. *"Ebony* Magazine's New Home."

63. "Salutatory," *Broad Ax*, July 15, 1899.

64. "Four Foundations Team Up to Buy the Historic Archives of *Ebony* Magazine," *Artnet*, July 25, 2019.

65. "Publisher Awarded Spingarn Medal," *Crisis*, August-September 1966.

66. "Ebony Magazine's Iconic Test Kitchen," *Chicago Tribune*, May 21, 2019.

67. "Plush Suite for Publisher," box 2, folder 1, BBP.

68. Reed, *Rise of Chicago's Black Metropolis*, 72; "Tearing Up a King's Castle," *Chicago Crusader*, November 20, 2017.

69. "In Memoriam"; "One More Thing on the Ebony/Jet Building," *WBEZ Chicago*, November 24, 2010.

70. "The Modern Spirits of Ebony and Jet," *New York Times*, December 3, 2015; "David Hartt, Stray Light," *MCA Chicago*, 2011, https://mcachicago.org/Exhibitions/2011/David-Hartt

71. Gayle, *Black Aesthetic*.

72. Smethurst, *Black Arts Movement*.

73. Neal, "Black Arts Movement," 29–30.

74. Smethurst, *Black Arts Movement*, 208.

75. "Any Day Now," *Ebony*, August 1969.

76. "Cover," *Ebony*, August 1969.

77. *"Ebony* Magazine's New Home"; Duberman, *Howard Zinn*, 73.

78. Hoyt Fuller to John Johnson, April 15, 1970, box 21, folder 17, HWFP; Hoyt Fuller to John Johnson, April 14, 1972, box 15, folder 22, HWFP; Hoyt Fuller to John Johnson, September 23, 1973, box 21, folder 18, HWFP.

79. "Afro-American Militants in Africa," *Black World*, February 1972; "Tanzania," *Black World*, March 1972.

80. "Black Cultural Nationalism," *Negro World*, January 1968.

81. *"Ebony* Magazine's New Home."

82. "*Ebony* Opens Its New Building," *Ebony*, October 1949.

83. Herbert Temple to Robert Blackburn, September 23, 1971, box 21, folder 19, HWFP; Hoyt Fuller to Edward Spriggs, September 10, 1971, box 21, folder 19, HWFP.

84. "The JPC Art Collection," box 15, folder 20, HWFP.

85. "JPC Art Collection Photopak," box 17, folder 8, LBJP.

86. "Swann Auctions Johnson Publishing Art," *Culture Type*, February 18, 2020.

87. "*Ebony* Magazine's New Home."

88. "Backstage," *Ebony*, September 1972.

89. Stange, "Photographs," 208.

90. "*Ebony* Magazine's New Home."

91. "Backstage," *Ebony*, September 1972.

92. Green, *Selling the Race*, 15.

93. "JPC-iana," box 22, folder 10, HWFP.

94. "Ebony at 50," *Chicago Tribune*, March 19, 1995.

95. "Failure Is a Word I Don't Accept," box 22, folder 10, HWFP.

96. Ibid.

97. "*Ebony* Magazine's New Home."

98. "Monroe Anderson," THM; "The Toughest Bosses in America," *Fortune*, August 1984.

99. "Backstage," *Ebony*, March 1972.

100. "John H. Johnson," *Washington Post*, September 14, 1980.

101. Sewell, "Opening the Boundaries," 72.

102. "Soul Survivor," *WBEZ*, January 14, 2013.

103. Georges' work for the photo essay was supplemented by contributions from staff photographers Isaac Sutton and G. Marshall Wilson. "Backstage," *Ebony*, November 1972.

104. "Backstage," *Ebony*, December 1970.

105. Johnson and Bennett, *Succeeding against the Odds*, 312.

106. Masthead, *Jet*, December 16, 1971; "Official Opening Ceremonies," box 15, folder 20, HWFP.

107. For more on Bennett and Johnson's relationship, see West, *Ebony Magazine*.

108. "New JPC Building Dedicated."

109. Ibid.

110. "Eight Million Dollar Home," *Los Angeles Sentinel*, October 5, 1972; "Johnson Building Debuts," *Pittsburgh Courier*, May 27, 1972.

111. "Black Journal Press Release," box 2, folder 2, BBP.

112. "Success Story," box 2, folder 2, BBP.

113. "New JPC Building Dedicated."

114. "New Office Building," box 2, folder 1, BBP.

115. "Striking Home for Johnson Publishing," box 2, folder 1, BBP.

116. Ibid.

117. "New Office Building," box 2, folder 1, BBP.

118. "Johnson's Office," box 2, folder 1, BBP.

119. "Interior Design," series 1, box C, HCB-AEA.

120. "Letters," *Ebony*, November 1972.

121. "Letters," *Ebony*, December 1972.

122. "New JPC Building Dedicated."

123. "The Top 100," *Black Enterprise*, June 1973.

124. "Chief of Ebony Named Publisher of the Year," *New York Times*, August 16, 1972.

125. "Johnny Johnson Does It Again," *New York Amsterdam News*, October 28, 1972.

126. Johnson and Bennett, *Succeeding against the Odds*, 324–26.

127. "John H. Johnson," THM.

128. Weems, *Business in Black and White*, 6.

129. For more on Black Power's philosophical diversity, see Joseph, *Black Power Movement*; Farmer, *Remaking Black Power*.

130. Weems, *Business in Black and White*, 120.

131. "New Group Here Attacks Nixon's Black Capitalism," *Chicago Defender*, January 18, 1969.

132. "Explaining OMBE," *Chicago Defender*, April 29, 1972.

133. James Brown to Bob Johnson, November 27, 1973, box 3, RNJP.

134. "Ebony Lavishes $8 Million."

135. "Letters," *Ebony*, December 1972.

136. "Backstage," *Ebony*, May 1972.

137. "Backstage," *Ebony*, June 1972; "Backstage," *Ebony*, August 1972.

138. "JPC Art Collection."

139. "Backstage," *Ebony*, April 1974.

140. Author correspondence with Charles Whitaker.

141. "White Kids in a Black World," box 2, folder 1, BBP.

142. "Johnson's Office: EBONY Superpad," box 2, folder 1, BBP.

143. "Johnson's Office," box 2, folder 1, BBP.

144. "Ebony Chief Aware of Poverty," box 2, folder 2, BBP.

145. Biles, "Rise and Fall of Soul City," 52.

146. Baradaran, *Color of Money*, 178–79.

147. "Johnson Shows 'Exhibit A,'" *Chicago Tribune*, May 17, 1972.

148. "Daley Lauds Publisher at Ribbon-Cutting Fete," *Chicago Defender*, May 17, 1972.

149. Haas, *Assassination of Fred Hampton*, 100.

150. Johnson and Bennett, *Succeeding against the Odds*, 315.

151. "Johnson Backs Daley," *Chicago Defender*, April 5, 1971.

152. "Chicago," *Black Enterprise*, May 1987; "Top Black Companies Choose Chicago First," *Chicago Daily News*, June 23, 1973.

153. Street, *Racial Oppression*, 121.

154. "Ebony Chief Aware of Poverty," box 2, folder 2, BBP.

155. "Worker, 77, Falls, Dies," *Chicago Defender*, July 30, 1969.

156. "Partners Make It Big in Business," *Chicago Defender*, March 27, 1971;

"Southside Oil Firm a Success," *Chicago Defender*, October 5, 1970; "Losing Comes Naturally," *Chicago Defender*, February 5, 1970.

157. "Ribbon Cutting," *Chicago Tribune*, March 15, 1970; "New Black-Owned Supermarket," *Chicago Defender*, February 21, 1970.

158. "Resident-Owned Grocery to Open," *Chicago Tribune*, February 22, 1970; "Jet Corporation Rises from Riot-Torn Streets," *Chicago Tribune*, September 24, 1970.

Conclusion

1. "Backstage," *Ebony*, November 1975.

2. "Backstage," *Ebony*, September 1974; "The B.E. 100," *Black Enterprise*, June 1975.

3. "The First 30 Years," *Ebony*, November 1975; "Washington Notebook," *Ebony*, November 1975.

4. "Abbott and History," *Chicago Defender*, May 5, 1975.

5. "5,000 Inspect *Defender*'s New Plant," *Chicago Defender*, May 14, 1921; "John Sengstacke," BJOHP.

6. "Defender Named Historic Site in Journalism," *Chicago Tribune*, May 6, 1975; "Journalist Society Honors Defender," *Chicago Tribune*, April 16, 1975.

7. "Miscellaneous Musings," *Chicago Defender*, March 26, 1910.

8. "Chicago Defender Now Nearing Its 30th Birthday," *Chicago Defender*, April 6, 1935.

9. Sandburg, *Chicago Race Riots*, 52.

10. "Dice Rattle Unheeded by Newspaper," *Chicago Whip*, December 19, 1922.

11. *Intercollegian Wonder Book*, 214; Wallace, *Media Building*, 3.

12. Baldwin, *Chicago's New Negroes*, 23–25; Trodd, "Black Press," 451.

13. "The Negro Press," *Time*, November 7, 1955; John Sengstacke to William Dawson, November 28, 1949, CABP.

14. "Abbott Spirit Strong," *Chicago Defender*, May 14, 1955.

15. *One Tenth of a Nation*.

16. "John H. Johnson," THM.

17. Wallace, *Media Capital*, 5.

18. "Our Office," *Chicago Defender*, January 6, 1912; "First Ten Years Are the Happiest," *Ebony*, November 1955.

19. Ward, "Black Press in Crisis," 34.

20. Michaeli, *Defender*, 472.

21. "Journalist Society Honors Defender."

22. Commission on Chicago Landmarks, "Johnson Publishing Company Building."

23. "Legacy on the Line," *Chicago Business*, June 22, 2009.

24. "Johnson Publishing Sells Historic Headquarters," *The Root*, November 16, 2010.

25. "Tearing Up a King's Castle," *Chicago Crusader*, November 20, 2017; "Johnson Publishing Company Files for Bankruptcy," *Washington Post*, April 10, 2019.

26. "Battered Bronzeville Looks to Future with Hope," *Chicago Tribune*, June 8, 1994.

27. Michaeli, *Defender*, 497.

28. "Black Chicago Fights to Save Historic *Ebony* Building," *Los Angeles Sentinel*, March 10, 2017.

29. "Brickbats Fired at City from Ruins," *Chicago Tribune*, April 28, 1984.

30. "A Missed Anniversary," *Chicago Crusader*, August 2, 2018.

31. "Back Home to Bronzeville," *Chicago Tribune*, May 27, 2009.

Bibliography

Archival Collections

Abbott-Sengstacke Family Papers, Vivian G. Harsh Research Collection of Afro-American History and Literature, Woodson Regional Library, Chicago Public Library, Chicago, Illinois

Allan Malcolm Morrison Papers, Schomburg Center for Research in Black Culture, Manuscripts, Archives, and Rare Books Division, New York Public Library, New York, New York

Barbara E. Allen Papers, Vivian G. Harsh Research Collection of Afro-American History and Literature, Woodson Regional Library, Chicago Public Library, Chicago, Illinois

Black Journalists Oral History Project, Columbia Center for Oral History, Columbia University, New York

Ben Burns Papers, Vivian G. Harsh Research Collection of Afro-American History and Literature, Woodson Regional Library, Chicago Public Library, Chicago, Illinois

Chicago Building Permit Street Index, University of Illinois–Chicago, Illinois

Chicago Urban League Records, Special Collections and University Archives, University of Illinois–Chicago, Chicago, Illinois

Claude A. Barnett Papers, Research Center, Chicago History Museum, Chicago, Illinois

Earl B. Dickerson Papers, Vivian G. Harsh Research Collection of Afro-American History and Literature, Woodson Regional Library, Chicago Public Library, Chicago, Illinois

Era Bell Thompson Papers, Vivian G. Harsh Research Collection of Afro-American History and Literature, Woodson Regional Library, Chicago Public Library, Chicago, Illinois

Harold C. Broderick / Arthur Elrod Associates Inc. Collection, The Lorraine Boccardo Archive Study Center, Palm Springs Art Museum, Palm Springs, California

The History Makers, Moving Image Research Center, Library of Congress, Washington, DC

Horace R. Cayton Papers, Vivian G. Harsh Research Collection of Afro-American History and Literature, Woodson Regional Library, Chicago Public Library, Chicago, Illinois

Hoyt W. Fuller Collection, Robert W. Woodruff Library, Atlanta University Center, Atlanta, Georgia

John W. Moutoussamy Papers, Research Center, Chicago History Museum, Chicago, Illinois

Lerone Bennett Jr. Papers, Archives and Special Collections, Chicago State University, Chicago, Illinois

Lerone Bennett Papers, Manuscript, Archives, and Rare Book Library, Emory University, Atlanta, Georgia

Robert and Naomi Johnson Papers, Manuscript, Archives, and Rare Book Library, Emory University, Atlanta, Georgia

Stephen Deutch Photograph Collection, Research Center, Chicago History Museum, Chicago, Illinois

U.S. Farm Security Administration / Office of War Information Collection, Prints and Photographs Division, Library of Congress, Washington, DC

W.E.B Du Bois Papers, Special Collections and University Archives, University of Massachusetts Libraries, Amherst, Massachusetts

William V. S. Tubman Photography Collection, Indiana University Libraries, Bloomington, Indiana

Other Sources

Adelman, Joseph M. *Revolutionary Networks: The Business and Politics of Printing the News, 1763–1789*. Baltimore: Johns Hopkins University Press, 2019.

Aiello, Thomas. *The Grapevine of the Black South: The Scott Newspaper Syndicate in the Generation before the Civil Rights Movement*. Athens: University of Georgia Press, 2018.

Alexander, Ann Field. *Race Man: The Rise and Fall of the "Fighting Editor," John Mitchell Jr.* Charlottesville: University of Virginia Press, 2002.

The American Newspaper Directory and Record of the Press. New York: Watson & Co., 1861.

Anderson, Benedict. *Imagined Communities: Reflections on the Origin and Spread of Nationalism*. London: Verso, 2006.

Bachin, Robin F. *Building the South Side: Urban Space and Civic Culture in Chicago, 1890–1919*. Chicago: University of Chicago Press, 2004.

Baldwin, Davarian. *Chicago's New Negroes: Modernity, the Great Migration, and Black Urban Life.* Chapel Hill: University of North Carolina Press, 2007.

Ballantyne, Tony. "Reading the Newspaper in Colonial Otago." *Journal of New Zealand Studies* 12 (2011). https://ojs.victoria.ac.nz/jnzs/article/view/488

Baradaran, Mehrsa. *The Color of Money: Black Banks and the Racial Wealth Gap.* Cambridge, MA: Harvard University Press, 2017.

Bates, Daisy. *The Long Shadow of Little Rock: A Memoir.* Fayetteville: University of Arkansas Press, 1986.

Bederman, Gail. *Manliness and Civilization: A Cultural History of Gender and Race in the United States, 1880–1917.* Chicago: University of Chicago Press, 1995.

Bekken, Jon. "Relations of Production at the *Chicago Defender*: Union-Busting, Contingent Labor and Consolidation in the Black Press." Unpublished paper, American Journalism Historians Association, 2020.

Belles, A. Gilbert. "The Black Press in Illinois." *Journal of the Illinois State Historical Society* 68 (1975): 344–52.

Berger, Maurice. *Seeing through Race: A Reinterpretation of Civil Rights Photography.* Berkeley: University of California Press, 2011.

Best, Wallace D. *Passionately Human, No Less Divine: Religion and Culture in Black Chicago, 1915–1952.* Princeton, NJ: Princeton University Press, 2005.

Bey, Lee. "A Century of Progress: An Alternative Tale." In *Chicago Architecture: Histories, Revisions, Alternatives,* edited by Charles Waldheim and Katerina Rüedi Ray, 124–28. Chicago: University of Chicago Press, 2005.

Biles, Roger. "The Rise and Fall of Soul City: Planning, Politics, and Race in Recent America." *Journal of Planning History* 4, no. 1 (2005): 52–72.

Birmingham, Stephen. *Certain People: America's Black Elite.* Boston: Little, Brown, 1977.

The Black Press: Soldiers without Swords, dir. Stanley Nelson (PBS, 1999).

Black's Blue Book: Business and Professional Directory. Chicago: Ford S. Black, 1921.

Blair, Cynthia. *I've Got to Make My Livin': Black Women's Sex Work in Turn-of-the-Century Chicago.* Chicago: University of Chicago Press, 2010.

Blakely, Robert J., and Marcus Shepard. *Earl B. Dickerson: A Voice for Freedom and Equality.* Evanston, IL: Northwestern University Press, 2006.

Blight, David W. *Frederick Douglass: Prophet of Freedom.* New York: Simon and Schuster, 2018.

Bone, Robert, and Richard A. Courage. *The Muse in Bronzeville: African American Creative Expression in Chicago, 1932–1950.* New Brunswick, NJ: Rutgers University Press, 2011.

Booker, Simeon. *Shocking the Conscience: A Reporter's Account of the Civil Rights Movement.* Jackson: University Press of Mississippi, 2013.

Boyd, Michelle R. *Jim Crow Nostalgia: Reconstructing Race in Bronzeville.* Minneapolis: University of Minnesota Press, 2008.

Broussard, Jinx Coleman. *Giving Voice to the Voiceless: Four Pioneering Black Women Journalists.* New York: Routledge, 2004.

Brown, Korey Bowers. "Souled Out: *Ebony* Magazine in the Era of Black Power." PhD diss., Howard University, 2015.

Buerglener, Robert. "Selling Automobility: Architecture as Sales Strategy in US Car Dealerships before 1920." In *Visual Merchandising: The Image of Selling*, edited by Louisa Iarocci, 157–74. London: Routledge, 2013.

Burg, David F. *Chicago's White City of 1893*. Lexington: University Press of Kentucky, 1976.

Burma, John. "An Analysis of the Present Negro Press." *Social Forces* 26 (1947): 172–80.

Burns, Andrea. *From Storefront to Monument: Tracing the Public History of the Black Museum Movement*. Amherst: University of Massachusetts Press, 2013.

Burns, Ben. *Nitty Gritty: A White Editor in Black Journalism*. Jackson: University Press of Mississippi, 1996.

Burt, Laura. "Vivian Harsh, Adult Education, and the Library's Role as Community Center." *Libraries and the Cultural Record* 44 (2009): 234–55.

Cairns, Kathleen. *Front-Page Women Journalists, 1920–1950*. Lincoln: University of Nebraska Press, 2003.

Camp, Stephanie. *Closer to Freedom: Enslaved Women and Everyday Resistance in the Plantation South*. Chapel Hill: University of North Carolina Press, 2004.

Campbell, James. *Middle Passages: African American Journeys to Africa, 1787–2005*. New York: Penguin, 2007.

Carby, Hazel V. *Race Men*. Cambridge, MA: Harvard University Press, 1998.

Carroll, Fred. *Race News: Black Journalists and the Fight for Racial Justice in the Twentieth Century*. Urbana: University of Illinois Press, 2017.

Census Data of the City of Chicago, 1934. Chicago: University of Chicago Press, 1934.

Centennial Newspaper Exhibition, 1876. New York: Geo. P. Rowell & Co., 1876.

Chambers, Jason P. *Madison Avenue and the Color Line: African Americans in the Advertising Industry*. Philadelphia: University of Pennsylvania Press, 2008.

Chicago and Its Resources, Twenty Years After. Chicago: Chicago Times Company, 1892.

Chicago Commission on Race Relations. *The Negro in Chicago: A Study of Race Relations and a Race Riot*. Chicago: University of Chicago Press, 1922.

Coburn, Leslie. "The Chicago Bee Building." In *Art Deco Chicago: Designing Modern America*, edited by Robert Bruegmann, 197–99. Chicago: Chicago Art Deco Society, 2018.

Colored People's Blue Book and Business Directory of Chicago, Ill. 1905. Chicago: Celerity Printing Co., 1905.

Commission on Chicago Landmarks. "The Black Metropolis–Bronzeville District." August 28, 1997.

———. "Chicago Orphan Asylum Building." Landmark Designation Report, December 4, 2008.

———. "Essex Inn." December 1, 2016.

———. "Johnson Publishing Company Building." October 5, 2017.

———. "Melissia Ann Elam Home." April 11, 1978.

———. "Motor Row District." Landmark Designation Report, April 3, 2000.

———. "West Town State Bank Building." November 14, 2002.

Cooley, Will. *Moving Up, Moving Out: The Rise of the Black Middle Class in Chicago.* Dekalb: Northern Illinois University Press, 2018.

Craig, Maxine Leeds. *Ain't I a Beauty Queen? Black Women, Beauty, and the Politics of Race.* Oxford: Oxford University Press, 2002.

Cygelman, Adele. *Arthur Elrod: Desert Modern Design.* Layton, UT: Gibbs Smith, 2019.

Dagbovie, Pero Gaglo. *The Early Black History Movement, Carter G. Woodson, and Lorenzo Johnston Greene.* Urbana: University of Illinois Press, 2007.

Daniel, Pete. *Deep'n as It Come: The 1927 Mississippi River Flood.* Fayetteville: University of Arkansas Press, 1996.

Davis, Frank Marshall. *Livin' the Blues: Memoirs of a Black Journalist and Poet.* Madison: University of Wisconsin Press, 1992.

Davis, Susan O'Connor. *Chicago's Historic Hyde Park.* Chicago: University of Chicago Press, 2013.

Detweiler, Frederick. *The Negro Press in the United States.* Chicago: University of Chicago Press, 1922.

Digirolamo, Vincent. *Crying the News: A History of America's Newsboys.* Oxford: Oxford University Press, 2019.

Dill, William. "Growth of Newspapers in the United States." MA thesis, University of Oregon, 1928.

Dolinar, Brian, ed. *The Negro in Illinois: The WPA Papers.* Urbana: University of Illinois Press, 2013.

Drake, St. Clair, and Horace Cayton. *Black Metropolis: A Study of Negro Life in a Northern City,* revised edition. Chicago: University of Chicago Press, 2015.

Drexel, Allan. "Before Paris Burned: Race, Class, and Male Homosexuality on the Chicago South Side, 1935–1950." In *Creating a Place for Ourselves: Lesbian, Gay, and Bisexual Community Histories,* edited by Brett Beemyn, 119–44. New York: Routledge, 1997.

Duberman, Martin. *Howard Zinn: A Life on the Left.* New York: New Press, 2012.

Duster, Alfreda, ed. *Crusade for Justice: The Autobiography of Ida B. Wells.* Chicago: University of Chicago Press, 1970.

Ericson, Staffan, Kristina Riegert, and Patrik Åker. Introduction to *Media Houses: Architecture, Media, and the Production of Centrality,* edited by Staffan Ericson and Kristina Riegert, 1–18. New York: Peter Lang, 2010.

Fagan, Benjamin. *The Black Newspaper and the Chosen Nation.* Athens: University of Georgia Press, 2016.

Farmer, Ashley. *Remaking Black Power: How Black Women Transformed an Era.* Chapel Hill: University of North Carolina Press, 2017.

Farrar, Haywood. *The Baltimore Afro-American, 1892–1950.* Westport, CT: Greenwood Press, 1998.

———. "The Black Press." In *Encyclopedia of African American History*, edited by Paul Finkelman, 231–41. Oxford: Oxford University Press, 2009.

Fenderson, Jonathan. *Building the Black Arts Movement: Hoyt Fuller and the Cultural Politics of the 1960s*. Urbana: University of Illinois Press, 2019.

Forman, James. *The Making of Black Revolutionaries*. Greensboro, NC: Open Hand Publishing, 1985.

Frazier, E. Franklin. *Black Bourgeoisie*. Glencoe, IL: Free Press, 1957.

Gallon, Kim. *Pleasure in the News: African American Sexuality and Readership in the Black Press*. Urbana: University of Illinois Press, 2020.

Ganz, Cheryl. *The 1933 Chicago World's Fair: A Century of Progress*. Urbana: University of Illinois Press, 2008.

Garb, Margaret. *Freedom's Ballot: African American Political Struggles in Chicago from Abolition to the Great Migration*. Chicago: University of Chicago Press, 2014.

Gardner, Eric. *Black Print Unbound: The* Christian Recorder, *African American Literature, and Periodical Culture*. Oxford: Oxford University Press, 2015.

Gasher, Mike. "Geographies of the News." In *Mediated Geographies and Geographies of Media*, edited by Susan Mains, Julie Cupples, and Chris Lukinbeal, 127–40. Dordrecht: Springer, 2015.

Gayle, Addison, ed. *The Black Aesthetic*. Garden City, NY: Doubleday, 1971.

Gellman, Erik. *Death Blow to Jim Crow: The National Negro Congress and the Rise of Militant Civil Rights*. Chapel Hill: University of North Carolina Press, 2012.

Glasrud, Bruce, and Laurie Champion. "Anita Scott Coleman." In *American Women Writers, 1900–1945*, edited by Laurie Champion, 77–81. Westport, CT: Greenwood Press, 2000.

Gooden, Mario. *Dark Space: Architecture, Representation, Black Identity*. New York: Columbia Books on Architecture and the City, 2016.

Grant, Colin. *Negro with a Hat: The Rise and Fall of Marcus Garvey*. Oxford: Oxford University Press, 2008.

Gray, Lee. "Type and Building Type: Newspaper/Office Buildings in Nineteenth-Century New York." In *The American Skyscraper: Cultural Histories*, edited by Roberta Moudry, 85–97. Cambridge: Cambridge University Press, 2005.

Green, Adam. "The Rising Tide of Youth: Chicago's Wonder Books and the 'New' Black Middle Class." In *The Middling Sorts: Explorations in the History of the American Middle Class*, edited by Burton Bledstein and Robert Johnston, 239–55. New York: Routledge, 2001.

———. *Selling the Race: Culture, Community, and Black Chicago, 1940–1955*. Chicago: University of Chicago Press, 2007.

Greenberg, Cheryl Lynn. *To Ask for an Equal Chance: African Americans in the Great Depression*. Lanham, MD: Rowman and Littlefield, 2009.

Greene, Lorenzo. *Selling Black History for Carter G. Woodson: A Diary, 1930–1933*, edited by Arvarh E. Strickland. Columbia: University of Missouri Press, 1996.

Grossman, James. *Land of Hope: Chicago, Black Southerners, and the Great Migration*. Chicago: University of Chicago Press, 1989.

Guarneri, Julia. *Newsprint Metropolis: City Papers and the Making of Modern Americans*. Chicago: University of Chicago Press, 2020.

Haas, Jeffrey. *The Assassination of Fred Hampton: How the FBI and the Chicago Police Murdered a Black Panther*. Chicago: Lawrence Hill Books/Chicago Review Press, 2010.

Haidarali, Laila. "Polishing Brown Diamonds: African American Women, Popular Magazines, and the Advent of Modelling in Early Postwar America." *Journal of Women's History* 17 (2005): 10–37.

Hale, Grace Elizabeth. "Black as Folk: The Southern Civil Rights Movement and the Folk Music Revival." In *The Myth of Southern Exceptionalism*, edited by Matthew Lassiter and Joseph Crespino, 121–42. Oxford: Oxford University Press, 2010.

Hall, James. "Fenton Johnson." In *Writers of the Black Chicago Renaissance*, edited by Steven Tracy, 218–32. Urbana: University of Illinois Press, 2011.

———. "On Sale at Your Favorite Newsstand: *Negro Digest/Black World* and the 1960s." In *The Black Press: New Literary and Historical Essays*, edited by Todd Vogel, 188–206. New Brunswick, NJ: Rutgers University Press, 2001.

Halliday, Aria. "Centering Black Women in the Black Chicago Renaissance." In *Against a Sharp White Background: Infrastructures of African American Print*, edited by Brigitte Fielder and Jonathan Senchyne, 240–58. Madison: University of Wisconsin Press, 2019.

Hartman, Saidiya. *Wayward Lives, Beautiful Experiments*. New York: W. W. Norton, 2019.

Hayner, Don. *Binga: The Rise and Fall of Chicago's First Black Banker*. Evanston, IL: Northwestern University Press, 2019.

Haywood, D'Weston. *Let Us Make Men: The Twentieth-Century Black Press and a Manly Vision for Racial Advancement*. Chapel Hill: University of North Carolina Press, 2018.

Haywood, Harry. *A Black Communist in the Freedom Struggle*. Minneapolis: University of Minnesota Press, 2012.

Hendricks, Wanda. *Gender, Race, and Politics in the Midwest: Black Club Women in Illinois*. Bloomington: Indiana University Press, 1998.

Henkin, David. *City Reading: Written Words and Public Spaces in Antebellum New York*. New York: Columbia University Press, 1998.

Henri, Florette. *Black Migration: Movement North, 1900–1920*. New York: Doubleday, 1975.

Herbst, Susan. *Politics at the Margin: Historical Studies of Public Expression Outside the Mainstream*. Cambridge: Cambridge University Press, 1994.

Hine, Darlene Clark. Introduction to *The Black Chicago Renaissance*, edited by Darlene Clark Hine and John McCluskey Jr., xv–xxxiii. Urbana: University of Illinois Press, 2012.

Hirsch, Arnold R. *Making the Second Ghetto: Race and Housing in Chicago, 1940–1960*. Cambridge: Cambridge University Press, 1983.

Holloway, Jonathan Scott. *Jim Crow Wisdom: Memory and Identity in Black America since 1940*. Chapel Hill: University of North Carolina Press, 2013.

Hooper, Lita. *Art of Work: The Art and Life of Haki R. Madhubuti*. Chicago: Third World Press, 2007.

Horne, Gerald. *The Rise and Fall of the Associated Negro Press: Claude Barnett's Pan-African News and the Jim Crow Paradox*. Urbana: University of Illinois Press, 2017.

Howard, Robert. "The Rise and Fall of Jesse Binga." In *Building the Black Metropolis: African American Entrepreneurship in Chicago*, edited by Robert Weems and Jason Chambers, 61–79. Urbana: University of Illinois Press, 2017.

Hricko, Mary. *The Genesis of the Chicago Renaissance*. New York: Routledge, 2009.

Hussain, Khuram. "Dreaming Differently about Freedom: Malcolm X and *Muhammad Speaks*." *Journal of African American Studies* 24 (2020): 319–36.

———. "Radical Black Media." In *Keywords in Radical Philosophy and Education*, edited by Derek Ford, 344–54. Leiden: Brill, 2019.

Hyra, Derek S. *The New Urban Renewal: The Economic Transformation of Harlem and Bronzeville*. Chicago: University of Chicago Press, 2008.

Ingham, John, and Lynne Feldman. *African-American Business Leaders: A Biographical Dictionary*. Westport, CT: Greenwood Press, 1994.

The Intercollegian Wonder Book. 2 vols. Chicago: Washington Intercollegiate Club of Chicago, 1929.

Jackson, Dennis. "The Outspoken Mr. Stone: A Conversation with Chuck Stone." *Black Scholar* 27 (1997): 38–57.

Jackson, Lawrence. *The Indignant Generation: A Narrative History of African American Writers and Critics, 1934–1960*. Princeton, NJ: Princeton University Press, 2011.

Jefferson, Margo. *Negroland: A Memoir*. London: Granta, 2016.

The Jews of Illinois. Chicago: Bloch and Newman, 1901.

Johnson, John, and Lerone Bennett Jr. *Succeeding against the Odds*. Chicago: Johnson Publishing, 1989.

Jordan, William. *Black Newspapers and America's War for Democracy, 1914–1920*. Chapel Hill: University of North Carolina Press, 2001.

Joseph, Peniel, ed. *The Black Power Movement: Rethinking the Civil Rights–Black Power Era*. London: Routledge, 2006.

Junger, Richard. *Becoming the Second City: Chicago's Mass News Media, 1833–1898*. Urbana: University of Illinois Press, 2010.

Keegan, Edward. *Chicago Architecture, 1885 to Today*. New York: Universe Publishing, 2008.

Kenney, William. *Chicago Jazz: A Cultural History, 1904–1930*. Oxford: Oxford University Press, 1993.

Knupfer, Anne Meis. *The Chicago Black Renaissance and Women's Activism*. Urbana: University of Illinois Press, 2006.

Kornweibel, Theodore. *Investigate Everything: Federal Efforts to Ensure Black Loyalty during World War I*. Bloomington: Indiana University Press, 2002.

———. *Seeing Red: Federal Campaigns against Black Militancy, 1919–1925*. Bloomington: Indiana University Press, 1998.

Kreiling, Albert. "The Commercialization of the Black Press and the Rise of Race News in Chicago." In *Ruthless Criticism: New Perspectives in US Communication History*, edited by William Solomon and Robert McChesney, 176–203. Minneapolis: University of Minnesota Press, 1993.

Krugler, David. *1919, The Year of Racial Violence: How African Americans Fought Back*. Cambridge: Cambridge University Press, 2015.

Leslie, Thomas. *Chicago Skyscrapers, 1871–1934*. Urbana: University of Illinois Press, 2013.

Lumpkins, Charles. *American Pogrom: The East St. Louis Race Riot and Black Politics*. Athens: Ohio University Press, 2008.

Mackintosh, Phillip Gordon. *Newspaper City: Toronto's Street Surfaces and the Liberal Press, 1860–1935*. Toronto: University of Toronto Press, 2017.

Mahoney, Olivia. *Douglas/Grand Boulevard: A Chicago Neighborhood*. Chicago: Arcadia Publishing, 2001.

Martindale, Molly. "Women in the Movement I." In *The Chicago Freedom Movement*, edited by Mary Lou Finley, Bernard LaFayette Jr., James R. Ralph Jr., and Pam Smith, 351–68. Lexington: University Press of Kentucky, 2016.

McCammack, Brian. *Landscapes of Hope: Nature and the Great Migration in Chicago*. Cambridge, MA: Harvard University Press, 2017.

McMurry, Linda. *To Keep the Waters Troubled: The Life of Ida B. Wells*. Oxford: Oxford University Press, 1998.

McWhirter, Cameron. *Red Summer: The Summer of 1919 and the Awakening of Black America*. London: St. Martin's, 2012.

Meier, August, and Elliott Rudwick. "Negro Protest at the Chicago World's Fair, 1933–34." *Journal of the Illinois State Historical Society* 59 (1966): 161–71.

Meriwether, James. *Proudly We Can Be Africans: Black Americans and Africa, 1935–1961*. Chapel Hill: University of North Carolina Press, 2002.

Michaeli, Ethan. *The Defender: How the Legendary Black Newspaper Changed America*. Boston: Houghton Mifflin Harcourt, 2016.

Miller, Wayne. *Chicago's South Side, 1946–1948*. Berkeley: University of California Press, 2000.

Mitchell, Melvin. *The Crisis of the African-American Architect: Conflicting Cultures of Architecture and (Black) Power*. New York: Writers Advantage, 2003.

Morris, Burnis. *Carter G. Woodson: History, the Black Press, and Public Relations*. Jackson: University Press of Mississippi, 2017.

Mullen, Bill. *Popular Fronts: Chicago and African-American Cultural Politics, 1935–46*. Urbana: University of Illinois Press, 1999.

Neal, Larry. "The Black Arts Movement." *Drama Review* 12 (1968): 28–39.

North, Louise. *The Gendered Newsroom: How Journalists Experience the Changing World of Media*. Cresskill, NJ: Hampton Press, 2009.

"Northwestern Terra Cotta Company Building." National Register of Historic Places Registration Form, December 22, 1988.

Olson, Liesl. *Chicago Renaissance: Literature and Art in the Midwest Metropolis*. New Haven, CT: Yale University Press, 2017.

One Tenth of a Nation. The Press. American Newsreel, 1953. https://www.loc.gov/item/mbrs01841243

Ottley, Roi. *The Lonely Warrior. The Life and Times of Robert S. Abbott*. Chicago: Regnery, 1955.

Pacyga, Dominic. *Chicago: A Biography*. Chicago: University of Chicago Press, 2009.

Paddon, Anna, and Sally Turner. "African Americans and the World's Columbian Exposition." *Illinois Historical Journal* 88 (1995): 19–36.

Pasley, Jeffrey. *The Tyranny of Printers: Newspaper Politics in the Early American Republic*. Charlottesville: University Press of Virginia, 2001.

Penn, I. Garland. *The Afro-American Press and Its Editors*. Springfield: Willey & Co., 1891.

Philpott, Thomas Lee. *The Slum and the Ghetto: Neighborhood Deterioration and Middle-Class Reform, Chicago, 1880–1930*. Oxford: Oxford University Press, 1978.

Picturesque World's Fair: An Elaborate Collection of Colored Views. Chicago: W. B. Conkey, 1894.

Pinder, Kymberley. *Painting the Gospel: Black Public Art and Religion in Chicago*. Urbana: University of Illinois Press, 2016.

Pruter, Robert. *Doowop: The Chicago Scene*. Urbana: University of Illinois Press, 1996.

Purnell, Brian, and Jeanne Theoharis. Introduction to *The Strange Careers of Jim Crow North: Segregation and Struggle outside of the South*, 1–42. New York: New York University Press, 2019.

Puth, Robert. "Supreme Life: The History of a Negro Life Insurance Company 1919–1962." *Business History Review* 43 (1969): 1–20.

Raiford, Leigh. *Imprisoned in a Luminous Glare: Photograph and the African American Freedom Struggle*. Chapel Hill: University of North Carolina Press, 2011.

Randall, Frank. *History of the Development of Building Construction in Chicago*. Urbana: University of Illinois Press, 1999.

Reed, Christopher. *All the World Is Here! The Black Presence at White City*. Bloomington: Indiana University Press, 2000.

———. *Black Chicago's First Century, 1833–1900*. Columbus: University of Missouri Press, 2005.

———. *The Chicago NAACP and the Rise of Black Professional Leadership, 1910–1966*. Bloomington: Indiana University Press, 1997.

———. *The Depression Comes to the South Side: Protest and Politics in the Black Metropolis, 1930–1933*. Bloomington: Indiana University Press, 2011.

———. *Knock at the Door of Opportunity: Black Migration to Chicago, 1900–1919.* Carbondale: Southern Illinois University Press, 2014.

———. *The Rise of Chicago's Black Metropolis, 1920–1929.* Urbana: University of Illinois Press, 2011.

———. "The Third Chicago School? Marking Sexual and Ethnic Identity." In *Chicago Architecture: Histories, Revisions, Alternatives,* edited by Charles Waldheim and Katerina Rüedi Ray, 163–75. Chicago: University of Chicago Press, 2005.

Renda, Mary. *Taking Haiti: Military Occupation and the Culture of U.S. Imperialism, 1915–1940.* Chapel Hill: University of North Carolina Press, 2001.

Rhodes, Jane. "The Black Press in the United States." *Oxford Bibliographies,* DOI: 10.1093/OBO/9780190280024–0046, last modified June 28, 2016.

Rhodes, Leara. *The Ethnic Press: Shaping the American Dream.* New York: Peter Lang, 2010.

Rice, Myiti Sengstacke. *Chicago Defender.* Charleston, SC: Arcadia Publishing, 2012.

———. "Robert Sengstacke Abbott." In *Building the Black Metropolis: African American Entrepreneurship in Chicago,* edited by Robert Weems and Jason Chambers, 44–60. Urbana: University of Illinois Press, 2017.

Richings, G. F. *Evidences of Progress among Colored People.* Philadelphia: Geo S. Ferguson Co., 1904.

"Robert S. Abbott House." National Register of Historic Places. Washington, D.C., 1976.

Roberts, Gene, and Hank Klibanoff. *The Race Beat: The Press, the Civil Rights Struggle, and the Awakening of a Nation.* New York: Vintage Books, 2006.

Roberts, John. *From Trickster to Badman: The Black Folk Hero in Slavery and Freedom.* Philadelphia: University of Pennsylvania Press, 1989.

Rocksborough-Smith, Ian. *Black Public History in Chicago: Civil Rights Activism from World War II into the Cold War.* Urbana: University of Illinois Press, 2018.

Rodgers, Scott. "Journalism: An Urban Affair." In *The Routledge Companion to Urban Media and Communication,* edited by Zlatan Krajina and Deborah Stevenson, 66–75. New York: Routledge, 2020.

Rolinson, Mary. *Grassroots Garveyism: The Universal Negro Improvement Association in the Rural South, 1920–1927.* Chapel Hill: University of North Carolina Press, 2007.

Rooks, Noliwe. *Ladies' Pages: African American Women's Magazine and the Culture That Made Them.* New Brunswick, NJ: Rutgers University Press, 2004.

Rudwick, Elliott, and August Meier. "Black Man in the 'White City': Negroes and the Columbian Exposition, 1893." *Phylon* 26 (1965): 354–61.

Russell, Thaddeus. "The Color of Discipline: Civil Rights and Black Sexuality." *American Quarterly* 60 (2008): 101–128.

Rutkoff, Peter, and William Scott. "Pinkster in Chicago: Bud Billiken and the Mayor of Bronzeville, 1930–1945." *Journal of African American History* 89 (2004): 316–30.

Sandburg, Carl. *The Chicago Race Riots*. New York: Harcourt, Brace, and Howe, 1919.

Schlabach, Elizabeth. *Along the Streets of Bronzeville: Black Chicago's Literary Landscape*. Urbana: University of Illinois Press, 2013.

Schrenk, Lisa D. *Building a Century of Progress: The Architecture of Chicago's 1933–34 World's Fair*. Minneapolis: University of Minnesota Press, 2007.

Semmes, Clovis. *The Regal Theater and Black Culture*. New York: Palgrave Macmillan, 2006.

Sernett, Milton. *Bound for the Promised Land: African American Religion and the Great Migration*. Durham, NC: Duke University Press, 1997.

———. *North Star Country: Upstate New York and the Crusade for African American Freedom*. Syracuse, NY: Syracuse University Press, 2002.

Sewell, Jessica. "Opening the Boundaries of Architectural History: Popular Culture, Imaginary Buildings, and the Influence of the Bachelor Pad." *Proceedings of the Society of Architectural Historians, Australia and New Zealand* 30 (2013): 67–79.

Simmons, Charles. *The African American Press*. Jefferson, NC: McFarland, 1998.

Singh, Nikhil Pal. Introduction to *Climbin' Jacob's Ladder: The Black Freedom Movement Writings of Jack O'Dell*, edited by Nikhil Pal Singh, 1–68. Berkeley: University of California Press, 2012.

Smethurst, James. *The Black Arts Movement: Literary Nationalism in the 1960s and 1970s*. Chapel Hill: University of North Carolina Press, 2005.

Snyder, Jeffrey Aaron. *Making Black History: The Color Line, Culture, and Race in the Age of Jim Crow*. Athens: University of Georgia Press, 2018.

Solomonson, Katherine. *The* Chicago Tribune *Tower Competition: Skyscraper Design and Cultural Change in the 1920s*. Chicago: University of Chicago Press, 2003.

Spear, Allan. *Black Chicago: The Making of a Negro Ghetto, 1890–1920*. Chicago: University of Chicago Press, 1967.

Stamm, Michael. *Dead Tree Media: Manufacturing the Newspaper in Twentieth-Century North America*. Baltimore: Johns Hopkins University Press, 2018.

Stamper, John. *Chicago's North Michigan Avenue: Planning and Development, 1900–1930*. Chicago: University of Chicago Press, 1991.

Stange, Maren. "Photographs Taken in Everyday Life: *Ebony*'s Photojournalistic Discourse." In *The Black Press: New Literary and Historical Essays*, edited by Todd Vogel, 207–227. New Brunswick, NJ: Rutgers University Press, 2001.

Stanley, Kimberly. "Dan Burley." In *Writers of the Black Chicago Renaissance*, edited by Steven Tracy, 141–49. Urbana: University of Illinois Press, 2011.

Stewart, Jacqueline. *Migrating to the Movies: Cinema and Black Urban Modernity*. Berkeley: University of California Press, 2005.

Stone, Chuck. *Tell It Like It Is*. New York: Pocket Books, 1970.

Street, Paul. *Racial Oppression in the Global Metropolis*. Lanham, MD: Rowman and Littlefield, 2007.

Strickland, Arvarh. *History of the Chicago Urban League*. Urbana: University of Illinois Press, 1966.

Teresa, Carrie. *Looking at the Stars: Black Celebrity Journalism in the Jim Crow Era.* Lincoln: University of Nebraska Press, 2019.

Thompson, Julius Eric. *Black Life in Mississippi: Essays on Political, Social and Cultural Studies in a Deep South State.* Lanham, MD: University Press of America, 2001.

Tinson, Christopher. *Radical Intellect:* Liberator *Magazine and Black Activism in the 1960s.* Chapel Hill: University of North Carolina Press, 2017.

Travis, Dempsey. *An Autobiography of Black Chicago*, revised edition. Chicago: Agate Bolden, 2013.

Trodd, Zoe. "The Black Press and the Black Chicago Renaissance." In *Writers of the Black Chicago Renaissance*, edited by Steven Tracy, 448–64. Urbana: University of Illinois Press, 2011.

Tuttle, William. *Race Riot: Chicago in the Red Summer of 1919.* Urbana: University of Illinois Press, 1970.

Tyre, William. *Chicago's Historic Prairie Avenue.* Charleston: Arcadia Publishing, 2008.

Tyson, Timothy. *The Blood of Emmett Till.* New York: Simon and Schuster, 2017.

Valle, Paul Della. *Massachusetts Troublemakers: Rebels, Reformers, and Radicals from the Bay State.* Guilford, CT: Globe Pequot Press, 2009.

Vogel, Todd. Introduction to *The Black Press: New Literary and Historical Essays*, edited by Todd Vogel, 1–14. New Brunswick, NJ: Rutgers University Press, 2001.

Von Eschen, Penny. *Race against Empire: Black Americans and Anticolonialism, 1937–1957.* Ithaca, NY: Cornell University Press, 1997.

Wald, Gayle. *Crossing the Line: Interracial Passing in Twentieth-Century U.S. Literature and Culture.* Durham, NC: Duke University Press, 2000.

Walker, Juliet. "The Promised Land: The Chicago Defender and the Black Press in Illinois, 1862–1970." In *The Black Press in the Midwest*, edited by Henry Lewis Suggs, 9–50. Westport, CT: Greenwood Press, 1996.

Wallace, Aurora. *Media Capital: Architecture and Communications in New York City.* Urbana: University of Illinois Press, 2012.

Ward, Francis B. "The Black Press in Crisis." *Black Scholar* 6, no. 1 (1973): 34–36.

Washburn, Patrick. *The African American Newspaper.* Evanston, IL: Northwestern University Press, 2006.

———. *A Question of Sedition: The Federal Government's Investigation of the Black Press during World War II.* Oxford: Oxford University Press, 1986.

Waters, Enoch. *American Diary: A Personal History of the Black Press.* Chicago: Path Press, 1987.

Watson, Jamal Eric. "John H. Johnson." In *Writers of the Black Chicago Renaissance*, edited by Steven Tracy, 233–41. Urbana: University of Illinois Press, 2011.

Weare, Walter. "Charles Clinton Spaulding: Middle-Class Leadership in the Age of Segregation." In *Black Leaders of the Twentieth Century*, edited by John Hope Franklin and August Meier, 167–90. Urbana: University of Illinois Press, 1982.

Weems, Robert. *The Merchant Prince of Black Chicago: Anthony Overton and the Building of a Financial Empire.* Urbana: University of Illinois Press, 2020.

Weems, Robert E., Jr., with Lewis A. Randolph. *Business in Black and White: American Presidents and Black Entrepreneurs in the Twentieth Century*. New York University Press, 2009.

Wells, Ida B., with contributions by Frederick Douglass, Irvine Garland Penn, and Ferdinand Lee Barnett. "The Reason Why the Colored American Is Not in the World's Columbian Exposition." University of Pennsylvania Digital Collections. https://digital.library.upenn.edu/women/wells/exposition/exposition.html

West, E. James. "Ben Burns and the Boundaries of Black Print in Chicago, 1942–1954." *Journal of American Studies* 53 (2019): 703–724.

———. *Ebony Magazine and Lerone Bennett Jr.: Popular Black History in Postwar America*. Urbana: University of Illinois Press, 2020.

Whitaker, Mark. *Smoketown: The Untold Story of the Other Great Black Renaissance*. New York: Simon and Schuster, 2018.

Williams, Jakobi. *From the Bullet to the Ballot: The Illinois Chapter of The Black Panther Party and Racial Coalition Politics in Chicago*. Chapel Hill: University of North Carolina Press, 2013.

Williams, Sonja. *Word Warrior: Richard Durham, Radio, and Freedom*. Urbana: University of Illinois Press, 2015.

Wilson, Clint C., II. *Whither the Black Press? Glorious Past, Uncertain Future*. Bloomington, IN: Xlibris, 2014.

Wilson, Dreck Spurlock, ed. *African American Architects: A Biographical Dictionary, 1865–1945*. New York: Routledge, 2004.

Wolcott, Victoria. *Race, Riots, and Roller Coasters: The Struggle over Segregated Recreation in America*. Philadelphia: University of Pennsylvania Press, 2012.

Wolseley, Roland. *The Black Press, U.S.A.* Ames: Iowa State University Press, 1971.

Woodford, John. "Messaging the Blackman." In *Voices from the Underground: Insider Histories of the Vietnam Era Underground Press*, edited by Ken Wachsberger, 91–98. Tempe, AZ: Mica Press, 1993.

Wright, Richard. *Native Son*. New York: Harper and Brothers, 1940.

Zucchino, David. *Wilmington's Lie: The Murderous Coup of 1898 and the Rise of White Supremacy*. New York: Atlantic Monthly Press, 2020.

Index

E. JAMES WEST is a research associate in American history at Northumbria University. He is the author of *Ebony Magazine and Lerone Bennett Jr.: Popular Black History in Postwar America.*

The University of Illinois Press
is a founding member of the
Association of University Presses.

———————————————

Composed in 10.25/14 Chaparral Pro
with Frutiger LT Std display
by Lisa Connery
at the University of Illinois Press
Manufactured by Sheridan Books, Inc.

University of Illinois Press
1325 South Oak Street
Champaign, IL 61820-6903
www.press.uillinois.edu